Policing Urban Poverty

Chris Crowther
Lecturer in Criminology
Buckinghamshire Chilterns University College
High Wycombe

Foreword by Alan Walker
Professor of Social Policy
University of Sheffield

Consultant Editor: Jo Campling

First published in Great Britain 2000 by
MACMILLAN PRESS LTD
Houndmills, Basingstoke, Hampshire RG21 6XS and London
Companies and representatives throughout the world

A catalogue record for this book is available from the British Library.

ISBN 0–333–74858–1

First published in the United States of America 2000 by
ST. MARTIN'S PRESS, INC.,
Scholarly and Reference Division,
175 Fifth Avenue, New York, N.Y. 10010

ISBN 0–312–22846–5

Library of Congress Cataloging-in-Publication Data
Crowther, Chris, 1968–
Policing urban poverty / Chris Crowther ; foreword by Alan Walker
; consultant editor, Jo Campling.
    p.   cm.
Includes bibliographical references and index.
ISBN 0–312–22846–5 (cloth)
1. Urban poor.   2. Poverty.   3. Crime.   I. Campling, Jo.
II. Title.
HV4028.C76   1999
364.4—dc21   99–40401
                                                                  CIP

This book is printed on paper suitable for recycling and made from fully managed and sustained forest sources.

10 9 8 7 6 5 4 3 2 1
09 08 07 06 05 04 03 02 01 00

Printed and bound in Great Britain by
Antony Rowe Ltd, Chippenham, Wiltshire

For Mum and Dad

Contents

Foreword

This important and timely book focuses on the policing of the urban poor and examines in painstaking detail the relationship between discourses on crime and poverty and practical issues of policy. The scope of the book is very wide – encompassing historical and contemporary analyses of the 'underclass', discussion of the debate on crime and poverty in the US, a rare analysis of the policy-making process in the police service, police responses to the riots in the 1980s, and recent criminal-justice policies. Chris Crowther successfully marshals this potentially overwhelming brief by building a firm theoretical foundation from sociological theory, particularly social constructionism and the analysis of power, and by addressing a consistent theme, the 'underclass', throughout the book. The result is an exemplary integration of social analysis and social policy and a clear demonstration that there is nothing as practical as good theory.

Chris Crowther's book is unusual in locating the discussion of crime and disorder in the context of an analysis of poverty and social exclusion. Moreover he brings the operation of the police service back within the purview of social policy, where it has been neglected for too long. The book also includes compelling verbatim extracts from his interviews with senior police officers.

His book emphasises that ideas about poverty and crime have very practical consequences with regard to police attitudes and behaviour. Thus the 'underclass' debate is part of the received wisdom with which police officers interpret everyday events and, in this case, interact with the urban poor. But, as Chris Crowther shows, there is not a simple correspondence between academic interpretations of the problematic concept of 'underclass' and those espoused by different strata of the police service. Furthermore, in practice, this notion may be employed by the service, at different times and in different locations, to justify contrasting approaches emphasising control or community development.

Chris Crowther traces discourses on poverty and crime from the nineteenth century to the present day, showing how the explanations employed by policy-makers have remained remarkably consistent even if the labels have changed. But it also reveals that senior police officers do not necessarily accept uncritically all that their political masters tell them. The simplistic and dogmatic contention that there were no links

between crime and poverty made by Conservative ministers in the
1980s was contested by many senior police officers who recognised the
important effects of economic, political and social exclusion.

Although the field research for this book was carried out when a Conservative government held power, it contains much of relevance to the
New Labour administration. The Prime Minister has used the term
'underclass' and the government is pledged to be 'tough on crime and
tough on the causes of crime'. However it must beware of the danger of
adopting an accusatory and moralising tone merely to appease the
right-wing headline writers, which would reinforce social exclusion and
get in the way of the balanced policies of care and control that are
required to tackle urban crime.

Chris Crowther's book is an important contribution to understanding
the complex relationships between poverty, crime and disorder and
policing, and I am very pleased to recommend it warmly to policy-makers
and students alike.

ALAN WALKER
University of Sheffield

Acknowledgements

Many people have contributed in a variety of ways towards the production of this book and it is not possible to mention everyone. The ideas I have tried to develop have been shaped by numerous individuals, although any lapses and shortcomings are entirely my own responsibility. I'm especially grateful to Alan Walker, who provided invaluable intellectual guidance and instruction as my PhD supervisor and his unstinting support during the early stages of my academic career. Robert Reiner and Simon Holdaway made some constructive comments and suggestions on how to improve the work on which this book is based. Mike King, Roger Hopkins-Burke and Martin Gill have also provided insightful comments with regard to certain aspects of my work. I am also indebted to the police officers who went beyond the call of duty: first, for agreeing to talk, secondly for talking so openly and thirdly for being so friendly and hospitable.

Numerous colleagues and students at Buckinghamshire Chilterns University College made the writing process bearable by inquiring about my progress, particularly Kevin Stenson and Max Travers. To those whom I have not mentioned, you know who you are. Marisa Silvestri also deserves thanks for listening to my whingeing about various things and for helping me to keep reasonably sane.

I have been blessed with many good friends over the years and it is always difficult to single out particular individuals, but the influence of some has been more enduring and unconditional than others. Gratitude to Mark Forshaw and Amanda Crowfoot, Monika Husemann, Suzanne Tose, Sam Keene, Anu Sethi, Martin Thornber, Andrew Leahy and William Harris, who have all shared with me some of the frustrations and many joys of life. I give my whole-hearted thanks to them for their love and care, feeding me, weekend breaks, evenings out and in, holidays in Rhodes and Zakynthos and for just keeping in touch when it mattered most. Many thanks to my new friends in High Wycombe too, but especially to Julian Matthews and Tony Morris, for their kindness, willingness to discuss ideas, appreciation of some of the absurdities of life and for sharing the good times.

Simon and Louise, thanks for being there. Above all, I dedicate this book to my Mum and Dad, with love. I hope the publication of this book repays some of the enormous debt I owe to you both, for your unwavering love, tolerance and support.

I would also like to acknowledge Annabelle Buckley and Karen Brazier at Macmillan for their respective contributions towards the publication of this book, and I'm grateful to Christine Suzman for carefully editing the typescript and waiting patiently while I made the necessary corrections. Finally, my thanks go to Jo Campling for her advice on the original proposal and for her encouraging and very helpful comments on earlier drafts of the book.

I would like to thank Perpetuity Press Ltd for permission to reproduce material in Chapter 9 which appeared in an earlier form in Roger Hopkins-Burke (ed.) (1998) *Zero Tolerance Policing* (Leicester: Perpetuity Press).

CHRIS CROWTHER
High Wycombe

1
Introduction

Decades and centuries come and go, but poverty is always in the news, and there is no reason to doubt that it will stay at the top of the agenda throughout the twenty-first century. This is quite a bold statement, given that in the UK in the mid-1990s, for example, its existence was denied by the Conservative Government of the day (Townsend, 1996: 11). Instead, less controversial concepts such as 'social exclusion', and politically contentious labels like the 'underclass', have been substituted for the notion of poverty. Indeed, a core concern of this book is the 'underclass'. Despite the attempts of some politicians to erase poverty from their lexicon of social problems, it has remained centre-stage in academic and public debate at an international level (Mingione, 1996; Room, 1995). This book explores the different meanings attached to poverty by senior police officers and its policy implications. At this point some of the key terms used in this book are defined.

Poverty

The issue of poverty has attracted the interest of many scholars from different perspectives (Alcock, 1997ab; Townsend, 1979; Oppenheim and Harker, 1996; Waxman, 1977; Holman, 1978; Donnison, 1982). Walker (1995: 102–3) provides a useful definition:

> The concept of 'poverty', as used in most policy discourse, has its origins in a liberal vision prevalent in Britain in the late nineteenth century. Within this paradigm, society was viewed as a set of individuals engaged in economic competition, which resulted in some having incomes large in relation to their needs while others risked destitution. Policy aimed to ensure that those in the latter category,

1

occupying the lowest position in the distribution of income to needs ratios, had the minimum resources necessary for survival.

A more commonplace definition refers to individuals who find it difficult to satisfy their basic needs, such as food, warmth and shelter. Clearly these resources are indispensable for survival in any society. Another perspective suggests that human beings should be able to participate in a wider range of social activities beyond eating and fighting off the worst excesses of the natural elements. The former is known as absolute poverty (Rowntree, 1901) and the latter relative poverty (Townsend, 1979). It is also worth noting that there are three types of poverty: 'transient, recurrent and permanent', which draws attention to the fact that poverty is a process (Walker, 1998 cited in Oppenheim, 1998a).

In Britain there is no official definition of poverty, and though there are plenty of indicators, the government refuses to accept them. The closest there is to an officially recognised indicator is the reference to those living on less than half the average household income. In the UK in 1979, 5 million (9 per cent of population) were living in poverty or beneath 50 per cent of average income after housing costs (HBAI). In 1994 the respective figures were 13.7 million and 24 per cent. The income of the bottom tenth of the population fell by 13 per cent, but rose by 40 per cent for the average, and 65 per cent for the top tenth. Children were hit the hardest: in 1979 1.4 million (10 per cent) were in poverty, but this had increased to 4.2 million (32 per cent) in 1994 (DSS, 1996 cited in Oppenheim, 1996: 139). The scale of poverty in America is much greater but there is a much higher proportion of working poor than in the UK (Fainstein, 1996).

Beyond poverty there is the issue of inequality of income. In the UK:

> The gradual, and uneven, reduction in the inequality of income ended in the late 1970s, and income inequality in the UK grew rapidly in the 1980s, more than reversing the previous post war fall. Meanwhile, the inequality of wealth distribution reduced substantially up to the mid 1970s, but has since levelled out (Hills, 1996: 14–5).

Social exclusion

In absolute terms, then, the 'growing divide between the rich and poor' has widened (Walker and Walker, 1997). What has happened in terms of relative poverty? Building on Townsend's (1979) work, the notion of 'social exclusion' became increasingly popular towards the end of the 1990s (Levitas, 1996: 7). This term:

has different, French origins. It derives from the idea of society as a status hierarchy comprising people bound together by rights and obligations that reflect, and are defined with respect to, a shared moral order. Exclusion is the state of detachment from this moral order and can be brought about by many factors, including limited income (Walker, 1995: 102–3).

This concept refers to poverty and inequality in terms of citizenship and whether or not citizens are included in society, especially the labour market. It also rests on the assumption that lack of income is just one form of exclusion, and individuals can be excluded if they are unable to participate in those activities that are taken for granted by the majority of citizens in a given society.

The 'underclass'

The 'underclass' is conceptually tied up with social class because it is said to 'acquire its meaning within the same framework of analysis' as the latter (Smith, 1992: 2–4). However, conventional class schema, based on the position of the individual in the labour market, is of limited utility for understanding the 'underclass' (Crompton, 1993; Westergaard, 1995; Marshall *et al.*, 1996; Devine, 1997). This is partly because the 'underclass' *captures* a much more *heterogeneous* population (Morris, 1995: 132). For example, the concept refers to: low educational attainment; a lack of adequate skills required to become a member of the labour force; shared spatial location; dependency on welfare, unemployment or joblessness and an unstable relationship with the labour market; pathological family structures and the inter-generational transmission of poverty; involvement in the unreported economy; and a predisposition to criminal and disorderly behaviour (Townsend, 1990; Walker, 1991ab; Westergaard, 1992). All of these criteria are not always joined together and are articulated in many ways, reflecting 'definitional' problems (Aponte, 1990) and difficulties in conceptualising and measuring the size of the 'underclass' (Edai, 1992; Ruggles and Marton, 1986). Each version is only relatively fixed and therefore open to 'deconstruction' (Gans, 1990).

According to Walker (1990ab) there are two main perspectives on poverty and the 'underclass' – the behavioural and the structural – which each have their own unique policy implications. Structural accounts tend to explain poverty and social exclusion in terms of the inadequacy of state provided welfare services, changes in the labour market and exclusion from social citizenship (Wilson, 1996ab; Dahrendorf, 1985).

Crime is an understandable response to the pressures arising from poverty and social exclusion (Young, 1998). Commentators such as Murray (1990) adhere to a behavioural perspective. The welfare state offers numerous incentives to rational human agents to choose not to work and make their own way in the world, and depend on state provided welfare instead. In terms of crime this view has its roots in Beccaria's classicism, and more recently, rational choice theory, which assumes that the individual enjoys free will. If an individual is presented with an opportunity to not work, or to commit a crime, it is their choice as to whether they take the opportunity or not. According to this school of thought, because action is an outcome of individual free choice, there is no point in searching for the causes of behaviour elsewhere. If behaving badly is too easy, the risks of being caught are remote, and the chance of sanctions being imposed significantly reduced, the potential rewards outweigh the costs (Roshier, 1989).

The proponents of the behavioural perspective argue that the cause of poverty rests with the individual, and structuralists, in the last analysis blame societal factors. These ways of seeing the social world belong to an old era and there has been a sea-change in terms of the interpretations of how individuals attempt to come to terms with their environment, both at an intellectual and practical level.

This book provides an analysis of the tension which exists between these different perspectives. It charts the emergence of a political consensus in government circles in the UK and the USA which, to varying degrees, is increasingly suspicious of the structural version. The key point here is that there is an unequal balance in terms of the weight accorded to the behavioural rather than the structural viewpoint. Take the election of New Labour in Britain on 2 May 1997 as an example. In the late 1980s Paul Gilroy and Joe Sim (1987) made a comment which (at the time of writing in 1998) has even more relevance with a supposedly left-wing party in power:

> The history of police differentiating between deserving and casual poor or between labouring and criminal classes, makes their modern attempts to sort reputable from slag citizenry appear less surprising. A left theory of policing will also have to contend with the legacy of Victorian moralism expressed in socialist writings which regards the existence of surplus labour (the lumpenproletariat) as an embarrassment to the idea of class analysis (Gilroy and Sim, 1987: 99).

This issue is revisited in Chapter 9.

Separating 'underclass' discourse into behavioural and structural categories is very helpful, but there is another significant characteristic. The structural category also includes a cultural dimension. Wilson (1993), for example, argues that 'either-or-notions of culture and social structure impede the development of a broader theoretical context in which to examine questions recently raised by the ongoing debate on the underclass' (1993: 22). The relative significance of culture in structural accounts of the 'underclass' is elaborated later on. The main point is that the 'underclass' is conceptually muddled. However, it is only by examining the complexity of the debate that the main themes can be identified. Moreover, the ambiguity of notions of 'underclass' may be a strength inasmuch that it can expose the confusing and complex nature of everyday life and draw attention to social injustice.

Poverty, unemployment and social problems

Within this book poverty, social exclusion and the 'underclass' are used interchangeably to refer to myriad groups, but especially those who are unemployed, lone parent families and those engaging in delinquent behaviour. On the basis of internationally agreed definitions, to be unemployed one must be actively seeking work. Individuals who are on government-supported training and employment programmes are classified as employed. By applying the actively seeking work criteria in the UK, only 20 per cent of people of working age can be classified as unemployed, and a significant group of workless and inactive individuals are therefore not counted (Gregg and Wadsworth, 1998). To further complicate matters unemployment, non-employment and inactivity are on a continuum and individuals move in and out of these different circumstances (Green and Owen, 1998).

A contemporary concern is with the anxieties about what may happen if work disappears from communities (Wilson, 1996a), particularly the impact of this transformation on family life and young men. In this sense the labour market is gendered. There is a perception that there is a connection between the economic redundancy of young males, their non-attachment to the nuclear family and high levels of deviant and disorderly behaviour (Murray, 1994; Campbell, 1993).

A plethora of scholars have focused on the enduring but ever-changing relationship between poverty and the individual's attachment to the labour market and welfare state in the UK and USA (Katz, 1989; 1993; Mann, 1992; Morris, 1994). This book also focuses on the links between a variety of debates about poverty and the distribution of welfare services, especially the contention that public welfare creates dependency and demoralises the poor. Despite mentioning the association of crime and disorder with the poor, or the 'underclass', the contributors mentioned above have not investigated this in any depth. Moreover, they have not taken stock of the influence of American ideas on British society. This contribution to the literature re-considers some of these issues by focusing on the relationship between crime, poverty, the provision of welfare services and policing from a comparative perspective.

Other scholars have also critically reviewed the concept of poverty in general, and specifically in relation to the so-called 'underclass' (Katz, 1993; Morris, 1994; Wilson, 1993). These accounts are historically informed and concentrate on the development of the welfare state in relation to different conceptions of citizenship. They also attempt to come to terms with the view that there is a shift from the 'welfare state' towards the 'state after the welfare state' (Clarke, 1996: 13). In doing this they make considerable advances inasmuch that they explore the condition of poverty in both British and American society. However, the issues of crime and disorder, and their policy implications are peripheral and crying out for further analysis.

Mingione's (1996) edited collection assesses debates about poverty, the social instability it creates and the attempts of various welfare regimes to restore social stability. Whilst the coverage of these issues is almost exemplary there are some notable omissions and missed opportunities. In particular, crime and disorder remain in the background of most of the essays. This book teases out these issues and suggests that the relationship between these phenomena needs to be moved front-stage as an issue within the social sciences and public debate. Mingione (1996) also reflects on the meaning of poverty in the USA and in different European countries (Buck, 1996; Fassin, 1996; Marcuse, 1996; Wacquant, 1996; Silver, 1993; Häussermann and Kazepov, 1992; Dangschat, 1994; Roelandt and Veenman, 1992); and further afield (Baum and Hassan, 1993; Bessant, 1995; Gordon, 1992). While this comparative approach is welcome, insufficient attention is given to the mechanisms which facilitate the cross-fertilisation of ideas between countries. This account considers the strong links between British and American society, particularly with regard to the response of policy-makers to poverty, social divisions, crime and disorder.

Poverty, which is seamlessly related to a number of other intractable problems, represents a serious challenge for policy-makers in all modern capitalist societies, mainly in the context of urban communities, but especially in the inner cities and on outer-city estates (Wilson,

1987; Keith, 1993; Campbell, 1993). Since the rapid expansion of urban areas in the UK during the nineteenth century, and the early twentieth century in the USA, the behaviour of the poor has been a talking point, particularly the fear that this behaviour is contagious, and that the 'roughs' will over-run respectable society (Morris, 1994; Katz, 1993). Without wishing to oversimplify two centuries of accumulated human experience as a glib observation, one of the most enduring themes has been the various attempts of policy-makers to understand and change the actions and circumstances of the individuals concentrated in these poor communities.

Crime and public disorder

Few topics cause more concern for governments and those who elect them than rising crime and disorder and, unlike poverty, nobody seriously disputes their reality and the extreme suffering they sometimes cause, particularly to the most vulnerable members of society (Donnsion, 1998). Official measurements show that crime rates increased dramatically between the 1950s and 1980s both in the US (US Department of Justice, 1993) and the UK (Home Office, 1998; Mirrlees-Black *et al.*, 1996). Due to the different ways in which crime is measured in different countries it is difficult to make international comparisons. What we do know about 18 countries, including Western Europe, the United States and Japan, is that they all experienced significant increases between 1987 and 1995. Indeed the figure for England and Wales (31 per cent) was the highest. Since 1995 there has been a reduction in two thirds of these countries. Although there has been a decline for some offences, the opposite is true for others. However, there is not time and space to dwell on the issues associated with crime statistics.

Instead, the preoccupation in this case is with riots and public disorder which seem to cause more concern than the mundane reality of most petty and not-so-petty crimes. It is also clear that there is a strong association between the intensive and insensitive policing of crime in certain poor locales, which on many occasions has resulted in urban unrest. In other words crime and disorder are interrelated (Waddington, 1992; King and Brearley, 1996). It was probably the Los Angeles riots in 1992 in the aftermath of the Rodney King affair which symbolised a long history of disastrous relations between the police and the poorest members of society. This episode apparently had resonance at a global level, and similar outbreaks of hostility between the police and poor were expected in other parts of the world, especially the UK (Keith, 1993: 254).

Significantly, the view that there is an association between these developments and poverty is widely held, although the explanations given for this relationship are varied and indeed sometimes contradictory (Pitts and Hope, 1998: 38–40; Cook, 1997). It is shown that the intellectual and practical response to these dilemmas is also characterised by a lack of agreement about the appropriate ways in which these problems should be tackled by the police. In this book the role of the police service or force is examined in relation to the political, economic and social context in which it is situated.

The police and policing

Bayley (1994) in the US, and Morgan and Newburn (1997) in the UK, provide accounts of the reform of the police service in the late twentieth century and the implications of these changes for the future of policing in these respective countries. They refer to the connection between poverty, crime and policing and the transformation of the welfare state, but their necessarily narrow focus precludes any detailed analysis of this dynamic relationship. This contribution opens up a different line of inquiry by exploring the police service's changing role in relation to other agencies within the welfare state.

Before going any further, there is an important semantic issue which needs to be addressed squarely, namely the distinction between the terms *police* and *policing* (Francis, Davies and Jupp, 1997: 5). Following Reiner's (1997: 1003–8) characterisation, the former refers to the specialised, formal state apparatus, endowed with the legitimate use of force, which is responsible for maintaining public order, controlling crime and various other quasi-social service tasks. The inception of the Metropolitan Police in the UK in 1829 by Sir Robert Peel is in some ways the archetypal model of police, and although its development in this setting clearly has a different history to that found in other parts of the world, there are some commonalities. Indeed the international dimension to studies of policing is at the forefront of analysis because similar trends affect all modern industrial societies (Brodeur, 1995; Mawby, 1990; Della Porta and Reiter, 1998). The mandate of police organisations is always being contested and there is little, if any, consensus on what it is or should be, but most discussions fall back onto two broad but symbiotic tasks (Bayley, 1994; Morgan and Newburn, 1997). On the one hand, the police are required to keep the peace and maintain public tranquillity. On the other hand, their job is to either prevent and detect crime or engage in crime-fighting. If anything, histories of the police tell us that the latter is much more difficult to achieve and indeed is an unrealistic objective (Morgan and Newburn, 1997: 202). Moreover, if the second task is prioritised above the first there are potentially calamitous consequences, such as the riots in the US during the 1960s which culminated in the LA riots in 1992 (Kerner, 1968; Davis, 1992; Srinvas, 1992; Yang, 1992), and the unrest in the UK since the 1980s (Scarman, 1981; Home Office, 1993a; Campbell, 1993). These issues are investigated more fully in due course.

The notion of *policing* is equated with the more nebulous notion of social control which 'connotes efforts to provide security through surveillance and the threat of sanctioning' (Reiner, 1997: 1003). This definition is elaborated by exploring how the police work with other state agencies – as well as players from local government, the informal and voluntary sectors – in performing these and a multiplicity of other tasks. The role of the police and policing in the twenty-first century is likely to have more in common with eighteenth century German notions of 'police science' *(polizeiwissenschaft)*, in which the police do more than fight crime and maintain public order, especially through their work with other agencies (Dean, 1994: 184–5). A key debate here is should the *police* alone, or this specialist organisation along with other agencies, be responsible for *policing* poverty. Of critical importance is the growing influence of American ideas about policing ('zero-tolerance' policing, for example) on the British police force, despite the different social problems that they experience.

Defining the field

This book investigates the policing of urban poverty by exploring critically the relationship between the different phenomena outlined above, especially how the links between them change across time and space. This narrative is thus written from an historical and comparative perspective, focusing specifically on the emergence of poverty, crime and the urban problem and the new police in nineteenth-century England (Graham and Clarke, 1996). This is more than just an academic exercise because contemporary discourses on poverty frequently refer to the past to justify present courses of action. Moreover, an attempt is made to come to terms with the view that 'what happens in the US will also happen in the UK.'

Regarding poverty, it is not unusual to hear that there is nothing new to say about the issue. For example, the English novelist, Martin Amis (1995: 171), has written that: 'Poverty said the same thing, century after century, but in different kinds of sentences.' The account that follows

tells an altogether different story. It argues that there have been profound changes to the nature of poverty, and not only in terms of the
ways in which it is conceptualised, defined and measured (Alcock,
1997a). Early studies of poverty in the nineteenth and early twentieth
centuries, such as those conducted by Seebohm Rowntree in the UK,
noted the qualitative differences between poverty in rural and urban
settings. The same happened in other parts of the world in the aftermath of the Second World War (Mingione, 1996: 7–10). In the twentieth century the main difference is the nature of the political response to
poverty, especially the forging of a new consensus on what is to be
done. At one time there were clear differences between the reaction of
those on the political left and right respectively, but this distinction no
longer holds, if it ever really did (Giddens, 1994).

To achieve the above objectives a disparate range of journalistic and
academic accounts, as well as some practitioners' – mainly senior police
officers – perspectives on the relationship between crime, social divisions, disorder and poverty are synthesised. By drawing on concrete
empirical examples the various responses of policy-makers to these
problems are analysed. The main focus is on some of the conflicts that
exist between central government and other key players involved in the
police policy-making process. This follows Reiner's prescription for
future analyses of the police:

> what is needed is more synthesis of research, not only in general
> texts (which has been attempted), but in general terms of projects
> relating themselves to broader theoretical issues as well as empirical
> work (Reiner, 1992a: 491).

In accord with this appraisal the policy implications of urban poverty
and the 'underclass' for the police and policing, requires more theoretical as well as substantive work.

The nature of the relationship between poverty, crime and policing
has been contested for a long time (Cook, 1997), but few authors have
addressed squarely, and at any length, the policy implications of this
controversy. Much of the empirical data used is based on developments
in policing in the UK, but thinking about both poverty and police policy has universal characteristics which transcend particular societies,
although contextually specific factors are of prime importance in the
last analysis. Bayley (1996: 40) has rightly pointed out that there is an
'international professional culture' and a fairly incestuous relationship
between 'flagship forces' such as the Los Angeles Police Department

(LAPD) and the New York Police Department (NYPD) in the US and London's Metropolitan Police (MP) in the UK. The case of 'zero tolerance' attests to this (Hopkins-Burke, 1998; Dennis, 1997). These issues are examined in Chapter 9.

Policing poverty – an interdisciplinary inquiry

Most studies have concentrated on the linkages between poverty and the welfare state and in doing so they have neglected the activities of the police service. Social policy has been chiefly concerned with the fields of health (including personal social services), income maintenance (social security and employment policy), education and housing (Hill, 1997). The omission of the police service is surprising because the operations of this organisation and the welfare state – and more specifically the academic disciplines of social policy and criminology – are in many ways inextricably related (Jones-Finer and Nellis, 1998). Hill has attempted to explain the lack of a connection between these two disciplines:

> internal law-and-order issues are only sometimes included ... [and defined as social welfare ones] ... and then only inasmuch that they interact with other aspects of social welfare. The pragmatic reason for leaving them out is that they involve specialised areas of study with a large specific literature (criminology and penology) which is often not very well related to the central concerns of the social welfare literature (Hill, 1996: 15).

The above assessment is only accurate up to a point, and whilst criminology is undoubtedly specialised, it shares some common ground with social policy. Taylor (1995: 407; 424 n3), for example, has argued that the relationship between changes in the labour market, state benefits, crime and deviance may be a rocky one, but these phenomena have not yet been divorced from each other. He also adds that by implication criminology is 'insulated' from social theory and some of the main concerns of social science in general. According to Ginsburg, it may also be possible to strengthen these interdisciplinary links by 'theoriz[ing] social policy as functioning to deal with the problem of order, social integration and social discipline in industrial societies' (1992: 10). This is the stuff of policing.

Although approaching these issues from ostensibly different disciplinary backgrounds there is a gap which may potentially be bridged. A central argument of this account is that in order to develop an adequate theoretical framework for the analysis of the policing of urban poverty, the nature of the relationship between the welfare state and the police needs to be teased out.

The book therefore aims to consider the policy implications and practical consequences of these different phenomenon for the workings of the welfare state in general and the police service in particular. It is written on the assumption that for many readers the territory covered in this book is likely to be unfamiliar, so considerable time and energy has been devoted to integrating a wealth of historical materials to put these issues in context. This has not been an easy task and the sheer volume of documentary evidence relating to these topics is more than daunting. It is not possible to even begin to reflect on the deep-seated complexity of these debates in any detail. Instead some broad themes are identified which ring true throughout modern industrial and capitalist societies.

By revisiting the history books this commentary attempts to provide some fresh and novel insights, not only into old debates, but also for looking into the future. The bulk of the literature written on these issues has been written by social scientists in American and British universities, but some of these accounts have not considered the relevance of the often high-falutin theories to practitioners working on the frontline. If nothing else, this book is a unique contribution inasmuch that it explores the practical relevance of these issues by including practitioners' own views, which should be of interest to academics, policymakers and the generally interested lay-person. Chapter 6 includes the views of senior police officers about certain aspects of their role in the policy-making process, and also considers the extent to which it could be said that they share a corporate identity. Chapters 7, 8 and 9 respectively, focus on their perceptions with the regard to the policy implications of the 'underclass' for the modern police service. Due to the sensitivity of the topics that are being examined the identities of the practitioners – who expressed their views in private – have been disguised in order to avoid compromising them in any way. Above all an examination of the interplay of everyday 'common sense' (Gramsci, 1971: 323–6, 419–24) thinking with the high-minded abstractions of the academy is timely.

Finding a starting point to begin writing about any issue in pubic policy is always a difficult and important decision but never an arbitrary one. The basic thesis of this book is very simple but one that is often overlooked in the hurly-burly of politics. Since time immemorial human beings have not only attempted to describe the phenomenon they see, but also to explain it to themselves and to others, primarily by searching for a cause. The same is true of poverty and crime. Before even starting to plan any strategy which aims to tackle any given social problem it is necessary to identify and specify its nature. This sounds fairly straightforward but a cursory glance at any account of policy-making processes shows that in reality it seldom is (Ham and Hill, 1993).

Summary

In sum, most narratives which focus on poverty rightly examine the relationship between this condition and the welfare state. However, in the majority of these accounts the role of the police service is neglected, despite the strong links between crime and poverty. This gap is particularly telling considering that many academic subjects within the social sciences focus on these issues from an interdisciplinary perspective, and yet not enough has been made of this line of inquiry. The book puts the welfare state closer to the centre of the police's response to the crimes of the poor. Moreover, the emphasis is placed on understanding how different government organisations work together with private and voluntary agencies to tackle social problems.

The structure of the book

For it to be possible to think critically about future developments it is necessary to take stock of the past. In Chapter 2 some of the key debates and themes are put into historical context, by reflecting on nineteenth-century conceptions of poverty and crime, and by describing the role the new police played in controlling these phenomena. There are continuities and discontinuities between that period and the twenty-first century. The abiding influence of the legacy of the nineteenth century should not be underestimated, and it continues to weigh on the minds of those carving out the future of government policy.

In late-modern capitalist societies (Giddens, 1990), the exchange of information is becoming increasingly rapid and those of us who are fortunate enough to have access to the global, information super-highway take this for granted. In Chapter 3 the focus is on the ways ideas travel more slowly, over the course of centuries, and back and forth between continents. The main focus is the relationship between what has been said in debates about poverty and crime in the US and the UK. Although the primary concern of this account is the UK, some familiarity with major developments in American social policy is indispensable, because of the impact the latter has had on the former.

Chapter 3 provides a brief historical overview of public policy in American society. It shows that the poor have borne the brunt of policy-makers' attention since the nineteenth century, culminating in the publication of the Moynihan (1965) report. This document identified a 'tangle of pathologies' concentrated in poor communities, especially those with large minority ethnic group populations. In the last quarter of the twentieth century many of the controversies contained in the Moynihan Report resurfaced, largely due to the writings of Murray (1984), whose ideas won the respective support of Presidents Reagan, Bush and Clinton. The changes Murray's ideas heralded in American public policy have also proven to be influential in policy-making circles in other parts of the world, especially the UK (Morris, 1994). Since the late 1960s crime has been central to political campaigns in the US. At that time, as the Great Society programmes such as the War on Poverty were introduced, law and order rhetoric was also mobilised to call for the displacement of social welfare by social control, hence the ongoing War on Crime implemented in the 1980s (Beckett, 1997: 11; Hahn, 1998; Donziger, 1996; Currie, 1998).

Prior to exploring the political and practical consequences of these international linkages in more depth, Chapter 4 outlines some of the key landmarks in discussions about the poor in the UK in the twentieth century. Again, this is not meant to be an exhaustive review, but one which picks up on some of the more novel and constant themes.

Given that there are some continuities between past and ongoing developments it is also suggested that it would appear that social policy in Britain is heading off in some new directions (Ellison and Pierson, 1998). As noted above, since the 1960s, but especially the mid-1980s, public commentary on social problems in America has been a powerful influence on a motley crew of journalists, policy-makers and academics in the UK, especially those subscribing to a behavioural perspective. However, scholars within British universities, who generally adhere to a structural explanation of poverty, have been busy providing a critique of the general thrust of thinking imported from across the Atlantic (Townsend, 1996; Lister, 1996). Amongst their criticisms is the view that these ideas are not necessarily transferable because of contextually specific factors, relating to differences in social divisions and the policy-making processes found in these societies (Donnison, 1998). In the UK, the articulation of class, race and gender with poverty, and the other 'pathologies' entangled with it, are markedly different. Later on in the book this is illustrated with reference to some concrete examples of specific forms of policing found in the UK.

Chapter 5 examines the practical consequences of thinking about poverty, specifically the far from straightforward relationship between theory and practice. By considering the relationship between discourse, or language, and material or social, economic, ideological and political forces and practices, it is intended to show how ideas are embedded in specific cultural and institutional contexts. It is demonstrated how ideas are utilised in many different ways by individuals and the organisational groups to which they belong. To paraphrase Karl Marx (1970), policy-makers, as much as philosophers, not only interpret the world in which they work, but also attempt to *change* it. Thus, practitioners draw on ideas from many different sources, add their own interpretations, and use these guide-lines for social action. In the case of this book the focus is on the intellectual and practical tasks involved in the policing of poor communities. In order to do this an analysis of the interaction between the different actors involved in the police policy process is required.

It is noted in the preceding chapters that since the 1980s a behavioural perspective on poverty and crime won the support of successive neo-liberal governments in the US and UK; and even the partial acceptance of New Labour in the latter (Lister, 1998: 222). However, at other levels of the policy-making machinery there may be conflicting ideas and values which call the government's version of events into question. At the heart of this chapter will be a discussion of the tensions between social structure and agency, or action, for understanding everyday social life and constructing common sense knowledge (Berger and Luckmann, 1967; Layder, 1997; Gramsci, 1971). An account is given of what takes place at different levels of the policy hierarchy. Although this chapter contains some rather abstract concepts, which may lead one into doubting their practical utility for understanding and responding to social problems, Chapter 6 illustrates their importance with reference to the police policy process.

The aforesaid chapter takes on board three closely connected issues. It begins by introducing some of the different definitions of the policy process in general, and more specifically, it denotes how these relate to a more specific interest in policing (Ham and Hill, 1993). The second section describes the formal structure of the police policy process and identifies those individuals and groups who participate in the determination of policy at different stages of this process (Grimshaw and Jefferson, 1987; Jones, Newburn and Smith, 1994; Morgan and Newburn, 1997). This is done by looking at the various players involved in formulating police policy, including acknowledgement of the other public, voluntary and private agencies, which work with the state or central government. Following that, the third section picks up on the issues raised in Chapter 5. It provides a critical analysis of the different levels of the police policy process, by concentrating on the issue of power and the conflicts and contradictions this creates (Bachrach and Baratz, 1970; Lukes, 1974).

Chapter 7 describes how changes in the ways in which crime and poverty are explained in political and public commentary may have an effect at certain stages of the policy process. Of central importance is the increased disenchantment expressed towards the public services in general and the welfare state in particular, mainly through the influence of neo-liberalism and the New Right (Taylor, 1991). This type of thinking, associated with the strategies of 'new public management' and marketisation, has led to a fundamental transformation of the postwar consensus on welfarism in British society (Clarke, Cochrane and McLaughlin, 1994; McLaughlin and Murji, 1997). Here it will be necessary to interrogate the view that these changes are bound up, in no simple way, with the movement away from social welfare to social control (Cohen, 1985).

By recognising the increasingly strong bonds joining criminal justice policy and social policy mentioned earlier on, the nexuses linking the police service and the welfare state and other related public, private and voluntary agencies are delineated. During the 1980s there was a shift of emphasis, in which central government abnegated its responsibility for solving social problems, and the buck was passed onto the other agencies mentioned above. This is reflected most tellingly by state attitudes towards poverty and crime, which underpin its dual strategy of blaming others for social problems. Firstly, these phenomena are the consequences of individualised behavioural factors and characterlogical deficiencies, not government policy. Secondly, following the introduction of the 'new public management', the agencies responsible for policing the poor are required to demonstrate their effectiveness and value for money by reducing the seriousness of these problems. If they fail to do this, then this is not due to the failure of government policy, but of the bodies who are obligated to respond to particular social problems.

Throughout the twentieth century the notion of community was an important reference point for policy-makers in aiding them to marshal ideas and resources to police the poor. In Chapters 7 and 8 some of the different usages of the rather vague and woolly idea of community in currency in police circles are scrutinised (Fielding, 1995; Skogan, 1995; Reiner, 1995a). By expanding on the themes contained in the other chapters, it is shown how the different players implicated in the police policy process have used the concept of community to organise their activities. This involves considering the relationship between communities as they are imagined at national, local and intermediary levels, and how these different perceptions enable and constrain police-makers to police the so-called 'underclass'. An analysis of several concrete examples of urban unrest and the state's reaction to these episodes form the backcloth to this chapter.

Chapter 9 explores the continued influence of American ideas in the aftermath of the election of New Labour in Britain on 2 May 1997. The rhetoric of the new government questioned neo-liberal and behavioural perspectives on poverty – recast as social exclusion – but there are continuities in practice. An attempt is made to predict what the future may hold in store for the poor and anticipate how policing will be adapted to perpetually changing forms of urban poverty. Amongst the most notable changes, and despite the concerted efforts of policy-makers, is that some members of society are likely to be out of work for prolonged periods of their adult lives (Dahrendorf, 1985; Wilson, 1996a). History tells us that there is a link between being out of work and poverty. More controversially, there is some evidence to suggest that certain types of crime and disorder are over-concentrated in poor communities (Cook, 1997). Debate about the causes of these phenomena continue to be divided between behaviouralists and structuralists, although there are some calls for a synthesis of these not necessarily incompatible perspectives on poverty and social exclusion (Jordan, 1996). However, given the profound changes that have affected social policy since the late twentieth century, key players in central government have attached overriding significance to behavioural factors. At lower levels some senior police officers have deemed structural factors to be more important. However, these counter-arguments are frequently ignored, which limits the capacity of practitioners to respond creatively to what may become intractable social problems.

The book concludes by arguing that our understanding of poverty can be enhanced by building on the existing ambiguity between the behavioural and structural distinction in discourses on social problems. For political, ideological and economic reasons, American and British governments are promulgating some of the key arguments of the former perspective instead of the latter. This is reflected in their agendas for the future of public policy; but the new political consensus has not secured the support of all players involved in the creation and of delivery services. Some practitioners have observed that central government activity, and indeed inactivity, may contribute to poverty, crime and disorder. They add that reliance on the free market and the neo-liberal disciplines of managerialism are not necessarily adequate replacements for state provided socialised services. By emphasising a 'common sense' (Gramsci, 1971) structural perspective on these social problems, police policy-makers highlight the extent to which they cannot coordinate an effective set of remedies to fix the problems of the exclusive society without more assistance from central government. The history books suggest that this would be a step in the right direction.

2
Historical Perspectives on Poverty and Crime

Discourses on the twin problems of poverty and crime are now put into historical context, beginning in the nineteenth century. The general consensus in the social sciences literature is that there are continuities between the nineteenth and twentieth centuries. As one writer put it at the beginning of the final decade of the last millenium there was a return to the nineteenth century:

> The stigmatisation of poverty, the battle over public and private control over essential utilities, the hope that voluntary services can provide from charity what the state will not provide by right, the battle over centralisation. Though the context has changed, there are many lessons to be learned from studying nineteenth century controversies. Some of the lessons are in danger of being forgotten (Jones, 1991: xi).

By reviewing some of these controversies several constant and novel themes are excavated, especially the interaction of behavioural and structural perspectives on poverty and crime. A recurring motif is that due to characterlogical deficiencies some disreputable individuals refuse to work and that this choice leads to dishonest, delinquent and disorderly behaviour. This perspective is of limited usefulness, though, because it overlooks the structural constraints on social action. However, it should be noted that what we now recognise as a structural perspective was much more difficult to conceive before the incremental growth of the social sciences during the nineteenth century.

The general thrust of the argument is that throughout history ideas about poverty and crime have been used by policy-makers to determine the general form and content of social policies. To illustrate this the chapter is split up into three parts. Firstly, the main representations of poverty in nineteenth century British society are introduced. In the second section the discussion focuses on the issues of vagrancy, the Poor Laws and the ideologies supporting them. Finally, thinking about crime and the creation of the New Police in 1829 in London by the then Home Secretary Sir Robert Peel is examined. Originally this bureaucratic and professional organisation was established to prevent crime and maintain public order only in London, but similar units were set up throughout the rest of England and Wales in 1856.

Nineteenth-century conceptions of the poor

This chapter analyses the main conceptions of poverty, property crime and disorder in currency in nineteenth century British society, which were a response to socio-economic and political changes, especially the growth of industrial capitalism and urbanisation. The labels used to classify the poor at that time included the 'residuum', the 'destructive' and 'dangerous classes', the '*lumpenproletariat*' and 'vagrants'. It is argued in Chapter 3, that although the terminology may differ, these ideas would appear to be of universal relevance and are frequently reference points to aid the comprehension of social phenomena in other modern societies, namely the USA. For example, Macnicol has observed that:

> The concept of an intergenerational underclass displaying a high concentration of social problems has been reconstructed periodically over at least the past one hundred years, and while there have been important shifts of emphasis between each of these reconstructions there have also been striking continuities. Underclass stereotypes have always been a part of the discourse on poverty in advanced industrial societies (Macnicol, 1987: 296).

There are undoubtedly continuities but the perspectives underpinning these reconstructions change over time and space, and poverty and crime are represented in terms of an ongoing interaction between behavioural and structural factors.

One legacy of the nineteenth century is the distinction between the 'worthy' or 'deserving' and 'unworthy' or 'undeserving' poor and the 'respectable' and 'rough' working class (Graham and Clarke, 1996: 145–53; Morris, 1994: 2; Stedman-Jones, 1971: 151). The 'worthy', 'deserving' and 'respectable' include those who were poor through no fault of their own. Respectability is closely bound up with the work ethic, religious values – principally Christianity – and a sense of duty and personal responsibility (Briggs, 1988; Foster,1988). The 'unworthy', 'undeserving' and 'rough', refer to some of the able bodied poor and the wilful idle or vagabonds. Moreover, 'The association of criminality with the indigent underclass was axiomatic' (Gatrell, 1990: 251).

More pertinently the 'dangerous classes' were a perceived challenge to social order and needed to be pacified (Steedman, 1984; Emsley, 1996a, 1996b). However, there is the *lumpenproletariat* to consider (Marx, 1930: 711; Engels, 1958). Although this concept is not entirely incompatible with the other ideas mentioned above, inasmuch that it focuses on crime and the personal and moral deficiencies which cause it, there is a difference because the *lumpenproletariat* shares values in common with the bourgeoisie. It also erodes working class solidarity and works against the mobilisation of a revolutionary proletarian movement.

The 'dangerous classes' inhabited areas, like the St Giles district in London, known as the 'rookeries', and buildings called 'flash-houses', 'beershops', and 'low theatres' which provided harbours of criminality and 'homes for the criminal class' (Foster, 1988: 77–8; Jones, 1988: 5; Hollingshead, 1986: xvii; Rude, 1985: 125; Tobias, 1967: 251–2; Wohl, 1977: 50; Morrison, 1891: 141). This spatial or physical division was reinforced by the ideological and symbolic separation of the poor from wider society. Some Social Darwinists went as far as comparing the poor with the different racial groups colonialists had encountered, and they were sometimes categorised as a 'race apart' (Richards, 1991; Mackenzie, 1979: xxxv; Graham and Clarke, 1996: 148). The existence of mobile and rootless 'vagrants', wandering from parish to parish, in some ways contradicts the claim that the poor were concentrated in geographical areas, but they share other traits in common.

There is a lack of consensus about the empirical veracity of the existence of a 'dangerous criminal class', but it is difficult to deny the imagined threat that this group posed to the status quo (Rude, 1985: 125; Phillips, 1977: 287). This was not necessarily because of a dramatic upsurge in the actual incidence of crime but a consequence of more profound societal changes. Criminality in the context of nineteenth-century society can be understood as symbolising deeply embedded fears about social change and public order. Indeed, as Tobias puts it, 'crime, and especially juvenile crime, in the first half of the nineteenth century was the crime of a society in violent economic and social transition' (Tobias, 1967: 255). This suggests that crime in itself does not cause societal breakdown unless it is related to other crises in authority.

For example, journalists and social commentators at that time tapped into public anxieties about the 'residuum' or the 'destructive classes' who could potentially overrun London, and there were calls for ameliorative action on the part of governmental and charitable organisations (Stedman-Jones, 1971: 320; Wrigley, 1973; Greenwood, 1873). Probably the most notorious commentator was Henry Mayhew, who identified four different classes in his 'natural history of the industry and idleness of Great Britain': Those That Will Work, Those That Cannot Work, Those That Will Not Work and finally Those That Need Not Work (Mayhew, 1861: 4). Under these headings Mayhew included the 'rich, the poor, the industrious, the idle; the honest; the dishonest; the virtuous; the vicious – each and all must be comprised therein' (Mayhew, 1861: 3).

Mayhew did nothing to dispute the existence of a 'dangerous class', characterised by poverty and criminogenic behaviour, but he was aware of the multiple motives and forces compelling individuals to behave badly, ranging from the resourceful who use their initiative and vitality to improve their lifestyle to those who are characterised by 'mental imbecility and low cunning' (O'Malley, 1966: 59–60). Unlike many of his contemporaries Mayhew made it 'impossible for any informed person to ignore the social cost of economic progress. His Londoners are never "hands" but always "people"' (O'Malley, 1966: 21).

Later on in the century Booth (1887, 1902) split the 'residuum' into three groups: (i) the 'loafers', (ii) the 'feckless and improvident' and (iii) 'irregular earners'. He suggested the first two categories should be sifted out from the city of London and transported to labour colonies. Such action could be justified on the basis that this segment of the poor were 'undeserving' of help because they were incapable of self-improvement and could not be reclaimed by civilised society. Marsden (1976: 298) cites Booth's description of a 'savage, semi-criminal class of people composed of occasional labourers, street sellers and loafers, who should be harried out of existence'.

Similarly, in his review of theoretical perspectives on poverty, Holman (1978) mentions Joseph Chamberlain's preoccupation with securing the support of the 'respectable' working class during the 1890s. This was imperative 'so the oneness between them could be promoted, with the poor cast as the undeserving, feckless outsiders' (1978: 205). At that time most anxieties were directed not so much at the material conditions endured by the poor, but rather because they were an eye-sore to members of respectable society. Dean and Taylor-Gooby summarise nineteenth-century discourses on poverty in the following terms:

In spite of competing diagnoses and prescriptions, there appears in Victorian England to have been something amounting to a consensus that the 'problem' had more to do with protecting the integrity and aspirations of the 'respectable' working class and the 'honest' poor than it did with the afflictions of the residuum itself (Dean and Taylor-Gooby, 1992: 31).

Some of these ideas were taken up by formal and informal providers of welfare and moulded to fit their respective views of the poor.

Vagrancy, the poor laws and Victorian values

The emergence of these images of poverty and crime are now described with reference to the English Poor Laws. In the nineteenth century the provision of welfare was underscored by the ideologies embedded in the Old Elizabethan Poor Law (1601), the Speenhamland System and the New Poor Law (1834) (Checkland and Checkland, 1973; Fraser, 1984). The Vagrancy Act of 1824 is also an important landmark and this is examined first (Chambliss, 1969). After that the legislation of 1834 and the formation of the modern police are discussed.

Vagrants – a rootless and wandering dangerous class

The term vagrancy refers to casual labourers, those who are not genuinely seeking work, and professional beggars and tramps. The vagrancy laws have a long history, and although it is not necessary to dwell for too long on this topic, some familiarity with its past is helpful because it shows how legislation was adapted in response to changing social conditions in order to reinforce control.

Chambliss (1969) maintains that some of the earliest legislation implemented in the fourteenth century was a reaction to the decimation of the population by the Black Death, and the subsequent requirement for labourers to sustain the fragile economy. If vagrants could be deterred from choosing vagrancy and if their mobility was restricted, or even curtailed, the recruitment of labour by landowners would be much easier. Thus the underlying rationale was to deter idleness and begging in order to engender economic growth. During the fifteenth century, as feudalism was superseded by capitalism, socio-economic conditions gradually stabilised. If capitalism was going to succeed, any behaviour which potentially jeopardised the advancement of economic and social progress had to be suppressed (Beier, 1985). This accounts for the references to the criminality of 'vagabonds' in the statute of 1530.

> Whoever man or woman, being not lame, impotent, or so aged or diseased that he or she cannot work, not having whereon to live, shall be lurking in any house or loitering or idle wandering by the highway side, or in streets, cities, towns, or villages, not applying themselves to some honest labour and so continuing for three days; or running away from their work; every such person shall be taken for a vagabond. (Quoted in Chambliss, 1969: 58.)

The Vagrancy Laws were reformed in response to changing perceptions of social problems in the early stages of the nineteenth century. The rate of vagrancy rose sharply as the veterans returning from the Napoleonic War met unemployment and high bread prices. Many resorted to begging and stealing to survive, and coincidentally the publication of the first official crime statistics in the first two decades of the 1800s showed, in terms of committals, that the rate of property crimes was increasing significantly. As well as the war veterans, there were also mounting concerns about the problem of juvenile delinquency. Parliamentary debate, talk amongst social reformers and public commentaries alike, started to attribute criminal behaviour to poor child-rearing practices and the failure of pauperized families to instil a sense of discipline in their youngsters (Chadwick, 1842; Gaskell, 1968; Greenwood, 1873; Hollingshead, 1986; Kay, 1850, 1969; Morrison, 1891; Murray, 1929; Wohl, 1977; Wrigley, 1973; Young and Handcock, 1956). A Select Committee Report (1815) stated that two thirds of London beggars were in fact children and were 'on course to becoming the very worst criminals' (cited in Rose, 1988: 5).

Demuth (1978) contends that the 1824 Act was passed into law to confront these problems, mainly by giving more power and responsibility to magistrates by further codification of the law. Enforcement of this law by the police proved to be problematic in some English inner cities in the late twentieth century (see Chapter 7). The overarching aim of the act was to tackle the problem of 'unmeritable wanderers' (Leigh, 1979: 97), by prohibiting the telling of fortunes, sleeping rough, exposing wounds as a means of begging, collecting alms under false pretences, indecent exposure, carrying offensive weapons, and being on enclosed premises for unlawful purposes. Section 4 stated:

> every suspected person or reputed thief, frequenting any river, canal, or navigable stream, dock, or basin, or any quay, wharf or warehouse near or adjoining thereto, or any street, highway, or avenue leading thereto, or any street (or any highway place adjacent to a street or

highway) with intent to commit an arrestable offence (Demuth, 1978: 11).

For these reasons the Vagrancy Act of 1824 was essentially a 'criminalising instrument' (Archaud, 1979: 21).

The Act also permitted the search of houses, ostensibly because of concern with housing conditions, but in actual fact because inhabitants of these 'dens of thieves and infamy' caused alarm in respectable society (Rose, 1988: 50). It was suggested that the existence of lodging houses: 'clustered in the labyrinthine rookeries, linked by secret passages and roof top escape routes', corrupted youngsters and led to them to becoming involved in vice and crime. The rookeries of central London were also considered to be 'hot beds', not only of disease, but also crime, political agitation, unrest and the 'dangerous classes' (Stedman-Jones, 1971: 167). These areas were often controlled by unscrupulous proprietors, some of whom acted as 'fences' who aided and abetted their criminal clients. Following legislation in 1851 lodging houses were subjected to regulations, to improve sanitation, as part and parcel of a general campaign against these 'harbours' of epidemics.

In the fourteenth and fifteenth centuries the problems of idleness and the avoidance of work were of detriment to economic growth, and legislation was passed to minimise vagrancy. This was replaced by a more specific commitment to address the deviant and delinquent behaviour of vagrants, mainly because their 'activities were offensive to the state' (Beresford, 1979: 144). Punitive measures were introduced to deter individuals from becoming vagrants. However, over-reliance on legal codes failed to recognise how due to adverse socio-economic conditions, vagrancy was one of the most viable means to the end of subsistence, or mere survival, for a sizeable section of the population.

The poor laws

It is not feasible to outline in detail the actual organisation and institutional structures involved in the provision of poor relief, but only to identify the fundamental principles enshrined in this legislation. The Poor Law of 1834 represented a 'watershed' in English social policy and set a precedent for welfare reform in Edwardian society, and eventually the post-war Welfare State in 1945. One should avoid overstating the presence of continuities in the course of history, but policies implemented in different historical periods present a set of pre-defined problems which are rarely dispensed with entirely, although they may be approached from a different strategic vantage point (Hogwood, 1992:

18). Before discussing the 1834 Act it is necessary to consider the Old Elizabethian Poor Law (1601).

Prior to that there was not so much a Poor Law, as 'laws against the poor and the rights of labour' (Fowles, 1881: 55). In 1536 a distinction was drawn between the 'poor impotent, sick, and diseased people, not being able to work, who may be provided for, holpen, and relieved' and those described as 'lusty, who having their limits strong enough to labour, may be daily kept in continual labour, whereby every one of them may get their own living with their own hand' (Fowles, 1881: 57). During the Tudor era there was a shift of emphasis and the distinction between the 'impotent poor' and the 'able bodied poor' was made explicit (Checkland and Checkland, 1973). The former category included infants, the elderly and others unable to support themselves, all of whom had a moral and legal claim to their impotence. The latter consisted of the 'victims' of economic crises and the concomitant decay of village and manorial life. There were also those known as the 'wilful idle' who were only begrudgingly given any support, if at all.

The 1601 Act was established in a rural society and administered by local parishes, who built almshouses for the old and infirm. Relief payments were given to the sick and unemployed of working age and there were apprenticeship schemes up and running for orphans. There were difficulties in the delivery of services because the sheer number of parishes and contrasting styles of administration inhibited the setting up of a co-ordinated system (Jones, 1991). There were additional problems relating to settlement and concern that the Act produced a deterioration of a sense of duty amongst the labour force and a decline of moral values (Fowles, 1881: 86–7). Throughout the seventeenth and eighteenth century the poor laws were frequently tweaked to adjust to changing socio-economic conditions.

Perhaps the most important change before the 1834 Act was the Speenhamland system, introduced in 1795 as a response to rising food prices and the costs incurred by the Napoleonic Wars. Its primary purpose was to make work compulsory and a condition for receiving benefit. The system was also intended to foster passivity among the population, thus enabling the lowering of their expectations and also to avoid mass starvation. It was based on calculations and allowances for relief of all poor industrious men and their families. The rate was fixed in accordance with the price of wheat and the number of family members. The actual outcome was rather different and wages fell below subsistence levels, rural unemployment increased, and labourers depended on casual work to supplement their income. To overcome this dilemma the

'Roundsmen' system was launched. Under this scheme overseers were obliged to assign unemployed parishioners to farmers who provided work on the condition that they could fix a price of their choice. This solution deprived workers of their independence, was demeaning and described by some as enforced slavery, all of which sharpened divisions amongst the poor (Jordan, 1973: 11). Hobsbawm described Speenhamland as a last ditch attempt to maintain traditional rural order in the face of a market economy, but it proved to be disastrous because it pauperised, demoralised and finally immobilised the labourer (Hobsbawm, 1959). There was also widespread disquiet because this system was a burden on the rates and it destroyed the sense of independence as a virtue amongst rural workers. Above all, it led to rioting and unrest, and as a result of this collective action the need for reform was recognised.

The New Poor Law

This was confused, lacking coherence and designed to be benevolent and malevolent in turns. However, it also included a set of core principles, reflected by the more bureaucratic, centralised and uniform administration that was set up. It:

> provided the services of a leaky umbrella. Underneath this miserable shelter there were crowded maternity cases, respectable old people, children in Poor Law Schools, young persons undergoing industrial training, the sick, the mentally defective, the work shy, and skilled men temporarily unemployed (Clarke, 1949: 107–8).

The principle of 'less eligibility' was of critical importance. This undermined the able-bodied poors' dependence on outdoor relief by providing indoor relief in the workhouse. This institution has a long history and has played a central role in the administration of the poor via a process of segregation, surveillance and stigmatisation. Most crucially, the purpose of the workhouse was to 'moralise' the poor and curtail the inter-generational and intra-generational transmission of behavioural problems.

These changes were a reaction to the perceived failures of the Old Poor Law which, if not exactly encouraging idleness, did not motivate everyone equally, because the material conditions of those receiving relief were not much worse than those actually in employment. Concern was expressed that being in receipt of poor relief may be a disincentive to work, explaining the cultivation of the principle of 'less eligibility'. This was invoked to reduce the attractiveness of idleness by ensuring that poor relief did not exceed the earnings of the lowest paid worker. The view that poverty amongst the able-bodied was caused by individual behaviour permeated the report. It was also felt that the visibility of the poor could demoralise not only those who were not able to secure work due to ill health or age, but also pauperised workers. This accounts for the significance of the workhouse test as a deterrent, and the workhouse itself, as a means of surveillance to regulate the behaviour of the poor (Digby, 1989).

The workhouse and the concomitant test, although not compulsory, was intended to provide indoor relief for the able-bodied worker rather than the outdoor relief available under previous legislation. This aim was not realised and outdoor relief continued to be the main style of welfare. However, the workhouse was an effective deterrent and it became a component of 'popular folklore' that stigmatised the condition of poverty and dependency on publicly provided services (Fraser, 1984: 50). Although the principle of outdoor relief remained intact the workhouse functioned as a watch and ward to control behaviour. For example, it was generally accepted by social reformers that this institution could prevent demoralisation among the children of paupers through education. If properly segregated, they could be moralised and protected from any temptations that may entice them into criminal behaviour. Within these institutions a concerted effort was made to inculcate a sense of personal responsibility, and where this was lacking, disciplinary measures could be called upon to achieve this end (Johnson, 1970: 116–9; MacClure, 1965: 44–9).

Perhaps the most important issue raised by the 1834 Act was the movement towards a more state-orientated form of administration, which clarified the nature of the relationship between local and central government. This is noteworthy, because the settlement laws created numerous problems under the control of the parishes by the Old Poor Law. If a degree of uniformity of the settlement laws could be achieved, many of the advantages that could be obtained by travelling from one parish to another would be diminished. One difficulty was the potential for abuse created by the phenomenon of vagrancy. The move towards centralising services would remove the incentives which made roaming between parishes a sometimes profitable exercise. Although there would appear to be some problems with the New Poor Law:

> There can be no doubt that the allowance system, as it was in being in 1834, went to the root of national well being. In checking it, and in restoring the threatened spirit of independence and industry, the

Commission, preserved, if they did not in part create, the Victorian doctrine of work on which the most characteristic achievements of the age depended (Young and Handcock, 1956: 683).

Victorian values

If one considers the linkages between the the Poor Law and other aspects of nineteenth-century society a much fuller and more detailed picture materialises. The activities of government and the impact of legislation do not emerge from a vacuum, but are rooted in beliefs and values or ideologies. In accord with *laissez faire* economic policy the state should only intervene in the lives of its subjects to a minimum, because it 'dwarfs its men and extinguishes vital power' (Mill, 1962: 250). Legislation was passed to ensure that it was the responsibility of able-bodied individuals to provide for themselves and their family, and the delivery of state relief was only made available to those who were incapable of work. Given that unemployment and under-employment had not been fully conceptualised in the Victorian imagination, it was relatively easy to claim that individual fecklessness and idleness were the prime causes of privation. Because explanations were couched in individualistic terms, the possibility that the behaviour of the 'dangerous classes' could stem from destitution and political marginalisation was not an acceptable exposition.

During the nineteenth century the evolution of the Poor Laws can be partly interpreted as an effect of Victorian values.

> In summary, we can say that the mainstream theory of the Victorian epoch had three essential features. Capitalism was not a transient social order, it was rooted in psychology, a human nature of eternal validity. Capitalists and workers had identical mainsprings of action, identical interests in maximising utility. Finally, if each actor sought his or her own interests, and was free to do so, no social barriers to social movement existed....This was an order to harmony and beneficence (Bellamy, 1988: 51).

When discussing this subject, one must be cautious and avoid distorting and over-simplifying the dynamic relationship between ideas and social practice over time and across space (Sigsworth, 1988: 1–8; Briggs, 1988: 25). In the ensuing chapters which consider conceptions of social problems in the twentieth and twenty-first centuries respectively, it is argued that especially since the 1980s, more up-to-date versions of Victorian values have been rejuvenated to justify and legitimate a number of social policies. For example, there are parallels between the work-house and government programmes, most notably 'workfare' in the US and 'welfare to work' in the UK (Jordan, 1996: 6; Digby, 1989). But as Walvin rightly suggests we should not lose sight of the fact that:

> Any attempt, in retrospect, to suggest that Victorians can readily be herded into one moral camp is to do gross injustice to the remark-able diversity of outlook, the conflict of opinions, the continuing arguments about moral issues, which permeated Victoria's reign (Walvin, 1987: 136).

For example, the centrality of the family and the values of obedience and thrift are not essentially Victorian but fit into much broader Christian, legal and traditional doctrines, but during this era these values were revered above others. These were imposed from above by the state, specifically against the 'rough' working classes. The work ethic, including punctuality and time keeping were useful rhetorical devices to back-up stories about the successes of self-made men. The importance of self sufficiency and individual responsibility was justified by appealing to Samuel Smiles's notion of 'self help', which proved to be invaluable in sustaining the principles of the New Poor Law:

> The spirit of self help is the root of all genuine growth in the indi-vidual; and, exhibited in the lives of many it constitutes the true source of national vigour and strength. Help from without is often enfeebling in its effect, but help from within invariably invigorates (Smiles, 1958: 35).

It is recognised that the need for succour is potentially infinite and it is impossible to provide enough resources to satisfy all human needs. Thus the value of self-help was of utmost importance, in the sense that individuals should anticipate periods of need, and make provisions for such occasions. Smiles assumed that if the working class possessed money then they were predisposed towards the activity of 'spree', or gratuitous spending (Briggs, 1988: 16). For those who were not so 'thrifty' the poor laws and various charitable organisations granted some support.

The Charity Organisation Society (COS) and Friendly Societies were important in the nineteenth century, particularly their concern with the 'poorest classes' and their 'veritable cesspool of anti-social habits' (Wootton, 1959: 51). To tackle these problems they advocated middle class values, such as the virtues of thrift, self-help and independence which were carried over into the next century. In carefully assessing individual needs to avoid wasting resources, the COS differentiated the 'deserving poor' from other kinds of poor people whose predicament was attributable to behavioural defects and bad habits acquired as a result of dependence on poor relief. A correlation was also discerned between physical defects and various forms of anti-social behaviour. The blind, for example, were considered to be 'deserving' because they did not engage in criminal or immoral behaviour whereas 'mental defectives' were fairly frequent offenders.

The Poor Law 1834 contains several references to criminality, regarded as symptomatic of human weakness and immorality (Checkland and Checkland, 1973: 148; 218; 351). Although paternalistic impulses have occasionally surfaced, the theme of individual responsibility has never fully disappeared. Those unable to work, such as the physically disabled and the aged and infirm, received some aid, but the authorities differentiated the 'deserving' poor from the 'undeserving' poor. The latter comprise vagrants, the 'dangerous classes', the 'residuum' and other elements who are disproportionately embroiled in criminal behaviour. The possibility that material need, arising out of the institutional and structural failings of a rapidly changing, industrialising and urbanising society, may have been a causal or contributory factor was generally rejected. Therefore if crimes are the acts of flawed and wicked individuals, the policies which tackle the problem are more likely to be based on individuals changing their own behaviour, human engineering as employed by Social Darwinists or by strengthening the state apparatus.

There is a paradox here because nineteenth century governments were committed to *laissez faire* economics and minimal government, but the maintenance of such conditions was dependent on a strong state to cushion society from the worst excesses of the free market. Thus the crime-prone poor were a potential menace, if not to the social order and status quo, to respectable society.

Thinking about crime and disorder

In the nineteenth century, thinking about disorder and crime was indoctrinated with the ideology of *laissez faire* liberalism. Individual liberty was prioritised above state interference in private lives. The values underpinning the Enlightenment project of modernity were also of critical importance, and attempts were made to restrain the often arbitrary and barbaric forces found in feudal society, by appealing to the values of rationality and civility. For instance, the imposition of the death penalty and the transportation of criminals to penal colonies came to be regarded, in some intellectual circles, as too punitive and severe. According to Gatrell (1990: 248) this change of mind reflected the influence of this '[l]arge intellectual current' on the key players in the criminal justice system. In essence, crime came to be considered as a social rather than biological problem. The 'materialist psychology' of Bentham, for example, posited that looking for the causes of crime in individual wickedness and 'original sin' neglected non-genetic and non-psychological variables. It is at this juncture that so-called classicist theories of crime have been applied, albeit with hindsight, to explain crime (Young, 1981: 253–66; Roshier, 1989). These ideas have been set in opposition to the positivist school of thought which claims that human behaviour is determined by immanent biological, psychological or environmental forces (Ferri, 1913; Garafalo, 1914). The former perspective had a major impact on American criminological thinking at the beginning of the twentieth century.

It has been claimed that the ideas now associated with classicism are somewhat misleading because they impose an artificial order on a disparate group of ideas which were not originally formulated to describe crime (Garland, 1997: 15–6). However, there are some common themes linking eighteenth- and nineteenth-century thinking with more recent reconstructions of these ideas. The classicist paradigm rested on four assumptions. Firstly, the human subject is rational and can exercise free will. The social order, rather than being a Hobbesian 'war of all against all', is arranged on the basis of a Social Contract. Classicism also has a strong allegiance with the political philosophy of liberalism, especially the Benthamite and Beccarian view that maximal individual self-responsibility and minimal state involvement is desirable. Fourthly, disorder and crime is an 'infringement of a legal code', and is defined as such within the legal process, 'that is by due process of law' (Young, 1981: 259). To ensure that the law is observed punishment existed as a deterrent, and was meant to be consistent rather than severe. Cohen (1994: 72) shows how the *offence* came to be regarded as more significant than the *offender*. The latter, in Cohen's (1994: 72) words is:

> the creature of free-market economics and the abstract legal subject of jurisprudence. He or she is amoral. Biography and social origin lose their explanatory and policy salience. Instead there is ... [the] ... reasoning criminal who sees opportunities and weighs up risks.

Disorder and crime were also viewed 'aggregatively' and related not only to individual but also community responses to squalor (Gatrell, 1990: 248). Harking back to the work of Archdeacon Paley and Patrick Colquhon (a Middlesex magistrate and key player involved in the evolution of the modern British police service), Gatrell suggests that a combination of economic, political, social and spatial factors – the architectural design of cities, industrialisation and urbanisation – presented opportunities for 'villainy' without detection. Gatrell (1990: 251) quotes the Royal Commission on the County Constabulary (1839): 'In scarcely any cases is [crime] attributable to the pressure of unavoidable want or destitution; . . . it arises from the temptation of obtaining property with a large degree of labour than by regular industry'. This kind of thinking complements the principles underpinning classicist theories of disorder and crime, which show that there is scope for the rational human subject to weigh up the benefits of committing a crime in relation to the risk of being caught and punished. Certain precepts of classicism are in many respects similar to what is now known as 'neoclassicism' or 'rational choice theory' (Henry and Milovanovic, 1996: 127–8; Cornish and Clarke, 1986).

Although there were many conflicting interpretations, the criminal continued to be identified as an 'emblem of assumed social changes for the worse' (Gatrell, 1990: 253–4). However, explanations of crime tend to be polarised. On the one hand, criminality was considered to be a consequence of 'poor human material', and on the other, a 'moral, deliberate declaration of war on society' (Wiener, 1990: 224).

Policing and poverty nineteenth-century style

Numerous commentators have examined the policing of the poor in nineteenth-century Britain (Brogden *et al.*, 1988; Cohen, 1979; Davis, 1989; Gatrell, 1990; Hagan and Palloni, 1990; McKenzie and Gallagher, 1989; Miller, 1977, 1979; Phillips, 1977, 1980, 1983; Reiner, 1985, 1992b; Silver, 1967; Steedman, 1984; Stevenson, 1977; Storch, 1975, 1976; Wiener, 1990; Wrigley, 1973). One of the foremost authorities on the police in the UK claims that:

> Studies of policing in all industrial societies and throughout modern police history show that the main grist of the mill of routine policing is the social residuum at the base of the social hierarchy. . . . [The] . . . basic organisation and mandate of the police in an industrial society tends to generate the practical concentration on policing

what has currently come to be signified as the underclass (Reiner, 1997: 1010–1).

The above quotation taken from Reiner shows that in this literature the word 'underclass' has replaced other 'core images' and 'archetypes' (Gatrell, 1990: 253), such as the 'residuum', 'criminal class' and the 'dangerous class'.

Prior to the nineteenth century, policing was provided at a local level by parish constables and urban watches who were appointed by local dignitaries. It was a haphazard enterprise and although few generalisations can be made, the bulk of police time was taken up by a wide range of activities, of which only a few were directly related to criminality. Dean (1994) illustrates this when referring to the German notion of 'police science' (*polizeiwissenschaft*), an important principle in eighteenth century European societies. In contrast to the more specialised function the police would perform in later periods they performed a dual role. On the one hand they maintained order by regulating the 'diverse [and] heterogeneous minutiae' of everyday life, ranging from morality and vagrancy to personal appearance and dress. On the other hand, the notion of 'cameralism' was important, particularly its bearing on household economy (Dean, 1994: 184–5). In terms of maintaining public order, the administration of the vagrancy laws was their main task (Chambliss, 1969). In the aftermath of the Gordon riots in 1780 and several other smaller conflagrations the parish constables were proven to be not very effective in quashing major disorder.

This form of policing was sometimes adequate in rural settings but since the eighteenth century industrialisation and technological innovations resulted in profound demographic changes, especially the growth of cities like London. At that time it was not the responsibility of the state to maintain law and order, because social stability could only be attained by allowing the free market to operate without any limitations and restrictions. This world view was gradually subverted by the belief that it was legitimate for the state to intervene in order to protect the interests of wider society against the failings of the market economy. Although J.S. Mill's belief that the province of the state should be limited to avoid the infringement of individual liberty, some government intervention was required.

The high concentration of the population in growing urban conurbations and the changes in the organisation of communities increased fears about the side-effects of over-crowding, and its assumed causal link with hedonistic behaviour, industrial unrest and poor discipline, as well as vivid memories of the Chartist movement. Stenson (1993: 377) describes the situation well:

> Programmes for new forms of police emerged amidst demands for rational methods to maintain order and provide a predictable basis of reduction of risks and promotion of security, allowing further developments of an industrial order. In this sense, Peel's New Police could be seen as taking the principle of (disciplinary) control beyond the institutional spheres out in the other social terrains, like the control of the recreational habits of the poor and so on. This extended the sphere of government into hitherto ungoverned spaces.

It was at this time, and with some reluctance, that some state intervention came to be regarded as a necessity. As indicated in the above quotation, the establishment of Sir Robert Peel's Metropolitan Police in 1829 is one example. This, in part, allayed the 'respectable fears' (Pearson, 1983) bound up with an '[altered] upper-class perception of routine crime . . . so that it came to seem symptomatic of a deeper threat to the social order as a whole, stemming from the '"dangerous classes", the rapidly growing urban poor' (Silver, 1967: 3). However, it must be said that the instructions given to the Metropolitan Police were to prioritise crime prevention above detection and punishment after an offence was committed (Critchley, 1978: 52–3). Concern was also expressed in government circles. For instance, in the Royal Commission on a Rural Constabulary (1836–9) – signed by Charles Shaw-Lefevre (Whig MP), Colonel Richard Rowan (the first Metropolitan Police commissioner) and Ewan Chadwick (a key architect of the Poor Law Commissioner's Report) – the fear of crime was described as forming a 'state of slavery' (1839: 648), creating a sense of insecurity in the face of a 'class of depredators, migrants or resident'. Although it recommended that state involvement should be kept to a minimum 'the suppression of vagrancy and mendicancy . . . is the business of the government to suppress or repress' (1839: 644). This illustrates the extent to which the police were preoccupied with crime prevention and public order. Along with Colonel Rowan, Richard Mayne (another one of the first Metropolitan Police commissioners) regarded the preservation of public tranquillity as more important than any other functions. Indeed on some occasions the force acted as a quasi-riot squad and was deployed to quell anti-Poor Law demonstrations, Chartist insurrections and other uprisings. However, there were delays in achieving this. After 1829 there was also considerable pressure from police reformers to transpose Peel's model into the provinces to further the centralisation, professionalisation and bureaucratic organisation of the police and policing. In 1856 the Home Secretary, Sir George Grey, passed into law the County and Borough Police Act, which made the creation of constabularies in all counties and boroughs in England and Wales compulsory.

To realise the objectives mentioned above, the tacit consent of, and the supply of information from, the community was a prerequisite. The General Instruction of the Metropolitan Police (1829) stated that the police officer 'will be civil and obliging to all people of every rank and class.' However, this was not necessarily put into practice and some sections of the populus experienced differential policing. After its inception the New Police was met with hostility, not only among the working classes, but also among the middle and propertied classes. Police were resisted by some of the occupants of positions of power and authority because as an arm of central government they were considered to be 'not English' and having more in common with the French police. There was also concern about the moral calibre of officers and their propensity for partiality and corruption, and the notion of 'good character' became an important criterion for recruitment (Gorer, 1969: 215).

By the 1860s the presence of police officers was accepted by the majority of the population and became a familiar feature of everyday life. The 'speed at which it was accepted by the propertied classes is astonishing. The reason is quite simply that the new police served their interests in rationalising social life by controlling a working class largely unaffected by factory discipline' (Hobbs, 1988: 40). Sections of the working class population remained very sceptical, particularly those living in areas susceptible to a higher level of police presence, and 'the less respectable sections of the [working class] were predominantly at the receiving end of the law-and-order campaigns' (Reiner, 1985: 61). But by the 1870s the police were welcome in most working class districts, a development closely related to material changes. The economic improvements of the 1870s and 1880s were contemporaneous with a marked decline in the number of assaults made on police officers. Although a number of gatherings created potential public order problems these were relatively infrequent, and the majority of crimes were committed by the hungry, against people from the same milieu. From the 1860s onwards there was a decline of property crimes. In sum, at the beginning of the nineteenth century, Britain was considered to be 'ungovernable', but by the end of the century was in possession of a reputation for collective tranquillity. According to Walvin (1987: 71–3): 'If Britain had become, by Victoria's death, more law abiding and

orderly, as the crime statistics indicate, it was largely the state's doing.'
Below are some studies which illustrate these trends.

Police histories and the 'underclass'

Davis's (1989) relational history focuses on the thematic connections
between the experiences of two communities in London which
although separated by a century have similar histories: the Jennings
Buildings and the Broadwater Farm Estate. Both experienced 'discriminatory policing'; against 'Irish immigrants' in the former and a 'primarily
black . . . underclass' in the latter (1989: 67). The latter is mentioned
again in Chapter 7 which analyses policing in the late twentieth century. The Jennings Buildings were perceived to be inhabited by paupers
and criminals and it was generally referred to by both police and public
as a 'rookery' (1989: 69). Few of the residents were actually involved in
crime, but because they were imagined to be so, police strategies con-
firmed this. Because these negative labels underlay police policy and
practice, Davis argues that 'it was inevitable that all the residents of the
Jennings Buildings came to be viewed by those outside as members of
the "dangerous classes"' (1989: 73).

Political upheaval on the continent also did not augur well for the
maintenance of social order in the Metropolis. Colquhon proposed that
stronger policing could suppress the criminality and the revolutionary
potential of the 'dangerous classes'. Crime thus came to be associated
with an 'underclass' whose members exercised their rationality to maxim-
ise their pecuniary gains through minimal effort, and who due to
their political ambitions and aspirations threatened the social and political order (Gatrell, 1990: 248–9). There are other dimensions to police
history.

Cohen's (1979) article is an important contribution to the literature. It
is of great interest not only because it is a major addition to historical
writing on policing, but also because it stands as a theoretical touchstone
for later analyses of race, riots and policing (Keith, 1993). It has also been
utilised to interpret the policing of the 'underclass' (Jefferson, 1990).

Cohen (1979) concentrates on the gradual changes which transformed the nature of police–community relations in Islington, North
London, between the 1870s and 1920s. Policing in the nineteenth century was based on antagonism between bourgeois law and proletarian
street cultures, often involving violent confrontations between the
police and the policed. After the First World War the nature of this relationship altered as a result of the restructuring of the labour market and
the working class, changing patterns of consumption and the effects of

this on the creation of a new political economy of policing. One of the emergent trends during this period was a reduction in the level of violence achieved through a process of 'urban pacification'. Structural processes also led to the gradual disappearance of the street cultures found in the nineteenth century. This was also related to the replacement of the rough lower working class by a skilled aristocracy of labour. The latter included the skilled, who were incorporated into the labour market. The former, which consisted of the unskilled and the young, remained unincorporated into the world of work. Increased economic opportunities and trade union membership, coincided with the respectable working classes' acceptance of a police presence in their communities. As mentioned above this happened unevenly and some youths continued to clash with the police, but this was on a much smaller scale in the 1920s than in the 1870s. This, in part, was also a consequence of changes in the pattern of policing.

The police perform a combination of 'expressive' and 'repressive' roles. On the one hand, they provide community and welfare services and on the other hand, they are law enforcers. This repressive role is more formalised, because as an arm of the state apparatus the police can legitimately use force. These sometimes interlocking and occasionally conflicting functions generate friction. To illustrate this, Cohen describes how police officers are expected to enforce the law without favouring one group above another, exactly in the same way as the judiciary. However, if the principles underlying formal legal rationality and statutory norms were applied on the streets as in the courts, then there would be mass arrests. To minimise the obvious difficulties that would arise if every law was enforced, including the threat to public order that this would pose, police officers exercise their powers of discretion. In Cohen's words:

> While statutory norms were still routinely enforced in the centre, in the new heartlands of the working-class city they were increasingly used only as an emergency measure, to justify the last resort of physical repression. In their place, a system of informal, tacitly negotiated and particularist definitions of public order were evolved which accommodated certain working class usages of social space and time, and outlawed others (1979: 131).

The main issue, therefore, is the effect of changes in the labour market on working class communities and the ways in which the division between the 'rough' and 'respectable' is forged. The latter had a stake in a society, whereas the former did not, and their behaviour attracted the attention of the enforcers of bourgeois law and order. However, the police had been able to negotiate a notion of 'public propriety' which was acceptable to the 'respectable' majority.

The developments detailed above should be understood, not simply as the impact of the authoritarian state apparatus on the poor, but as a reaction to improved material conditions, which instilled in the working class a 'clear appreciation of the benefits to be gained from keeping within the law' (Walvin, 1987: 79). Although the state had laid the foundations for governing certain aspects of individual and collective behaviour, urban life did continue to be affected by poverty and the crimes of the poor, but criminality was separated from a belief in the existence of a dangerous, criminogenic 'underclass'.

Reconstructing the Criminal

By the latter years of the nineteenth century the extent and seriousness of criminality had been reduced, if not contained, symbolised tellingly by the presence of police stations and regular fifteen minute patrols in the 'rough' and 'dark' parts of town. The vitality and initiative of the criminal was seized by professional law-breakers and crime-fighters, leading to a marked decline in the size of the 'criminal classes'. This was largely an effect of the increasingly centralised, professionalised and bureaucratic organisation of the police. Contemporaneous with this reduction in lawlessness, the criminal was considered to be a feeble character who was weak-willed and whose delinquency and criminality was determined by hereditary and environmental factors. The overt moral significance which had been accorded to criminal behaviour was abandoned and explanations rested on the assumption that it was 'poor human material' instead of a 'moral . . . deliberate, declaration of war on society' (Wiener, 1991: 224).

Concluding remarks

A diversity of readings of a poor, criminogenic and dangerous underclass have appeared in various guises at different moments in history. In the nineteenth century these ideas were a reaction to the profound social changes associated with industrialisation and urbanisation. The growth of cities and large towns resulted in socio-economic and political turmoil and upheaval. These environments were also conterminous with the problems of property crime and public disorder. In Victorian society the 'dangerous classes' threatened to overrun respectable society. The cause of this was not poverty but essentially wicked behaviour. Govern-ments throughout this period approached the problem by attempting to reform the moral economies of the poor and through enhancing the means of surveillance and social control.

Throughout most of the nineteenth century policies were imple-mented under the auspices of the Poor Law administration in order to tackle poverty and criminality. This system, and the principles on which it was built, was not an altruistic or charitable expression but an intervention to repress pauperism. The New Poor Law (1834) stated that able-bodied individuals were responsible for providing for themselves and their families. The principle of 'less eligibility' was introduced to ensure that the position of the idle pauper must be made less pleasant than that of the independent labourer, however poor. Intimately linked to this was the introduction of the workhouse test as a replacement for outdoor relief, which had been proven to be unsuccessful in ameliorat-ing pauperism. The emphasis on individualised explanations of poverty neglected unemployment and the extent to which need sometimes played a part in producing deviant, delinquent and disorderly acts. Another agency would be needed to confront these problems.

Before Peel's reforms in 1829, the police performed a wide range of activities, but since then they have been expected to perform more spe-cialised tasks. The ability to prevent crime was important but the pro-motion of 'good order' and security became a priority. Despite a hostile reception the police were gradually accepted by most of the public and they also succeeded in eroding the seriousness of the threat posed by the 'dangerous classes'. The police were in essence a symbolic repres-entation of order and respectability and the majority of the population eventually consented to and accepted their omnipresence, but force could be exercised legitimately against communities which resisted their attentions. By the late nineteenth and early twentieth century, the level of disorder and disorganisation that had stirred up so many 'respectable fears' had been quelled. This was because most of the work-ing class had been incorporated into respectable society when they acquired the trappings of economic and political citizenship (Marshall, 1972; Cohen, 1979).

3
Debating Poverty and Crime in the US: from Moynihan to Murray

There is a view amongst many academics and policy-makers that 'what happens in social policy in the United States will happen in the UK.' The accuracy of this statement is assessed by reviewing debates which focus on the links between poverty and crime in America, beginning in the late nineteenth century. Then, moving on to the twentieth century, broad developments in social policy are delineated, beginning with Franklin D. Roosevelt's 'New Deal'. This embodied the belief that the government had at least some responsibility for redistributing income from the rich to the poor by providing welfare services, in the form of various means-tested programmes, social insurance schemes and human capital programmes. At that time Aid For Families With Dependent Children (AFDC) was implemented, a combined state and federal programme, which provided services for unmarried mothers to assist them with childcare. A landmark in the history of public policy in American society was the Moynihan Report (1965). This controversial account posited a causal link between the behaviour of poor families, especially units headed by lone female parents, and a 'tangle of pathologies', including welfare dependency and crime and disorder. These problems were disproportionately concentrated in minority ethnic communities, thus suggesting that there was a correlation between 'race' and poverty. Katz (1993), for example, has pointed out how 'race and sexuality became fused with the usual stigma attached to welfare, and African-American women raising themselves became the new undeserving poor' (1993: 11). Moreover, the causes of poverty were no longer socio-economic but located in the individual's psychological make-up. This led to the restructuring of social provision as part of the neo-liberal project of the New Right, who were pivotal in constructing a political consensus on welfare issues which rendered the distinction found in traditional politics between left and right redundant (Giddens, 1994: 23). There were economic and political causes: the oil crisis of 1973 for the former and the end of the Cold War towards the end of the 1980s for the latter. Equally important was the manifestation of the view that 'government is not the solution to our problem, government is the problem' (Reagan, 1981: 211), thus accounting for the description of social policy in the US in relation to the 'reluctant American welfare state' (Janssen, 1993). Instead, government expenditure should be cut by making individuals, rather than the state, responsible for their own welfare.

Since the 1980s President Lyndon Johnson's and President J.F. Kennedy's respective 'War on Poverty' and the 'Great Society' programmes – launched in the 1960s – have been usurped by a 'War on Crime' and 'zero tolerance policing', oriented towards regulating the behaviour of the poor (Piven and Cloward, 1993; Bratton, 1997; Silverman, 1998). As Simon (1993: 3) has observed, this trend is hardly novel, because since 'the Jacksonians in the 1830s to the presidential campaign of 1988, crime has recurrently been a privileged site in the American conscience for expressing deep anxieties about class, race, and social order.' However, there was a new impetus. Informed by the ideas of Charles Murray (1984; also see Gilder, 1982; Mead, 1986; 1992) Presidents Reagan, Bush and Clinton, have resurrected and built on some of the arguments contained in the Moynihan report, culminating in Bill Clinton's strategy to 'end welfare as we know it'. The emphasis was placed on the centrality of the family, personal responsibility for one's actions and, most importantly, the work ethic. Eligibility conditions were tightened in order to minimise welfare dependency by reducing government responsibility for providing welfare services. At the same time there were concerted efforts to include all 'able-bodied' individuals in the labour market, even unwed mothers. Thus the backbone of the United States's residual and means tested welfare system, namely AFDC, came under attack. Throughout the 1980s a behavioural interpretation of social problems, manifest in the form of the 'underclass', was popularised, particularly with regard to minority ethnic groups. It is shown that welfare reforms have been successful in budgetary terms but that the resultant, more restrictive, welfare programmes have failed to address the problems of poverty and crime (Beckett, 1997). The conclusion briefly sets up the next chapter which shows that some American ideas about social policy have won support in the UK.

American history – the 'disreputable poor' and the 'underclass'

There are parallels, as well as differences, between the provision of poor relief in American and British society (Katz, 1989; Morris, 1994). In the former the dominant political ideologies – for both the Republican Party and Democratic Party, but especially the former – were individualism, self-help, *laissez faire* economics, patriotism and the Benthamite principle of the greatest happiness of the greatest number. As Trattner (1974: 47) puts it:

> Since wealth was a primary source of happiness, unfettered self-interest and the accumulation of wealth (and property) was the ideal; the economic welfare of the nation was not a matter of predetermined policy, but one of free and natural growth.

American conservatives are also suspicious of big government. In the US the welfare state is a residualised safety net, based on selective rather than universalist principles, such as those which characterised the British welfare state (Katz, 1986). This is consistent with Esping-Andersen's (1990) characterisation of the welfare state in the US as 'Liberal', which means that welfare is closely related to labour market forces. Those in work prosper because they are able to satisfy their needs through the market, whereas those out of work are less secure, because they have to rely on the family and minimal state welfare services.

Unlike European states the American state was not so strong and was less centralised (Fraser and Gordon, 1994: 320). This reflects the belief that individuals are responsible for their own destinies, not the state. Thus, explanations of poverty rest on moral and psychological explanations which highlight deficiencies in the character of individuals. During the first half of the nineteenth century, for instance, the distinction between the 'able-bodied' and 'impotent' poor was moralised, hence the 'deserving' and 'undeserving' poor (Katz, 1993: 6).

In a society in which unemployment was inconceivable for the abstemious, able-bodied and assiduous, those individuals who had not secured employment were 'voluntarily idle', and thus 'unworthy'. The social position of the latter group was a reflection of their inherent indolence, extravagance, immorality and other flaws in their character (Trattner, 1974: 51). The notion of 'moral blamelessness' is relevant here. The blind, deaf mutes and 'curable insane', along with orphans of the Civil War were 'blameless' and 'deserving'. In contrast to this group were the paupers who were held responsible for their own actions and also their socio-economic circumstances. This was easily legitimated because of the association of 'undeserving' paupers with crime and delinquency (Handler and Hollingworth, 1971: 17–9). Indeed crime was perceived to be seamlessly connected with pauperism. Matza links these ideas explicitly to the class structure of American society.

Matza's (1966) notion of the 'disreputable poor' consists of four categories: the (i) 'dregs', (ii) 'newcomers', (iii) 'skidders' and (iv) 'infirm'; consisting of immigrants in particular and various other groups of poor people. The 'disreputable poor' is equivalent to Charles Brace's (1872) 'dangerous classes' who live in 'regions of squalid want' and 'wicked woe' (Matza, 1966: 302). Warner and Srole's (1945) 'lower lower class', which rested beneath an 'upper lower class', is another reference. The latter are the 'deserving' and the former the 'undeserving'. Membership of such groups is not permanent and their make-up changes regularly because of frequent and relatively profound transformations in the economy, and the effect these transitions have on the level of unemployment. Also, because of behavioural problems the 'disreputable poor' may be a 'persistent' presence which makes the task of reform very difficult (Matza, 1966: 290–2).

Due to rapid social changes which have occurred in American society Matza's explanation is somewhat deficient. By focusing on the links between migrant labour and poverty, other dynamic forces underlying the process of pauperisation – such as lone parenthood, the concentration of unemployment in particular geographical areas and changes to the welfare system at state and federal levels – are neglected. More fundamentally there is no empirical evidence to back up Matza's claims that immigration creates the sort of class structure he sketches. Wilson's (1987) thesis – which is reviewed later on – implicitly refutes many of Matza's arguments, by 'link[ing] structural, social-psychological, and cultural arguments (Wilson, 1993: 22). However, some of Matza's insightful comments continue to be relevant, given Simon's (1993: 256) claim that the: 'return of dangerous classes is a worldwide phenomenon linked to the disempowerment of the industrial working classes in the face of a new global economy.'

As shown in Chapter 2 similar terms were used in Victorian Britain to assess the merit and desert of the poor to those used in America, but their practical consequences are different because of their distinctive welfare systems. What is the relationship between these discourses on poverty and public policy in the US?

From poor relief to the 'War on Poverty'

To trace the evolution of public assistance in America, one must begin in the nineteenth century and then move on to the 'crisis of welfare' associated with public assistance programmes such as the Aid to Dependent Children (ADC) – which following the Social Security Act of 1935 became Aid to Families with Dependent Children (AFDC) – and the controversies associated with the 'War on Poverty' in the 1960s (Moynihan, 1969).

Since the nineteenth century there has been the gradual development of a 'two-track' welfare system in the United States. Programmes in the 'first track' are based on the contributory principle, such as unemployment benefits and pensions, and ear-marked wage reductions. The 'second track', consisting of public assistance programmes, funded out of general tax revenues, were originally implemented to keep Southern blacks dependent on low wages. This system has proven to be significant in reinforcing the distinction between the 'deserving' and 'undeserving' poor (Fraser and Gordon, 1994: 321–2).

The hegemonic social and political groups at that time created conditions under which public policy-makers could absolve any responsibility for the 'casualties of capitalism'. Handler and Hollingworth (1971) show that in Wisconsin, for example, there was poor relief, in principle, but the actual provision of assistance was inconsistent and dependent upon administrative discretion. Concerted efforts were made to ensure that relief was not expected automatically as a right to avoid undermining self-responsibility. The administration of public policy was centralised and rationalised, and there was a move away from the provision of relief at the level of the town to the county; hence the County Poorhouse Act, 1824. These almshouses, alternatively known as 'poor farms' and 'infirmaries', accommodated the old, young, sane, insane, epileptics, feeble minded, blind, alcoholic, the hardened criminal and juvenile delinquent (Monkonnen, 1993: 343).

Children in particular were perceived to be susceptible to becoming paupers and engaging in criminal behaviour. Following the Civil War there was an increase in the number of orphans, and at the same time, the Child Saving Movement was founded. Children, who were once considered to be entirely blameworthy, became blameless. The cause of the problem was no longer interpreted as hereditary, but misfortune instead. They were also regarded as 'pre-delinquent' and amenable to treatment. This, as well as other factors, led to the provision of Aid for Dependent Children (ADC) which, among other things, aimed to prevent children embarking on a delinquent career (Handler and Hollingworth, 1971: 20–6).

The status of the child's mother was also important, hence the distinction between mothers who were widowed; the 'deserving', and those who had not married; the 'undeserving'. The latter were expected to work and provide support for themselves and their children. If the mother failed to find a job, and assistance was not made available from elsewhere, her children were then institutionalised in public sector hostels or foster homes.

At a federal level the Quincey Report on American Public Relief (1821) and the Yates Report (1824) vocalised concerns about the workings of poor relief, especially its impact on the character of the voluntary idle. The values held by this minority group were the antithesis of those cherished by the religious and respectable majority. Until the 1870s the provision of outdoor relief, which was regarded as a disincentive to industriousness, exceeded indoor relief, but this was gradually reversed thereafter (Morris, 1994: 59–60).

Continuities in the twentieth century

There were many other changes to the American welfare system and it is beyond the scope of this review to mention all of these (see Katz, 1993 for a full discussion). The programme which represents – especially for Moynihan's (1965) and Murray's (1984) thinking – the 'basis for welfare explosion in the 1960s, and the contentious focus for much of the subsequent "underclass" debate' is AFDC (Morris, 1994: 64). This has been scrutinised in some detail elsewhere (Ellwood, 1988), and only a few background details are sketched here.

The AFDC, an afterthought to the Social Security Act (1935), was initially a residual programme. It was introduced to provide short-term assistance to widows, intended to be replaced by a social insurance scheme. It was jointly funded by a matched contribution of federal and state governments, although the poorer states were given some additional support where necessary. Later on, its coverage was extended to cater for other populations. The main difficulty was that despite more prosperity and a reduction in the number of people registered as poor, there were also more AFDC beneficiaries. In 1936 there were 0.5 million recipients, but by 1973 the case-load was in the region of 12.5 million (Rein, 1970: 89). Due to a combination of demographic, economic, political and social changes there was an increase in the number of one parent families. In the 1950s it supported 110 000 families but a further 800 000 were added in the 1960s (Morris, 1994: 65).

Reviewing this period, Handler and Hollingworth (1971: ix) argue that some awkward questions were raised, concerning the issue of whether the AFDC system of relief was an example of the effectiveness and generosity of state welfare or indicative of a moral breakdown and anomie. Additionally the AFDC lacked support amongst the public and was an embarrassment to policy-makers. The Moynihan Report brought this to the forefront of public debate and created a sense of national emergency in policy-making circles (Rainwater, 1970: 408).

The *American dilemma:* the 'Negro' family, illegitimacy and 'disorganised matrifocal family life'

The Moynihan Report (1965) is the key document for understanding poverty in American society, particularly the condition of the black family, and it set the tone for later debates such as the underclass (Piven and Cloward, 1993). Although the root cause of the problems discussed in the report is generally considered to be the matriarchal family structure, or those units headed by the mother rather than the father, other scholars have argued that unemployment amongst black men is the main issue (Katz, 1993: 11). The report claimed that the impoverished black family was economically, psychologically and socially disadvantaged. Moynihan pointed out that the 'black bourgeoisie' (identified by E. Franklin Frazier (1962)), which had been co-opted into mainstream society was not an issue, adding only that the comparative success of this group concealed the level of disorganisation and disadvantage among those in lower-working-class communities. In other words Moynihan notes the tension, later elaborated on by William Julius Wilson (1978), between the primacy of 'race' and class as an explanation of poverty.

Moynihan focused on a group which came to be spatially concentrated in northern urban regions following their migration from the rural south in search of work. O'Hare and Curry-White (1992) have questioned the assumption that poverty is no longer a problem in the rural south, and they claim that blacks there are actually poorer and more economically and socially disadvantaged than blacks in larger cities found in the urbanised and industrialised north. However, in the north past experiences of slavery, discrimination and urbanisation are exacerbated by the inability of migrant labourers to find employment in these conglomerations. Within these communities Moynihan talked about a 'cycle of failure', which was echoed by Otto Kerner a few years later in his report into the aftermath of the Watts riots, when he wrote that the 'employment disabilities of one generation breed those of the next' (1968: 252).

The combined effects of poverty, social isolation, marginalisation and separation were causal factors leading to the involvement of young black males in various forms of criminal and delinquent activity.

Moynihan alluded to the consensus in the extant research literature which indicated that crime rates were highest in places inhabited by non-white minority ethnic groups. Additionally a number of sociological and psychological studies revealed a linkage between delinquent behaviour among black American male youth and mother-headed households (Moynihan, 1965: 84–6).

The disintegration of this family structure was linked to an unprecedented expansion of public assistance and welfare programmes. The AFDC (which as noted above was initially a residual programme) was overwhelmed by the burden of a rising rate of claims for assistance made by the black family (Moynihan, 1965: 12–14). According to questionable calculations the rate of illegitimacy had increased disproportionately in black families: almost a quarter of births in black families were to unmarried mothers, and eight times as many black than white families were headed by females. Only a minority of black children reached the age of 18, having lived for a prolonged period with both of their parents. This trend was not mirrored by changes in family structure in the white population. Thus the black 'matriarchal' family structure failed to conform to that of wider society and consequently the progress of the group as a whole was retarded, creating a burden on the black population, but primarily on black women (Moynihan, 1965: 45).

The general thrust of Moynihan's thesis is that the number of female headed households and the rate of illegitimacy are disproportionately over-represented in black rather than white communities. In other words there are 'race' specific connotations. The assumption that there is 'tangle of pathologies' inherent in the structure of female headed households underpins the report. In sum there are multiple problems, and explanations of these involve considerable tension between structural and behavioural perspectives, but more significance is attached to the latter:

> at the centre of the tangle of pathologies is the weakness of the family structure. Once or twice removed, it will be found to be the principal source of most of the aberrant, inadequate or anti-social behaviour that did not establish, but now serves to perpetuate the cycle of poverty and deprivation (Moynihan, 1965: 76).

Matriarchy is regarded as a problematic feature of black American family life, because this type of family structure makes women responsible for transmitting the culture through their role in socialising their offspring.

The response to the report has sometimes been critical and many liberal scholars were reluctant to contemplate its controversial claims (Wilson, 1993: 2). Even Moynihan indicated that he was aware of the politically sensitive issues that he had stirred up, and substituted the term 'illegitimacy' with 'no fathers' (Rainwater and Yancey, 1967: 162–3). Moynihan also made a sweeping generalisation which did not consider any historically specific or controlled regional analysis about the group he described. Further research in these areas was discouraged, and throughout the 1970s official measurements did not make any distinction between black and white lone parents. However 'race' and ethnic divisions remained an implicit item on policy-makers' agendas and by the mid-1980s they were referred to explicitly again (Brown, 1989: 64; Wilson, 1993). Some scholars also focused on 'non-black' minority ethnic groups, particularly Latinos and Hispanics (Massey, 1993) and Mincey (1988) has raised an important question by asking 'is there a white underclass?'

Public policy and the culture of poverty

At the time of the Moynihan report discussions about public policy were echoed in the academic world by Oscar Lewis's ideas (1968). Lewis's 'culture of poverty' thesis, and the closely related conceptions of 'lower class culture', 'low income lifestyle', 'lower class Negro culture', 'culture of unemployment', 'culture of the uninvolved', 'slum culture' and 'dregs culture', are all examples (Valentine, 1968: 13). Lewis (1968) argued that disadvantage is intergenerationally transmitted, especially when methods of child rearing fail to socialise children correctly to enable them to adapt to specific environmental and socio-economic conditions. In coming to terms with finite opportunities and as part of a survival strategy, non-conformist behaviour is necessary, hence the formation of distinctive and self-perpetuating sub-cultural systems. Valentine (1968) and Leeds (1977) subjected Lewis's thesis to detailed scrutiny and rejected the premise that the problems of poverty are rooted in the psychological make-up of the poor:

> it may distract attention from crucial characteristics of the stratified social system as a whole and focus it instead on alleged motivational peculiarities of the poor that are of doubtful validity or relevance. Several investigations of the problem of class cultures suggest the cultural values of the poor may be much the same as middle class values, merely modified in practice because of the situational stresses. The view has been presented that such putative lower class characteristics

as self-indulgence or inability to defer gratification are better explained by situational variables then by determinants of class affiliation (Valentine, 1968: 17).

Valentine is right to direct our attention to the structural position that the poor occupy rather than just the behaviour of individuals, because sub-cultures are a trait of all social groups, the poor and rich alike. The actual characteristics of these sub-cultural formations is not so much an issue of psychology, socialisation and individual pathology but of cultural and structural constraints.

The policy implications of these various contributions to thinking about poverty are now identified in the context of the 'War on Poverty'. Between 1964 and 1972 the Community Action Programme (CAP) was set up (Moynihan, 1969: xv–i; 75–100). This diverse assemblage of local and federally financed neighbourhood-based anti-poverty agencies was oriented towards relieving poverty by facilitating the participation of members of communities, or to use the jargon, 'maximum feasible participation'. These programmes aimed to benefit minorities and women, in legal and normative terms, but the commitment to tackling inequality was minimal. The failure of these programmes to create the conditions necessary for participatory democracy without compromising the actualisation of both participation and democracy was later cast as a 'debacle' (Moynihan, 1969: 203). In line with Morris's (1994: 67) review, the problems the 'War on Poverty' was designed to tackle had not been lain to rest, most notably the pathological structure of the black family. In Moynihan's (1969: 203) words, 'All this will be part of a past that has already shaped the future.' These words, probably for different reasons than Moynihan may have intended, seem set to continue to resonate in the twenty-first century. It is also worth noting that at this time the sound-bite 'War On Crime' was coined by President Johnson's Commission on Law Enforcement and the Administration of Justice (established in 1965), although it would have a different meaning later on under the leadership of President Ronald Reagan.

The 'underclass' – Moynihan revisited

In November 1995, Newt Gingrich (at that time the Republican Speaker of the House of Representatives) addressed Republican state governors in New Hampshire. In his speech he made a link between the murder of a woman and her children with the funding of the welfare state:

Now, a country which has this kind of thing going on – and this is not an isolated incident: there's barbarity after barbarity; there's brutality after brutality. And we shake our heads and say 'Well, what's going wrong?' What's going wrong is a welfare system which subsidised people for doing nothing; a criminal system which tolerated drug-dealers; an educational system which allows kids to not learn and which rewards tenured teachers who can't teach, while destroying poor children who it traps in the process with no hope. And then we end up with the final culmination of a drug-addicted underclass with no sense of humanity, no sense of civilisation and no sense of the rules of life in which human beings respect each other (*The Independent*, 23 November 1995).

Many of the problems Moynihan had concentrated on three decades earlier are reiterated here, although the 'new' issues here are those of crime and drugs (Davis, 1988; Beckett, 1997). Indeed it is shown shortly that the 'War On Crime' superseded attempts to solve social problems through publicly provided welfare services.

Throughout the 1970s poverty still existed in the United States, but it was a relatively short term experience for the majority of people (Garfinkel and McLanahan, 1986). Also at that time Wilson (1978) turned away from the issue of 'race' towards class and spatial factors like place of residence, to explain the differential black employment rates and the 'tangle of pathologies' related to this.

For several political commentators the arrival of the 1980s signalled profound changes in the rate of welfare dependency (Jenks, 1992). Anxieties about the pathological structure of lower working class cultures and subcultures also came into the minds of populists and politicians alike. Following an article in *Time* magazine (29 August 1977), Auletta (1982) introduced the notion of an 'underclass' onto the political agenda to describe a population of criminals, delinquents and the 'passive poor.' The existence of this group was purportedly an outcome of over-generous welfare benefits, which encouraged a lack of self-discipline amongst adults and the inadequate socialisation of their children (Morris, 1994: 81). It was argued that welfare undermines the motivation to work, contributing towards dependency on the state and eventually profound social dislocation. In certain respects Auletta's work, along with that of Gilder (1982), Mead (1986; 1992) and Murray (1984), reconstructed Moynihan's and Lewis's (1968) ideas. Rather than focusing on structural factors, they stigmatised the poor and 'blamed the victim'. The poverty of the 'underclass' is therefore a manifestation of individualised shortcomings situated in the culture of the lowest social stratum and some minority ethnic groups.

A disadvantaged ghetto underclass

Other voices, particularly William Julius Wilson (1987, 1996a) also gained an audience. Writing from a liberal and structuralist perspective, Wilson did not, initially at any rate, refute the existence of an 'underclass'. A superficial glance at his work could lead one into thinking that he is restating Auletta's (1982) and Moynihan's (1965) views. However, Wilson focuses on the real problem of poverty in the form of a structurally disadvantaged 'underclass':

> [the underclass is] individuals who lack training or skills and either experience, long term unemployment or are not members of the labour force, individuals who are engaged in street crime and other forms of aberrant behaviour, and families that experience long-term spells of poverty and or welfare dependency (Wilson, 1987: 8).

Instead of focusing exclusively on cultural and personal defects among the inhabitants of black neighbourhoods other variables are more salient. For instance, educational under-achievement in black communities means that opportunities for employment are few and far between. This is not only a reflection of a 'culture of poverty', but also structural and spatial constraints. The work young black males are qualified to do exists outside their own neighbourhoods, and due to the lack of transport and its cost, they are prohibited from taking up these jobs, even on those rare occasions that they are actually offered employment. This denial of opportunity is confounded by other economically determined restrictions such as the lack of mobility, and young black males tend to become locked into ghettos and are therefore isolated from mainstream society.

In his later work Wilson (1996a) refers to the 'weak institutional infrastructure' found in these geographical areas. Although there are informal relationships within these locales, like those found in the family, which provide social control, a 'strong organizational capacity or an institutional resource base that would provide an extra layer of social organization', is lacking. Here Wilson is referring to the absence of the church, voluntary agencies, schools, community centres and private business organisations which could exert a strong and co-ordinated influence on communities. In these neighbourhoods parents are frequently too over-burdened to socialise their children, which coupled with the absence of an 'institutional infrastructure' in the civil sphere, increases social isolation and the attending social problems (1996a: 64). In a similar vein, Jencks (1992: 123) has referred to the skills/spatial 'mismatch hypothesis'. This notion describes those places where the work available is exceeded by those available for work. Wilson's and Jencks's respective explanations are arguably more subtle than those found in the commentaries of conservatives, like Murray, who sustain an hegemonic image of an 'underclass', composed 'of people with serious character flaws entrenched by a welfare subculture and who have only themselves to blame for their social position in society' (Wilson, 1989: 182).

In contrast to Wilson's structural account, Murray (1984) focuses principally on individual behaviour and contends that the provision of welfare erodes the work ethic and fosters dependency and vice by encouraging male irresponsibility, particularly among black American men. Using medical metaphors he argues that welfare encourages behaviour which infects the respectable poor like a disease. This disease is spread by a minority of deviants and threatens to become the cultural norm in some communities, unless the government indicates that it is not prepared to tolerate their lifestyles. Murray also contends that the AFCD mother is not only a 'proxy' for the non-employed father, but that the system which supports her is a cause of his unemployment. For example, in the aftermath of the Social Security Act (1961), AFDC coverage was expanded to cover not only lone parents but also families with unemployed fathers, although only twenty four states did this (Morris, 1994: 64–5). Although it was not enacted universally, the majority of the twenty four states in which it was implemented were clustered in cities in the Midwest and Northeast where male unemployment and poverty was high (Wilson, 1993: 14). In 1970 only 1 in 10 families were claiming AFDC but by 1990 a quarter of families were in receipt of this benefit, and 50 per cent of families have spent at least some time on AFDC. There were also fears that the growth of lone teenage parent populations would lead to school drop outs and the reproduction of poverty. Above all else the AFDC was a manifest failure which had not resolved the problem of poverty: half of children in America are below the official poverty line and the poverty rate amongst lone mothers stood at 54 per cent (Waldfogel, 1997: 11–12).

Thus Moynihan's (1965) thesis – the welfare dependent mother is the key cause of male unemployment – is rewritten two decades later in different kinds of sentences, albeit with new nuances.

The discussion now focuses on a more specific analysis of Murray's ideas about single mothers. McLanahan and Garfinkel (1989) and

Wilson (1993) scrutinise the relationship between the weak attachment of this group to the labour force and the concomitant social isolation. They approach the problem by re-examining the enduring and complicated question of whether the provision of welfare services ameliorates or increases the intergenerational transmission of poverty.

Is there an 'underclass'?

McLanahan and Garfinkel (1989) reject the utility of Murray's 'rational choice' model for explaining poverty, which argues that people weigh up the pros and cons of particular courses of action and make a conscious decision to behave in a certain way. Joblessness is of central importance to their analysis of lone parenthood, but as Wilson argues (1993), non-participation in the labour market must also be related to family formation and welfare. This is necessary to explain the 'matrix of constraints and opportunities' which produces a diversity of behavioural outcomes instead of a single one (Wilson, 1993: 7).

There is another dimension to McLanahan and Garfinkel's argument. Like the Moynihan Report (1965) there is the implicit suggestion that the intergenerational transmission of poverty may become acceptable if single parent families are perceived to be the norm. There is a correlation between this argument and Murray's assertion acknowledged above that such values are contagious and can effect whole neighbourhoods. McLanahan and Garfinkel (1989: 101) postulate that the AFDC does create a number of disincentives because many women would be worse off in employment than remaining on welfare. They concede that there may be a small number of individuals who may fit Murray's portrayal of an 'underclass', particularly the 'one parent family formation [which] tends to focus on what is described as the growth of the proportion of out-of-wedlock babies, particularly among black women' (Brown, 1989: 65). For example, in 1994 'illegitimate births' totalled 22 per cent among whites and 66 per cent among blacks (*The Times*, 29 May 1995).

In the US there is a preoccupation with the 'tangle of pathologies' caused by deficiencies in the black family structure. This has proved to be a persistent feature of public policy debate on poverty. Unwed black mothers are the 'undeserving poor' who represent the 'American Dilemma' of an 'underclass' (Myrdal, 1964). Various research projects have questioned this generally behavioural perspective on these topics (Wilson, 1987; 1991a; 1991b), but in terms of the construction of policy poor female headed households have continued to take the brunt of the blame.

Since the 1980s the radical right have promoted values which shore up the traditional family structure. The importance of marriage and the two parent family, consisting of a male breadwinner and female home-maker, bolstered by Christian morality, have been consistently advocated by organizations such as the Institute for Cultural Conservatism. Concerted efforts have also been made to persuade single mothers to go out to work instead of staying at home. Attempts by the Federal government to eliminate AFDC as a supplement to low wages, and the enforcement of a work requirement in 'workfare' programmes, have also been accelerated. The long term effects of these debates and policies in practice remain to be seen (Harris, 1993). However, President Clinton praised an article in the *Wall Street Journal* penned by Murray as 'essentially right' (*The Times*, 29 May 1994). It is now appropriate to consider the policy implications of some of these debates.

The new welfare reform consensus

By the end of the twentieth century the already blurred distinction between the Democrats and Republicans was becoming even fuzzier, and it would appear that there is now a growing cross-party political consensus. In the field of social welfare there is broad agreement that through a policy of retrenchment, costs should be reduced, eligibility restricted and the behaviour of recipients reformed. The organising principle of the Republican reforms was to get the poor to do more to help themselves. During this period there was evidence of a growing divide between the poor and the rich, and between 1977 and 1992 the poorest tenth lost 20.3 per cent of their post-tax income whereas the equivalent income of the top 1 per cent of earners had grown by 135.7 per cent. President Clinton pledged in the 1992 Presidential campaign that the Democrats would 'end welfare as we know it.' Over the course of the final decades of the last millenium this project was achieved in three ways. As to the first, by 'restructuring social provision'. Secondly, as noted above, Murray, Mead and Gilder 'shifted the welfare debate.' Thirdly, a core project of successive governments has been to consolidate the newly formed welfare reform consensus (O'Connor, 1998: 51).

The Reagan years

Following the election of President Reagan, there were major changes in American economic and social policy which prompted policy-makers to question the efficiency and overall utility of state welfare. The main aim was to further dismantle the already reluctant welfare state and restructure the provision of services by reducing taxation and public expenditure on services and investing more money in defence (Pierson, 1994).

The 'restructuring of social provision' involved the process of market-isation, benefit substitution, modification of the form of financing, especially regressive taxation, and alterations to the administrative mechanisms in the form of 'New Federalism'. The Omnibus Budget Reconciliation Act of 1981 (OBRA) set about achieving this goal. This devolved administrative responsibility for the allocation of welfare resources from a federal to a state level, thus designating a more residual role for central government, particularly in the delivery of AFDC (O'Connor, 1998: 53–4). It was assumed that AFDC should only exist as a 'safety net' to assist the 'truly needy'. To achieve this, eligibility criteria would have to become more restrictive and people were given incentives, such as work expenses and earnings disregards, to find employment (Atherton, 1994: 272).

During the second Reagan administration, which commenced at the end of a recession, the then President argued that the amplification of crime and poverty was a consequence of the 'welfare culture' (Gross, 1982). These problems would be addressed by strengthening families, principally those in receipt of AFDC, by increasing parental responsibility for their children. The most momentous piece of social policy legislation was the Family Support Act 1988, which was the baby of the then New York Senator, Daniel Moynihan. There were four elements to this Act.

Child support orders were to be enforced against errant parents, and in 1990, the Child Support Enforcement Office was able to withhold the wages of absent fathers in order to collect child support. Secondly, states were required to develop Job Opportunities and Basic Skills (JOBS) programmes, which equipped the unemployed with the necessary training and skills to enter the labour market. Thirdly, child care and health care benefits were still available to families for a year after finding employment. Benefits were also improved by raising the earned income and childcare disregards. Finally, some families with two unemployed parents were entitled to claim AFDC (as noted above this used to be optional), but one of the parents had to work for at least sixteen hours a week in order to receive it. An assessment of the success or failure of the FSA is difficult, but it is clear that due to economic problems, demand for employment exceeded supply, and the JOBS programme was in competition with other welfare services. Also, work requirements and training alone do not broach the structural forces which produce unemployment (Atherton, 1994: 274–5).

Although there have been reductions in domestic spending and significant welfare reforms, one of the unplanned consequences of these changes is a larger federal bureaucracy. Moreover, states have not been given any extra income to help them to perform their additional duties. Despite aims to the contrary there have only been 'cosmetic changes in welfare'. Indeed Reagan's tax reforms led to a greater degree of inequality, although at the expense of the federal deficit, and between 1980 and 1988 the number of poor people increased by 3 million (O'Connor, 1998: 51).

There was not any social policy legislation of note during the Bush administration and he remained committed to minimising public expenditure. In the 1990 budget negotiations Bush said: 'Read my lips: No new taxes!'

The Clinton record

In his 'Quiet Revolution' in public policy President Clinton pledged to 'end welfare as we know it', by tackling welfare dependency, as well as crime and disorder (Glazer, 1995: 21). Over the course of his first term in office (1992–6) Clinton was involved in a struggle over welfare issues with the Republicans who had taken control over Congress. Indeed it was not until just before the national elections in November 1996 that the Compromise Bill was signed in the August of that year. There were continuities with what the Republicans had done, such as the concern with programme cost, the relative significance of state authority and family responsibility, as well as the notion of 'time limits' to reduce the duration of welfare dependency. The latter shortened the period of time one could be in receipt of AFDC, compelled recipients to work, and stressed the importance of recipients' obligations as part of the eligibility tests to obtain benefits. Clinton built on his predecessors' commitment to giving individual states greater responsibility by granting 40 states the permission to experiment with welfare reform. Also the Personal Responsibility and Work Opportunity Reconciliation Act of 1996 ended 61 years provision of federal cash assistance to the poor (O'Connor, 1998: 57).

O'Connor (1998) argues that Clinton's reforms consisted of three areas of change: (i) state authority, (ii) personal responsibility and family values and (iii) work. In relation to state authority, the entitlement status of AFDC was terminated and converted into a block grant called Temporary Assistance to Needy Families (TANF). This fixed the level of funding from the federal government and made individual states responsible for determining expenditure. To encourage personal responsibility a five year lifetime limit was placed on welfare benefits. Claimants were only allowed to receive TANF for up to two years, unless they were working. The five year lifetime limit could affect up to one-third of the caseload, even if women were working. It could also result in 1 million children being cast into poverty. States also had the option to impose harsher sanctions if they so wished. Unmarried teen parents continued to be high on the political agenda, and where deemed appropriate they were forced to stay on at school and live with an adult to be eligible for assistance. Mothers were also given the choice of co-operating with the state, by identifying the father of their children, or losing 25 per cent of their benefit. It has been estimated that this could push between 1.1 and 3.5 million children into poverty (O'Connor, 1998: 58).

The third organising principle of Clinton's welfare reform package was to end welfare dependency by making work pay and placing time limits on welfare. Building on the Family Support Act 1988 (FSA), the Work and Responsibility Act of 1994 (WRA) made employment the central goal. The overall success of this legislation depended on the ability of individual states to help recipients to find and remain in gainful employment. However, more cash was needed to make welfare-to-work a success, and more problematically, there was no money available to pay for child care for those women leaving AFDC. In Wisconsin, for example, welfare was replaced with an employment programme, 'Wisconsin Works', which stated that everyone except those with pre-school children under three months of age should work. This intensified the demand for child care and lone mothers could spend as much as half of their earned income on this commodity. The market rate also meant that mothers with especially young children paid a relatively higher fee compared to those with older children. Furthermore, states were not given any money to invest in creating employment opportunities, although if they failed to meet federally set employment goals, the welfare block grant was reduced (O'Connor, 1998: 58; Waldfogel, 1997: 14).

In sum, Clinton's reforms were implemented to tackle a multitude of problems. Consistent with the preoccupation with family values, the first goal of federal and state policy was to move lone mothers from welfare to work. It would appear that welfare-to-work schemes had some success, but it is not clear if this was down to other factors. It is also likely that benefit cuts will have a negative effect on the poor, due to the introduction of time limits, and also if there are no provisions to support those unable to work. Finally, the importance of job creation and the provision of child care should not be neglected because of its expense. It would initially be expensive, but the long term pay-offs would be great, given the potential savings made on the welfare budget (Waldfogel, 1997: 14).

Handler and Hasenfeld (1997; Handler, 1996) challenge some of the 'myths' which helped to mould the welfare-to-work policies of successive governments in the US. They begin by providing evidence that expenditure on social security is not the main drain on welfare expenditure, by pointing out that more is spent on Social Security Retirement Pensions and Medicare. Next, the young single mother is not the typical welfare recipient. Also, despite popular convictions to the contrary, the work ethic is strong amongst the poor, and people drift in and out of welfare and low paid jobs.

There are four obstacles to the likely success of welfare to work. In the first place jobs are not necessarily an escape route from poverty, because many people enter into low paid occupations. Secondly, lone parents are especially prone to poverty when they are in work because in comparison to two parent families they are disadvantaged, mainly due to the cost of childcare and because the majority of lone parents, who are women, earn less than men. A third problem is that being in employment is potentially damaging to children, because they spend more time apart from their parents. Lastly, employment is not available in some areas, and where it is, the pay may be low. Thus lone mothers are poor if they work and poor if they stay with their children (Handler and Hasenfeld, 1997).

It is beyond doubt that public expenditure on welfare between 1965 and 1992 increased by 800 per cent, but it would appear that its impact on reducing poverty has been negligible (Woodson, 1995: 6). Perhaps one of the problems is that 'the way the (current) debate is framed – "welfare" as contrasted with "work" – is obsolete and counterproductive' (Handler, 1996: 33). Disillusionment with social policy is now rife and criminal justice policy is seen as the panacea for America's social problems.

From social policy to crime policy

Back in 1990 a retired senior police officer described an:

> underclass... [of] ... sexually exploited teenage mothers on welfare ... illiterate, undereducated, unemployable. Drugs and alcohol are their methods of escape. They are unskilled and unpromising. Their self esteem is at rock bottom after a life time of being told that failure is their fate. They are victims of racism and are very likely to have been abused as children. Finally they've been shaped into muggers, thieves and vandals, and society insists they be destroyed. Rehabilitation

doesn't have a high priority in the midst of strident cries for blood (Bouza, 1990: 193).

Within the first few pages of this chapter it was pointed out that the work of historians of crime shows that these phenomena have been a major issue in American politics at least since the nineteenth century, a point which was not lost on those participating in the President's Commission on Law Enforcement and the Administration of Justice (1968). The late 1970s are a watershed period inasmuch that the rhetoric about crime and the rapid expansion of the institutional apparatus to control crime was unprecedented (Fattah, 1997: 5–6). Reagan and Bush successfully tapped into public anxieties and worries about street crime and drugs. Inspired by the work of one of his policy advisers, the right realist criminologist, J.Q. Wilson (1975) – and one of his protégés, Charles Murray – Reagan questioned the view that crime had any socioeconomic causes. In accord with neo-classical criminology, the decision to commit a crime is based on rational choices made by individuals with innate psychological deficiencies. Also dismissed was the view that state welfare could reduce poverty and in turn tackle crime. The central thesis is that people are responsible for their own actions and any attempt to blame external forces is unwarranted. In other words, spending money on the poor would be unwise and ultimately be a waste of finite resources (Beckett, 1997: 46–52).

There is a curious twist to this tale, though, because politicians were not averse to fortifying the law and investing more resources into the police, prosecutors and prisons. Perhaps this is not surprising since in 1989 crime was estimated to have cost the United States $61.4 billion, so some concerted action was called for (Zedlewski, 1989: cited in Taylor, 1997: 296). Since the late 1970s the emphasis has been 'To Get Tough' with criminals, which has been augmented by President Clinton's Violent Crime Control and Law Enforcement Act of 1994. Prior to being elected, President Clinton expressed views about crime and disorder which were in line with those of Wilson (1993; Sampson and Wilson, 1993), and he was critical of the Republican's decision to focus on the behaviour of the poor in isolation from their socio-economic location. For example, in 1994 Bill Clinton echoed W.J. Wilson's (1996a: 64) claim, discussed above, that the 'weak institutional infrastructures' of some communities needed to be strengthened:

> When Clinton proclaimed that 'we have to rebuild the bonds of society' with 'community development banks' and 'empowerment

zones', he referred [to] a revitalised 'civil society' – 'parents, churches and community groups and private business people and people at the local level' (*New York Times*, 22 October 1994 cited in Silver, 1996: 117).

However, Clinton's liberalism was short-lived, and there was an 'about-face on crime related problems', and the liberal position of the Democrats came to resemble the conservative views espoused by the Republicans (Beckett, 1997: 61). There was also an ideological realignment in relation to the crime problem.

Currie (1996; 1998) shows that as expenditure on welfare was being reduced the billions of dollars spent on 'correctional activities' climbed sharply. The number of people detained in federal and state prisons rose from 196 000 in 1974, 462 002 in 1984, to 1 100 100 in 1995. If local prisons containing people awaiting trial and those serving short sentences are included, then the figure in mid-1997 stood at almost 1.6 million. This means the rate of incarceration of Americans is 550 per 100 000. For African-Americans, the figure is 1947 per 100 000, which is six times higher than whites (Rutherford, 1998: 118). The fact that 33 per cent and 11 per cent of black and white people respectively are below the poverty line is overlooked by those responsible for formulating criminal justice policy (Sudo, 1994).

The introduction of 'three strikes you're out', means that anyone who has two convictions for violent offences and is convicted for a third offence, faces the prospect of a twenty-five years prison sentence. This may further expand the prison population, and it has been estimated that by 2020 it may be somewhere between 3 and 7 million (Rutherford, 1998: 130).

The evidence on the effectiveness of these 'Get Tough' policies is inconclusive and depends on the political standpoint of individual commentators and the respective criteria they use to evaluate success and failure (Hahn, 1998). Firstly, due to the existence of contradictory evidence it is not at all clear if crime has continued to rise, or decline, as the prison population has swelled. For example, there is the *National Crime Survey*. Since 1972 this survey has examined victims' experiences of certain crimes, and concluded that by 1992 the rate for most offences was not rising but stabilising (US Department of Justice, 1993). However, reports about specific crimes at different moments in time and space tell another story. For example, the rate of black-on-black homicides in some American communities, such as Los Angeles, where each year there are more homicides than in Britain as a whole, despite their respective populations of 3.5 million and more than fifty million (Mann, 1993 cited in Young, 1997: 478). Secondly, Murray (1997) has argued that even if crime is continuing to rise this may be an effect of previous policies, and the problem of crime in the late 1990s was a result of the reluctance of criminal justice professionals to give offenders custodial sentences in the 1960s and 1970s (for a summary of these debates and relevance to the UK context see James and Raine, 1998: 12–18).

The policy implications of crime and poverty for the police in American society are examined in Chapter 9 which critically evaluates the notion of 'zero tolerance policing'.

Conclusion

In the USA debates about crime and poverty have been conducted in the context of the 'reluctant welfare state'. One of the powerful driving forces is the work ethic, which does not entertain the idea that people may be unemployed. There is a tendency to blame the behaviour of those out of work for their non-attachment to the labour force, and to reject the suggestion that this may be due to the restructuring of the labour market and a scarcity of jobs in some geographical areas. There is a strong belief that individuals should look after themselves and their families' own needs and not rely on state provided welfare.

In Chapter 2 the evolution of the welfare state in the UK was traced and although there are some striking similarities between what happened there and what happened in the USA there are fundamental differences too. Firstly, the similarities. The distinction between the 'deserving' and 'undeserving' poor is evident in both societies, as is the influence of liberalism on social policy. There are far more differences. For economic, cultural, political and social reasons, American society lacks the kind of foundations of a welfare state which the English Poor Laws provided. Moreover, the already scarce services that were once provided are now being eroded. Also, poverty and crime in the USA is racialised and black mother-headed families have been blamed for most of the nation's social problems, ranging from welfare dependency to delinquency and violent crime. To address these problems individuals have been given the responsibility to secure employment and to pay their own way in life. There has traditionally been minimal state support for those who are unable to achieve this, but the eligibility criteria are rapidly becoming increasingly stringent, and consequently the size of the excluded underclass is expanding. Unemployment and poverty are more or less synonymous in urban areas, and although the relationship between both relative and absolute poverty and crime is complex, the two would appear to go hand in hand, especially violent crime and drugs related offences. Since the 1960s successive American presidents have given up on the 'War on Poverty', and marshalled their rhetoric and resources to fight a 'War on Crime'. Both of these wars have been lost and amongst the casualties are the homeless, the workless and the working poor and a burgeoning prison population. Meanwhile in the UK some commentators have shown that they are prepared to embrace American ideas, particularly Murray's version of the 'underclass'.

4
Poverty and Crime in Britain

The aim of this chapter is to outline discussions about poverty and crime in Britain. It emphasises the significance of some of the themes contained in the narratives reviewed in Chapters 2 and 3. First, although there are striking parallels between the nineteenth and twentieth centuries there are some newly emergent themes. Secondly, since the 1960s American thinking has had a profound influence on British policy-makers. Although, compared to the former, 'race' has not been as significant a factor for the latter, there are some similarities, particularly the influence of the behavioural perspective. The issue of family structure and the tendency to blame unmarried mothers for the crimes of unemployed males has also been at the top of the agenda. These assumptions underscored certain aspects of government policy-making between 1979 and 1996, but as the latter half of the book shows the structural perspective on social problems has won more support amongst some key players at lower levels of the policy-making machinery. Beginning from where Chapters 2 and 3 left off, this chapter focuses on some twentieth-century notions of poverty, the historical continuities linking these ideas to the nineteenth century, and the impact of thinking from across the Atlantic on Britain prior to 1997. It is argued that the distinction between behavioural and structural approaches for understanding the 'underclass' and poverty, needs to be made much clearer in the minds of policy-makers.

Poverty and pathology in Britain – the nineteenth-century legacy

Marsden (1976) acknowledges the legacy of Marx and Mayhew evidenced in the early twentieth-century notion of 'problem families'. This referred to a relatively small and socially disorganised group of families which were somehow left behind by the rising tide of respectability and affluence (Marsden, 1976: 298–9). According to Marsden, Stacey's (1960) work adds to the tradition of subdividing the population into several layers, including the 'respectable', the 'ordinary', and the 'roughs'. The first category consists of secure, tightly knit and privatised family units. The second shares some of the first group's qualities, such as the work ethic, keeping regular hours and paying their own way, but they lack other more visible signs of affluence and respectability. The family is central to this analysis, especially the importance of dual parenting for the socialisation of children. The issue of family structure is expanded later on in this chapter. The 'roughs' consist of those who are ostracised from the other two segments of the working class, incorporating the 'work-shy', 'feckless' and that highly popularised 'folk devil', the 'scrounger' (Deacon, 1976). What were the practical consequences of such thinking for early twentieth-century social policy and how do these relate to later developments? The next section examines the Eugenics movement and then changes in social security policy.

The Eugenics movement

This system of thought referred to the biological, hereditary and behavioural characteristics of the poor. In terms of policy, the solution to poverty involved intervening in the ways in which the poor reproduced (Barnes, 1977: 60; Macnicol, 1987; Wood, 1929, 1931). At a later date the movement's position was reappraised, and cultural and psychological explanations replaced biological ones. To address the problem of poverty and its concomitant 'pathologies', it was argued that household maintenance, personal relationships and mental health required improvement (Wootton, 1959: 56).

The condition of poverty, therefore, arose out of serious psychological defects in individuals who were situated in a particular cultural milieu. To eliminate 'social problem groups', individual responsibility and autonomous self-government were encouraged. Wootton criticised these accounts because they ignored the circumstances of particular families, neighbourhoods and individuals. The neat categories of 'roughness' and 'social problem groups' do not explain or describe the complexity of social reality:

we thus reach the near tautological conclusion that the proof of the psychopathic personality or emotional immaturity of a problem family is to be found in part at least in the characteristic behaviour which merits its inclusion in this class. Yet none of these labels – low intelligence, emotional immaturity or psychopathic personality – can have any meaning except in terms of criteria which are themselves independent of the behaviour which they are invoked to explain (Wootton, 1959: 62).

Wootton's critique is generally well based and it is difficult to disagree with the general thrust of her reasoning. However, in the case of establishing merit and desert in social security policy the differentiation of the population into 'deserving' and 'undeserving' populations is arguably, as will be indicated later on, not always so problematic.

Social security – the 'scrounger'

Deacon (1976) outlines the development of the 'genuinely seeking work test'. This was introduced to limit the financial burden placed upon the state for the relief of poverty during periods of economic inactivity. A common misconception is that following World War I social policies made generous concessions to the unemployed, but the reality is quite different. As in the case of the Poor Laws, many policy-makers were preoccupied with the negative disincentives and the 'personal demoralisation' arising from dependence on state-provided financial assistance. Fears that claimants would grow accustomed to the dole and that many of the unemployed were not actively seeking work to the best of their ability were also prevalent (Deacon, 1976: 87–90). There was concern that the idle would receive the same income as the active and that the former would come to regard their inactivity as a soft option. It was felt that individual responsibility would be eroded, especially the obligation to seek employment. The 'genuinely seeking work test' was introduced as a remedy, which required the unemployed to provide evidence of their efforts to find a job. Thus the principle of 'less eligibility' embodied in the Poor Laws was retained, albeit in a slightly modified form.

The state of the individual claimant's mind was also assessed by officials to determine whether or not they were predisposed to working or living on benefit. Furthermore, this enabled the distinction between the 'deserving' and 'undeserving' to be sustained and legitimated on the grounds that: 'The object of good administration should be to exclude the undeserving altogether, not cut down the rate of the deserving' (Deacon, 1976: 54).

The 'scrounger' has continued to be a popular image in media accounts in the context of the post-war Beveridgean welfare state, and other terms such as 'welfare scroungers', 'benefit swindlers' and the 'work shy' can be added to this list (Donnison, 1976). Such notions also continue to have repercussions on the administration of social security

(Howe, 1985; Dean and Taylor-Gooby, 1992). Howe addresses similar issues to those raised by Deacon in a study of a Social Security Office, by focusing on the assessment of claimants' needs. Although the 'deserving/undeserving' distinction is not explicitly mentioned there are other closely related, implicit assumptions. On the one hand, there are the 'greedy', 'grasping', 'difficult', and on the other hand, the 'nice', 'polite' and 'grateful'. Howe contends that the categories 'deserving and undeserving' are mobilised in discourse (though not necessarily in practice) to explain the behaviour of the poor (Howe, 1985: 66).

Research undertaken by Dean and Taylor-Gooby (1992) refers to a notional hierarchy which social security officers use in their day-to-day work to determine the pattern of service provision. The elderly are generally held in the highest regard, recipients of child benefit in the middle and single parents and the unemployed the lowest. The authors claim that: 'Implicit in public opinion are distinctions between deserving and undeserving groups of social security recipients. Attitudes to state welfare dependency, if they are not inconsistent, are somehow selective' (Dean and Taylor-Gooby, 1992: 169).

Some method of ascertaining the merit or desert of individuals has therefore been an enduring feature of social policy, and it is hard not to agree that it is necessary to lay down some ground rules to guide the allocation and distribution of finite resources. It is also arguably justifiable to criticise certain kinds of behaviour because full citizenship is justifiably based on balancing the mutual obligations and rights of the individual citizen and the state. However, care must also be taken to avoid the 'near tautological' reasoning Wootton (1959: 62) highlighted earlier, in which accounts of behaviour are severed from any wider societal context. The reasoning individual cannot always weigh up the relative advantages and disadvantages of certain courses of action under specific social conditions, and they may sometimes make the wrong choice. In short, there are individuals whose actions are rightly criticised, and the distinction between the 'deserving' and 'undeserving' is necessary, but there are many contingencies in social life, and under some circumstances these labels are too clear-cut and inappropriate. It is beyond the scope of this discussion to resolve this dispute here, which is something that still perplexes moral and political philosophers.

The 'underclass' in modern British society

The 'underclass', in one form or another, is a persistent theme in discourses on poverty and other kinds of social exclusion. The term itself was first coined by the Swedish sociologist, Gunnar Myrdal (1964), to explain poverty in American society. It has been in currency in Britain since the 1970s but was relatively unknown until it made the headlines in the late 1980s. Since then, numerous attempts have been made to define, measure and conceptualise the 'underclass', and although there is a lack of agreement regarding its make-up, the following phenomena are its main criteria: low educational attainment, a lack of adequate skills required to become a member of the labour force, shared spatial location, dependency on welfare, unemployment and under-employment or an unstable relationship with the labour market, pathological family structures and the inter-generational transmission of poverty, involvement in the unreported economy and a predisposition to criminal and disorderly behaviour (Westergaard, 1992: 576). As one can see, the 'underclass' is a complex notion which refers to many different phenomena. This, for some scholars, is indicative of its conceptual incoherence. In Morris's (1995: 132) view, for example, 'The common usage of the concept of an underclass in fact captures a population far too heterogeneous to constitute a social group in any sense other than receipt of state benefit; a civic status rather than a class position'. However, Morris recognises that there are other uses of the idea. This is an important point because some commentators, particularly those writing about policing, and some senior police officers, have used the concept of an 'underclass' to capture this heterogeneity, thus serving as a critique of the political economy and the hegemony of New Right and neo-liberal ideologies (Reiner, 1997: 1038–9).

The main schools of thought

Westergaard has identified three versions of the concept of an 'underclass', namely those of 'moral turpitude', 'outcast poverty' and 'rhetorical' (Westergaard, 1992: 576). For the purposes of this chapter Walker's (1991a) more straightforward distinction of behavioural and structural versions will be used to structure the argument. The reason for adopting this approach is that these two schools manage to embody the main political values which uphold representations of the 'underclass'. The political lens through which the 'underclass' is viewed is also an important factor in assessing its policy implications. Another reason for this choice is that Westergaard's threefold distinction refers to different ways of seeing and describing the 'underclass' rather than explaining it. Westergaard's (1992: 576) typology, though important, would seem to be flawed because it leads to the rejection of the utility of the 'underclass'. He suggests that if I am right the concept will not really hold up in either main version. I hope I am right in my impression that, as a fashion, underclass talk has been media-commentary-led rather than social-science-led. Among sociologists in this country, I suspect, scepticism about even the structural version of underclass theory has tended to prevail over enthusiasm (Westergaard, 1992: 580).

On one level of analysis the above assertion is essentially right, but in the same article, Westergaard (1992: 581) concedes that the idea of an 'underclass' will continue to attract attention, and so long as there is 'close testing by the twin professional criteria of consonance with discoverable fact and of conceptual coherence' it need not be rejected outright. Reiner (1994: 726), for example, has drawn attention to social injustice by arguing that policing is overwhelmingly concentrated on a structurally excluded 'underclass'. This kind of analysis may not be damaged by Westergaard's (1992) critique. To minimise the conceptual incoherence that sometimes characterises talk about the 'underclass', Walker's (1991) behavioural/structural distinction will be addressed more squarely in the narratives on policing addressed later on in the book. What is the significance of this difference of perspective?

Structural accounts tend to combine different types of quantitative and qualitative data to provide various indicators of poverty, material deprivation, social exclusion and patterns of inequality. The inadequacy of state provided welfare services, changes in the labour market, and exclusion from citizenship are the factors underlying 'underclass' formation. In contrast, the behavioural perspective as represented by Murray (1990) relies on impressionistic and anecdotal evidence. Such accounts hold the individual to be culpable for their own poverty. It is argued that the provision of welfare undermines individual responsibility by giving rational human agents incentives to not work and provide for themselves, thereby creating welfare dependency. Moreover, citizens treat welfare as a right, without recognising that responsibilities and obligations are the other side of the full coin of citizenship.

The division of poor communities along the lines of the 'rough' and the 'respectable' is one example of the behavioural approach. The former includes the 'undeserving', 'unworthy' and the 'disreputable' poor, and the latter, the 'deserving', 'worthy' and 'reputable' poor. The leitmotif coming out of these debates is that the 'underclass' is a section of the population which has become detached from wider society, due to a mixture of dynamic structural processes and changing patterns of individual and group behaviour.

Some old and new debates

In a speech made at Birmingham on 19 October 1974, the then Conservative Secretary of State for Education, Sir Keith Joseph, remarked that mothers in social class V (referring to the Registrar-General's class categories) should be held responsible for 'producing problem children, the future unmarried mothers, delinquents, denizens of our borstals, subnormal educational establishments, prisons, borstals for drifters' (quoted in Ward, 1989: 64). A £500 000 grant was awarded to the then Social Science Research Council (SSRC), to assess Joseph's contention that there are inter-generationally and intra-generationally transmitted 'cycles of deprivation'. Joseph attached more importance to behavioural than structural factors, arguing that deprivation is rooted in the individual, and that seeking other causal factors found at a wider societal level is futile. Rutter and Madge's (1976) review of the evidence stands as a rebuttal of Joseph's arguments, showing that the transmission of 'cycles of deprivation' was the exception rather than the norm:

> At least half of the children born into a disadvantaged home do not repeat the pattern of disadvantage in the next generation. Over half of all forms of disadvantage arise anew each generation. On the one hand, even where continuity is strongest many individuals break out of the cycle and on the other many people become disadvantaged without having been reared by disadvantaged parents (1976: 304).

Other commentators have focused on structural factors. Giddens's (1973) definition of the 'underclass' incorporates the low paid, the 'chronically unemployed or semi-employed'. Writing at a time when the UK capitalist economy was undergoing rapid structural change in the aftermath of the oil crisis, Giddens focused on socio-economic divisions in the labour market. On the one hand, there is a relatively secure 'core' group of workers, and on the other, an insecure and low paid group that is peripheral to the world of work. In addition to this structural dimension, Giddens also refers to cultural factors such as ethnicity, thus indicating that the formation of an 'underclass' is a result of more than socio-economic factors. Overall Giddens's account of the 'underclass' is relatively superficial and has not been elaborated.

'Race', class and the 'underclass'

There are similarities between Giddens's (1973) and Rex's (1973) descriptions of an 'underclass'. The latter argued that:

we have created in this country an underclass, whose membership is largely drawn from the immigrant community. It has become identified particularly with certain areas of the city, which it would be wrong to call ghettoes because they are by no means confined to single ethnic groups, but it is the immigrants in those residential areas who form the prime target of attack in racist speeches. Increasingly too, these areas become socially segregated from the rest of the city, the more so neighbouring slum areas are cleared away (Rex, 1973: 165).

Rex adopted Weber's concepts of status, market situation and class, to explain how resources are allocated through distributive networks. The idea of an 'underclass' was used to explain the complex articulation of 'race' and class, without collapsing 'race' into class or vice versa. Rex's usage of the 'underclass' is based on Myrdal's (1964) definition. According to Rex's interpretation, the 'underclass' is a section of the population situated in the context of a capitalist, free market society, in which the values of competition and choice are promoted at the expense of other principles. The majority of the population can meet their needs by legitimately exercising freedom of choice in the market place. Members of the 'underclass' are not sufficiently motivated or do not have the necessary opportunities to enter into this social system and fail to realise these aspirations. They remain caught up in a tangle of pathologies living in a culture of poverty in which families transmit deprivation to their next of kin. By falling outside the conventions of mainstream society the 'underclass' exists as a surplus population that contributes nothing positive towards society as a whole. Of particular significance is the legacy of the colonial period. This structural dimension continues to have an impact on the implementation of various public and social policies, coupled with the action of individual actors at work and on the streets, in differentiating groups along the lines of 'insider' ('white') and 'outsider' ('black') status.

Rex (1973) also examined housing, the labour market and welfare issues. The concept of 'housing classes' referred to the patterns of social stratification arising out of local government policies devised for the allocation and distribution of housing, particularly the proclivity of local authorities to house minority ethnic groups in poor quality accommodation concentrated in 'twilight zones'. In the context of the labour market, minority ethnic groups are employed in the less desirable and more unacceptable roles such as low paid and unskilled manual work. Rather than basing his explanation on the economically reductionist logic of certain strands of Marxism, Rex considered the part played by the indigenous labour force in creating social divisions. Throughout the course of their struggle to improve their market situation the 'white' labour force often entered into antagonistic relations with 'black' labourers. The segregation of 'white' from 'black' workers is thus shaped by individual attitudes and actions. As such, racism and racial discrimination are not just an outcome of impersonal, structural factors but also an effect of social actors. At this point the tension between 'race' and class surfaces as an important dimension.

From a 'neo-Marxist' perspective, Westergaard and Ressler (1975: 11) argued that although there is stratification by colour this does not necessarily replace stratification by class, but rather that the divisions of class, ethnicity and 'race' co-exist and create a sub-proleteriat within the working class. This section of the population, including Catholics in Northern Ireland and black minority ethnic groups in the inner cities, is predisposed to political protest and violence as a reaction to their oppression. Significantly, the potential violence and disorder of the 'underclass' is an issue which sets a precedent for later narratives on the notion in the aftermath of the inner city riots of the early 1980s.

Other 'neo-Marxist' writers such as Sivanandan (1982) have also incorporated social class into their analysis of a racialised 'underclass'. Attempts have been made to demonstrate a linkage between the 'underclass' and 'race', by focusing on the socio-economic, historical and political forces which have created a 'black underclass'. The main argument is that social class is divided along the lines of 'race'. The intersection of 'race' and class creates conditions under which the formation of an 'underclass' or 'sub-proletariat' has taken place. Sivanandan claims that British society has an atomised working class that is fractured to such an extent that the 'hierarchies within are based on "race" and nationality to make conflicting sectional interests assume greater significance than the interests of society as a whole' (Sivanandan, 1982: 114). This is explained as an effect of institutional racism which serves the interests of the dominant class and creates a marginalised 'sub-proletariat' made up of minority ethnic groups. The capitalist system is dependent upon the exploitation of 'black' labour to facilitate the accumulation of profit which ensures the continuation of the capitalist economy. This overtly functionalist account regards the 'black' labour force as instrumental in the maintenance of the status quo. In Sivanandan's terms, for the growth and continued success of an exploitative mode of production: 'Capital requires racism not for racism's sake but for the sake of capital' (Sivanandan, 1980 quoted in Gilroy, 1987: 21).

Rex's (1973) earlier work was a reference point in Lord Scarman's (1981) inquiry into the Brixton disorders, which in turn was reflected in Dahrendorf's (1985) conception of an 'underclass'. In the view of the latter, this population is excluded from economic, political and social citizenship. It is an 'amorphous' group that stands outside a more well defined and clearly recognisable majority class. This 'underclass' consists of somewhere between 10 per cent and a third of society. By contrast with the majority class, or the 'two-thirds', this 'one-third' is excluded from full citizenship. Dahrendorf (1985: 104) stated that:

Probably the only inclusive way to describe it is negatively. The 'underclass' consists of those whom the full citizens of society do not need. They are either not citizens, or no longer citizens, or no longer full citizens or not yet citizens.

The first of these categories refers to minority ethnic groups; the second the elderly; the third are the 'drop outs'. Added to these groups are the sick, those who come into conflict with the police and the fourth and most important category, the young. It should be noted that not all of the young are part of an 'underclass', but only some of those who are concentrated in geographical areas with high levels of unemployment. Due to structural changes in the labour market, in the context of the work society that is running out of work, many young people are excluded from employment. Combined with the increasingly large gap between leaving home and school, and finding full-time employment, this has created a 'no-man's land' for many young people. Exclusion from citizenship means that young people no longer have the opportunity to conform to the norms and values of mainstream society and fail to fulfil their obligations and responsibilities to the wider community. One of the outcomes of this is that some individuals choose, albeit not under circumstances of their own choosing, to act in an antisocial fashion, hence the crime and disorder of the 'underclass'. The behaviour of this 'underclass' typically includes involvement in rioting and participation in violent activities such as football hooliganism and other petty criminal offences. Dahrendorf (1987: 15) contends that if a significant minority of the young are not given a stake in society, then society gives off the impression that it has given up on its stake in the future. To counter these tendencies it is necessary that members of society receive full citizenship.

Halsey (1989: 16) has also described the 'underclass' as a ghettoised group consisting of those falling outside the labour market, especially

youth drawn from minority ethnic groups. This racialised group is characterised by social pathologies such as, educational failure, illiteracy,
broken families, high crime rates, poor housing and spatial concentration in the inner city. The social contract of citizenship is virtually non-
existent and this layer of the population does not have any real stake in
society. Halsey shares similar views to other 'ethical socialists' (Dennis
and Erdos, 1992; Dennis, 1993) who lament the decline of the nuclear
family, particularly the growing proportion of children born into
fatherless single parent families. To remedy this Halsey argues that it is
necessary to teach men how to be husbands and fathers, and to enable
them to return to a traditional family. In his own words, 'We've also got
to have a tremendous drive to teach men how to be husbands and fathers.
The project as understood by feminists is making women more like men
but it ought to be making men more like women' (Halsey, 1993).

Other commentators have argued that 'race' is of declining significance. Field's (1989) conception of an 'underclass' – a stratum beneath
the working class, including single parent families, the long term unemployed, and the poor elderly – is one example. The emergence of this
'underclass' is a consequence of structural changes at a macro level. The
transformation of the class structure is caused by a number of interrelated dynamic processes at work in the labour market, which affect the
pattern of income distribution. In addition to these factors, the impact
of the authoritarian populism of 'Thatcherism' on public attitudes led
to the erosion of the values underpinning economic, political and
social citizenship.

As indicated earlier, crime, delinquency and disorder are also traits of
the 'underclass' debate (Cook, 1997). Runciman (1989: 27), for example,
refers to a small group within one of his fourfold divisions of social
classes into 'systacts', which consists of 'outlaws, mendicants, vagabonds,
captives, drop-outs, criminals and so forth whose roles are stigmatised
by the ideology of those located above them'. This is an adjunct to
Runciman's main concern, namely the division of society into seven
classes, each of which are related to the type of employment an individual
is able to find. Concerning the 'underclass', Runciman (1990: 388)
argues that:

> The term must be understood to stand not for a group or category of
> workers systematically disadvantaged within the labour market but
> for those members of British society whose roles place them more or
> less permanently at the economic level where benefits are paid by
> the state to those unable to participate in the labour market at all.

Towards the end of the 1980s there was a shift of emphasis in the 'underclass' debate, and the hegemony of the structural school of thought (underpinned by 'neo-Marxist' and Weberian theory), was replaced by the behavioural perspective, especially of Murray, referred to earlier. This is normally associated with the ascendancy of the New Right, which has gathered momentum since the 1980s. Significant structural changes were also occurring at this time, such as a rise in the number of long term unemployed, a burgeoning lone parent population and increased welfare dependency. The New Right judged these changes to be the unintended consequences of the post-war consensus on the Welfare State. Rather than referring to the structural problems facing welfarism, they focused on the damaging effects of state provided social services on the individual's character and behaviour.

New dimensions of an old debate

Murray (1990, 1994) has introduced his version of an 'underclass' – or the 'new rabble' – from America into the British debate. One of the most unique aspects of Murray's work is that it is gendered and it highlights the so-called crisis of masculinity. There is also a significant point of departure from the debate in the United States and previous disputes in the United Kingdom inasmuch as the 'underclass' is deemed to be both white and black. Another novel dimension is that, in Westergaard's (1995: 117) words, this 'newer variant is distinct by the resoluteness of its conception of class as a matter of voluntarily adopted life-styles – good versus evil – essentially unconditioned by economic structure.' This kind of thinking, actively promoted by the New Right, therefore signalled a profound change from the kind of analyses in vogue until the late 1980s.

Murray's 'underclass' is recognisable by three interrelated characteristics; crime, illegitimacy and voluntary unemployment. According to this behavioural perspective the 'underclass' is not a description of the condition of poverty *per se* but an explanation of a certain type of behavioural (not cultural) adaptation to it. Young men's involvement in crime and disorder is one example. Another causal factor is the 'dismembered family' and the inadequate parenting of boys provided by young unmarried women. These factors contribute to the voluntary idleness of men whose rationally made decision not to participate in the labour market is combined with a refusal to take on board the responsibilities of parenthood. These individuals are labelled as 'barbarians' whose incivility is a reflection of their exploitation of the rights of social citizenship without fulfilling their obligations and duties to the wider community.

  According to Murray (1990: 2), since the 1960s all of the poor have come to be regarded 'equally as victims [who] would be equally success-ful if only society gave them a fair shake'. Murray rejects the view that poverty can be solved by social policies which redirect and redistribute money to target specific individuals and groups. In his view the poor have been 'homogenised', and consequently, useful labels such as the 'ne'er-do-well poor person' have disappeared. Other categorisations such as the 'undeserving', 'unrespectable', 'depraved', 'debased', 'disrep-utable' or 'feckless' have been replaced by the more benign idea of a 'culture of poverty'. Murray claims that these tags were important because they looked beyond the issue of the 'degree of poverty', by focusing on a 'a type of poverty' instead. Murray claims that it is atom-ised individuals who are culpable for their own predicament, rather than any other social agent or agency.

  As noted earlier on, Murray's polemic is based on anecdotal evidence. In one account, which makes a distinction between respectable and unrespectable poor families, the main arguments are illustrated by draw-ing on impressions gained during the author's own childhood in 1950s Iowa. The latter are responsible for all of their own problems and the pos-sibility that other factors may be at work in the construction of poverty are not taken into consideration. More significantly, no attempt is made to acknowledge that 1950s American society is very different to British society. The perception that 'what happens in the United States will hap-pen in Britain' neglects the salience of the specific spatial and temporal contexts in which the social phenomenon the 'underclass' describes are embedded. Murray argues that the family is the site out of which social problems arise, particularly where there are unemployable males who fail to perform an adequate socialising function for their male offspring. Thus, in 1950s Iowa, for certain types of poor people, the family struc-ture *per se* was pathological. By the late-1980s-early-1990s the family was still the main source of trouble, but illegitimacy or unwed mothers are the best indicator of an underclass in the making. There were:

  1.3m (up from 840 000 in 1979) single parents. Most (52%) are bringing up children alone as a result of divorce or separation, but those who have never had a partner comprise the fastest growing group (rising from 160 000 in 1981 to 430 000 in 1991). The propor-tion of births outside marriage has increased from 6% in 1961 to 39% (*The Sunday Times*, 14 November 1993).

In the last analysis, Murray (1990: 13) argues that 'The key to an underclass is not the individual instance but a situation in which a very large proportion of an entire community lacks fathers, and this is far more common in poor communities than in rich ones.'

Of great concern is the way in which various configurations of single parent families, poverty, welfare dependency, crime and delinquency are gendered (Campbell, 1993). The connections between these different factors were made explicit at the time of the 'outer city' riots and community disorders in the summers of 1991 and 1992. At that time Murray (1992) argued that inadequate socialisation, particularly of those male children lacking the necessary role models for them to grow up into decent fathers, was a key causal factor of the riots. Fatherhood is prioritised above all other factors as the main antidote to criminality. This contradicts Murray's earlier arguments mentioned above, where even some fathers in two-parent families are deviant and contribute nothing to the socialisation of their male progeny. Thus the blame is shifted onto unwed mothers. More cogently, even where there are fathers who are out of work and who may not set their children the right example, this is a consequence of voluntary redundancy. In sum, Murray argues that if a father does not go to work it is his choice and, moreover, any patterns of behaviour that may be associated with not working are also a matter of individual free will, rather than a reaction to structural constraints.

The traditional family is the place from where free society originates. Without it, it is not possible to inculcate into the minds of children the need for self-government. This is imperative if the institutions on which the functioning of a free society is dependent are to continue. Wootton (1959) had shown on a previous occasion that these arguments went against the grain of the available research evidence. Likewise, Rutter and Madge's (1976) rejection of the general thrust of Sir Keith Joseph's 'cycles of deprivation' thesis in the mid-1970s is suppressed.

How does Murray's polemic measure up against other arguments? In the next section his views on unmarried mothers, and the part this vulnerable group has purportedly played in creating criminogenic and disorderly communities, is reviewed. After that his thinking about unemployment is questioned.

Lone parenthood – 'dismembered families?' and 'moral panics'

In Britain lone parents – of which 90 per cent are female – stand in stark contrast to the 'couple centred', traditional or bourgeois family structure, consisting of a male breadwinner as head of the household, and a female whose main priority is child rearing (Hardey and Crow, 1991). The former participates in the public sphere and the latter in the private sphere. The fact that not all family units conform to the variant of familist ideology outlined above stirred up a debate in common sense, academic and public policy discourses before Murray appeared on the scene (Finer, 1974). Although the bourgeois family is presented as natural and unchanging, a common criticism is that the single earner, high fertility family of the 1950s is, from an historical perspective, more exceptional than it is sometimes perceived. There are, for instance, some middle-class (Renvoize, 1985; Hardey and Crow, 1991: 18) and lesbian women (Leonard and Speekman, 1986 in Hardey and Crow, 1991) for whom single parenthood may be the preferred option. Single parents may also be held culpable for many social ills, but it is not lone parenthood *per se* which is deemed to represent a serious dilemma. The widowed, the separated and the divorced, especially since the Divorce Reform Act of 1969 which made the process much simpler, signify problems, but these are of a different nature to single unwed mothers (Hardey and Crow, 1991).

'Unmarried mothers', 'unwed mothers', 'unsupported mothers', 'fatherless families' and 'incomplete families' are included among the many interchangeable terms used to describe lone parents. These labels denote a household with one resident parent, and are sometimes used to stigmatise women by stereotyping them as 'undeserving', 'unworthy' and 'rough'.

Parenting may be linked by common fertility and the child rearing cycle, but definitions of the kind Murray outlines neglect complicated changes connecting parenthood, marital status and other relationships between parents over a longer period of time (MacDonald, 1956; Spence, 1954 cited in Wootton, 1959: 36–8). Although the number of unmarried pregnant women had increased by 100 000 from 753 000 in 1981 to 853 000 in 1991 (OPCS, 1994), this conceals a diversity of family structures. Bradshaw and Millar (1991) support Brown's (1989: 10) claim that:

> The image of a typical lone parent as a young single mother beginning lone parenthood with the birth of a child and continuing in that status until the child is 16 or 18 is no longer valid – if that ever was. Such lone parent families do exist, but as a small minority.

The OPCS (1994) shows a significant increase in teenage mothers between 1981 and 1991. Oppenheim also provides figures showing that in 1979 the rate of teenage births for girls aged 11 to 14 was 7.9 per 100 000, but by 1993 the rate had risen to 10.8 per 100 000. In 1993, 7200 under-sixteen-year-old girls were pregnant. The rate of conceptions within this group was 8.1 per 1000 girls. According to the OPCS in 1990 the equivalent rate was 10.1 per 1000. Thus there has been a 20 per cent decline between 1990–1993 (OPCS, 1995). For young women between the age of 15 and 19 there was a sharp increase in the 1980s and 1990s, and in 1993 there were 21 724. However, OPCS data shows that the overall number of teenage conceptions declined for the first time in seven years from 115 000 in 1990 to 103 000 in 1991 (OPCS, 1994). In 1993 there were 87 000 teenage pregnancies of which 91 per cent were outside marriage. Thirty five per cent of all teenage conceptions were terminated by an abortion (OPCS, 1995).

The story is much the same now as it was in the first half of the century when Wootton (1959: 301) concluded that there was not much concrete evidence to corroborate the view that the consequences of illegitimacy are necessarily negative. Despite this the statistics mentioned above provide much scope for anxiety. In accord with these figures, and repeating Brown's (1989) earlier findings, Oppenheim (1994: 28) argues that within the category of lone parent families the number of single mothers is increasing, but they are only a small part of a larger group. Nevertheless, various 'moral panics' have been constructed in response to this particular 'folk devil'.

Of particular concern is the connection between single parent families, poverty and welfare dependency (Walker and Walker, 1997) as well as crime and delinquency (Cook, 1997; Coote, 1994; Dennis and Erdos, 1992; Dennis, 1993). Throughout history the majority of unsupported mothers have been poor (Holman, 1970). Official statistics (DSS, 1993) and independent research (Bradshaw and Millar, 1991) duplicated this finding two decades on. In 1994, the DSS (drawing on Family Expenditure Survey [FES] data) showed no change in this trend. If the 'unofficial' poverty line (defined by the CPAG as below half the average income after housing costs) is used to measure the extent of poverty amongst this group the figure in 1979 was 28 per cent and in 1991/2 it was 75 per cent (DSS, 1994). In 1979 45 per cent (310 000) of all lone mothers were in receipt of Supplementary Benefit. By 1989 72 per cent (740 000) were on Income Support (IS) which replaced Supplementary Benefit in 1988 (DSS, 1991 cited in Millar, 1994: 26). Thirty per cent of people of working age receiving Income Support are lone parents and 60 per cent of children living in families on this benefit are headed by a lone parent (Millar, 1994: 26).

Unemployment – structure or agency?

There are other more fundamental difficulties with Murray's work, such as the lack of empirical evidence to show that structural exclusion from the labour market results in the emergence of 'underclass'-type groups. Marshall *et al.* (1996), and especially Gallie's (1994) work, assess both the utility of 'conservative' and 'radical' notions of the 'underclass' – equivalent to behavioural and structural versions respectively – focusing on the location and experiences of the unemployed in the UK labour market, especially the long-term unemployed. Gallie's (1994) research refutes the 'conservative' perspective (epitomised by Murray) which claims that as a consequence of their behaviour those out of work are unemployable. The unemployeds' past experiences, and the level of employment stability, measured in terms of the frequency of changing jobs, and the period of time people spent in the job they held for the longest, was similar to people currently in employment. Likewise, the suggestion that the unemployed have different attitudes to work than the employed is not supported by the evidence.

The 'radical' account posits a link between exclusion and marginalisation from the labour market with material deprivation and cumulative disadvantage. The evidence certainly supports the view that the long term unemployed experience a particularly high level of cumulative disadvantage. Even when factors such as age and class are controlled for, they are much more likely to endure financial hardship and a lack of adequate social support. Unemployment is not the choice of individuals but an outcome of changes in the labour market, technological innovation, as well as employer and government policies which 'disproportionately' affect the manual working class, but especially non-manual workers. Importantly, the unemployed do not respond to their predicament by developing a 'distinctive subculture'. Marshall *et al.* (1996: 40) make a similar point when they argue that:

> as regards the so-called underclass our results are consistent with those obtained by other researchers, who have been unable to identify an underclass in terms of particular attitudes to work, job search behaviour, degree of social marginalization or participation. Against this background, the concept itself looks increasingly flawed, and certainly fails to provide a platform from which to launch a convincing critique of class analysis because of its 'missing millions'.

The research evidence thus finds the main arguments of both schools of the 'underclass' debate to be deficient, particularly with regard to the view that non-participation in the labour market contributes, in any simple way, to the creation of a distinctive sub-culture amongst the poor.

Is there an underclass?

In the 1980s, with the exception of the 'conservative' viewpoint, expressed by Sir Keith Joseph, the behavioural perspective was virtually absent from narratives about poverty. Despite Westergaard's (1992) scepticism about the concept of an 'underclass', on those occasions when it is used by academics, a structural version is the dominant one. This account rests on the premise that there is a structurally generated 'underclass' that is surplus to the requirements of the labour market and which is excluded from social citizenship. It may be possible to synthesise these different approaches, but further research is required before this can be attempted. In the meantime, Gardiner's (1995: 372) observation, written from a criminological perspective, is a helpful guide-line. He has indicated that both the behavioural and structural approach are problematic:

> It can be a very useful phenomenon to use in examining state control of the bottom groupings in the social hierarchy, but when the use has become widespread and diverse without foundation in rigorous empirical evidence, the use of such a term beyond a popular metaphor is limited. Underclass simplifies a complex range of social relations and processes and runs the danger of leading to ideological obfuscation of the social processes which cause poverty and deprivation.

The above criticisms do not necessarily mean that the concept of an 'underclass' should be jettisoned, but that it must be used with more caution. In the literature that examines policing, for example, the 'underclass' is used as a rhetorical device to criticise the neo-liberal strategy of inequality (Reiner, 1997: 1038–9). Any attempt to highlight the very real effects of this development are welcome, especially the all too real problems of crime and disorder which affect poor communities. However, it ought to be remembered that as yet the 'underclass' is not an empirically defined section of the population with a concrete existence. Moreover, it does not always adequately capture the heterogeneity of the phenomenon it describes. It may therefore be more appropriate to say, at this stage, that there are groups in 'underclass'-type positions.

The concept of an 'underclass' may still be useful, but a cautionary note regarding recent changes in the political sphere should be added.

In contrast to previous occasions when an 'underclass' has been identified, scant attention has been given to the influence of structural factors
on its formation. Before the election of New Labour in May 1997, individual inadequacies and bad behaviour, and not wider structural factors, caused the emergence of an 'underclass'. It is imperative that
further work is done to make the distinction between behavioural and
structural versions of the 'underclass' more explicit. Failure to do this
may result in explanations of social problems and social divisions that
emphasise the immorality or innate deficiencies of individuals rather
than structural constraints.

'Respectable fears' – the view from Parliament

'Our Ministers do not refer to the underclass' (Willetts, 1992: 42).

Since Murray's polemic appeared on the scene in late 1989 and its
re-emergence in 1994, and despite criticisms (Lister, 1996), media-led
commentaries on social policy show that a degree of consensus on
Murray's thinking, not necessarily intentional, has been exhibited at
various levels of the state and civil society.

In July 1993 *The Sunday Times* focused on the then Conservative Secretary of State for Wales, John Redwood, and his visit to the St Mellons
estate in Cardiff. This serves as a clear example of the consensus which
Murray played a part in shaping or tapping into. The statistic that six
out of ten children belong to unmarried mothers is used to explain the
'fact' that delinquency, disorder and crime is rife on that estate. The
'underclass' was not emerging or about to arrive but had over-run the
estate. To exacerbate this, its contagious nature threatened to spread
even further afield. As Peter Lilley argued (then Conservative Secretary
of State for the Department of Social Security), rising crime and the
associated disintegration of the nuclear family structure permeates large
swathes of society. Kenneth Clarke, former Conservative Chancellor of
the Exchequer (1993–7) referred to the 'underclass' in his 1994 November Budget speech:

> My second priority has been to use this [economic] recovery wisely,
> to encourage the creation of more jobs particularly for people who
> have been out of work for some time. We must combine greater pros-
> perity for the majority with measures to prevent the emergence of a
> deprived underclass excluded from the opportunity to work and
> dependent on welfare (*The Daily Telegraph*, 27 September 1995).

Tony Blair, then leader of the Labour Party in opposition, also mentioned the idea. Talking about the social divisions which emerged during the period of Conservative government he said, 'The Tories never cared about the underclass. Now they have sold out on the middle class too' (*The Times*, 6 February 1995). Some individuals whose work involved direct contact with government departments also alluded to an 'underclass':

> Top civil servants believe government policy is creating "islands" of poverty, disaffection and social division, reports *The Sunday Telegraph*. The permanent secretaries of eight departments blame ministers for the growth of an underclass in Britain. The warning was delivered at a meeting called by Sir Robin Butler, the cabinet secretary (*The Times*, 12 February 1995).

Unlike in media circles, where Murray circulates more freely, 'Murrayism' does not explicitly inform the perspectives quoted above in any simple way. However, in Chapter 9 it is shown that due to the formation of a new political consensus and following the election of New Labour in May 1997 some of his ideas are still influential. The legacy of nineteenth-century Victorian moralism has interfused the thinking of Fabians, ethical socialists and communitarians. It would also appear that New Labour share some very similar assumptions about the poor to their neo-liberal predecessors (Deacon and Mann, 1997; Driver and Martell, 1997; Hughes, 1996).

The 'underclass' – an old tale about poverty with new twists in the story

As illustrated by the comparison of developments in American and British social policy, the 'underclass' debate has a long history, and has been employed for many different purposes. Despite these variations there are cultural and political continuities between the two respective countries, and ideas adopted from the former by the latter have proven to be congruent with discussions taking place in both social contexts. The threads that are woven together in this section pertain to the British situation, for reasons which are made clear shortly. The most important theme is that the idea of an 'underclass' has been offered as an explanation for the condition of poverty and other inter-related social problems.

There are structural and behavioural perspectives on poverty and the 'underclass' but the latter perspective has received more publicity.

'Murrayism', for example, focuses on the rational social actor, an agent who consciously chooses a particular way of life. If an individual is poor it is not a result of government policy and macro-economic forces but the outcome of a personal decision. Views of this kind echo New Right thinking and practice. For example, Marshall's principle of (1972: 15) 'democratic-welfare-capitalism', and the political and cultural values underpropping it, have been questioned by the neo-liberal values of New Right ideologists.

Advocates of free market principles and individual choice (Friedman, 1980; Hayek, 1973; 1986) have reappraised the role of government, particularly the welfare state. The proposed remedial action is minimal government involvement and maximal personal responsibility. Proponents of this philosophy are not concerned either with the redistribution and reallocation of resources or rebuilding destroyed economic and social structures, but maximising the ethic of personal responsibility and self-government. It is argued that market forces are a far more efficient and responsive mechanism to preserve social order than inefficient and unresponsive state-run bureaucracies. However, the state sometimes intervenes in the formation of policy relating to the poor and their families.

Take poverty as an example. It is not the job of the state to accept responsibility for it's 'strategy of inequality' (Walker, 1991b), and amelioration of the worst effects of poverty must come from elsewhere, namely the individual. The poor individual is blamed for his material circumstances rather than any all encompassing abstract concepts such as the state, the government and society. By focusing on individual human action, and by neglecting or understating the salience of structural constraints, this explanation tends to 'blame the victim'. Such views have been a feature of many different political ideologies which, at various times, have differentiated the poor into those who are on the one hand 'respectable', 'deserving' and 'worthy', and those on the other hand, who are 'rough', 'undeserving' and 'unworthy'.

While it is arguably necessary to use such terms to establish an individual's merit or desert in formulating social policies, the material circumstances in which the poor find themselves must not be ignored. In the case of children, lone parents and a significant majority of the unemployed, such labels are unfair. A minority of the unemployed and those responsible for crime and disorder may deserve such tags, but we still must not lose sight of the unpropitious social conditions under which such behaviour sometimes happens.

Since 1979, outside of the academic world, such distinctions have been almost entirely based on behaviour and deployed to widen social divisions with more conviction and on a greater scale than ever before (Walker and Walker, 1997). Categorisations of this type create social divisions on the basis of subjective impressions and stereotypes, and Murray, for example, has refused to consult or even acknowledge the existence of research evidence that contradicts his claims.

Changing conceptions of poverty are also mediated by various other factors. These are socially constructed divisions, including class, age, ethnicity/'race', sex and gender dimensions. Ethnicity and 'race', for instance, are sometimes a feature of the 'underclass' debate and these variables interact in different ways. Under certain circumstances 'race' and ethnicity, instead of class, are key factors at work in redrawing the conceptual boundaries of the 'underclass'. At other times, the reverse is true. The fact that configurations linking ethnicity, 'race' and the 'underclass' are perpetually changing creates confusion and uncertainty. It is possible to highlight one determining factor, though. Although 'race' and ethnicity are not a permanent feature of discussions about the 'underclass', the frequency with which they coexist, in one form or another, suggests that the 'underclass' has 'race' specific connotations. Unlike some Marxists, no attempt is made to collapse 'race' into class. Instead the unique status of 'race' and class is recognised at particular moments.

Lone parenthood is another issue. This categorisation lacks a clear meaning and many different groups are subsumed under this term, consisting of the divorced, the separated, the widowed and single unmarried or unwed mothers. Throughout history the latter group has been most prominent in public debate, thus indicating that the 'underclass' has been gendered. This interconnects with the other main social divisions of age, ethnicity, 'race' and wider changes in the class structure of late modern society. These variables are interlocked and create many complex configurations.

The reaction to mother-headed households has revealed one of the paradoxes of the ideology of neo-liberal and New Right ideologies. Under certain circumstances minimal state intervention is preached but not practised. Where the maximal role of autonomous self-government is out of step with the expectations of the strong state there has sometimes been a clash of interests. Striking a balance between the two principles has consistently posed problems. For instance, Murray's (1990) recommendation for minimising and curtailing the role of central government and to increase self-government is contradicted by the call for a strong state to remove children from unwed mothers.

Campbell (1993, 1994), Cook (1997) and the collection of essays edited by Coote (1994) have shown that behind many of the commentaries on female-headed households is a discussion about male irresponsibility: read crime, delinquency and disorder. In Campbell's words (1993: 302–3):

> the external themes of discipline and punishment, and sexuality, legitimacy and wedlock – or, put another way, motherhood and the fatherless family. Neither sexuality nor style created mass unemployment or the so called underclass. They were not to blame. But in the mind of the old respectability and New Right it was not mass unemployment that was to blame for the underclass … it did not see a masculine response to an economic crisis – it saw instead a failure of the mothers to manage the men.

In other words, then, single unwed mothers are blamed for many social problems. Dependency on state welfare has weakened their dependence on a male breadwinner. Their independence from men has been shifted to a dependence on the state, thus undermining traditional conceptions of masculine identity. Poverty, illegitimacy, voluntary unemployment and criminality become part of the same phenomenon, namely the 'underclass'. Some of the most vulnerable women in society are held to be responsible, not only for being unmarried, but also for the criminal and disorderly acts of some men. 'New Right' and 'rational choice' commentators alike argue that this is not the consequence of structural factors and institutionalised discrimination, but deficiencies rooted in the individual subject. In Chapter 9 these issues are considered in the context of New Labour's response to these social problems.

5
From Theory to Practice

[A]ll studies of crime and deviance, however deeply entrenched in their own technical traditions, are inevitably grounded in larger, more general social theories which are always present (and consequential) even as unspoken silences (Gouldner, 1973: ix).

A key objective of this chapter is to show that thinking about poverty and crime has practical consequences. Ideas do not exist in a vacuum but are the creation of individuals and the various social groups to which they belong, and they are also used to change the world in which people live and work. The nature of the relationship between ideas and practice is highly complex and extreme care needs to be taken if it is to be examined appropriately. Some of the theoretical debates which relate to the issues addressed in the rest of the book are introduced. The 'underclass' debate is taken as an example. The contention that the police *police* an 'underclass' has often been posited in academic texts, but the theoretical assumptions on which such arguments are postulated need to be clarified.

The main focus is on the relative significance of behavioural and structural versions of the 'underclass' in police discourse and in the police policy process. Murray (1990), for example, has attributed the behavioural version of the idea to police officers:

The people who deal most intimately with poor communities in their daily lives use the same distinction among the poor that I use. The managers of council estates, policeman in poor neighbourhoods, social workers, nurses, and physicians, may or may not bridle at the term 'underclass', but if the topic of conversation is not whether this American reactionary is right, but rather a leisurely discussion of

how these people go about their work and what life is like in the
communities where they work, the distinction between the good
folks and the underclass shines through after the first five minutes
(Murray, 1990: 70).

The purpose of this commentary is to show something rather different,
namely that a socially constructed idea of an 'underclass' is embedded
and made meaningful by some senior officers from a distinctive structural perspective. The 'underclass' is often rejected as fundamentally
flawed by most sociologists because it distorts social reality (Westergaard, 1992: 580), and as noted in the previous chapter, a small minority
of criminologists have questioned its utility too (Gardiner, 1995: 372).

Despite these warnings, some versions are useful for people working
in other stables. Thomas's (1923; 1951) observation that if something is
regarded as real *then it is real in its consequences* is a useful guide-line.
This may be illustrated by drawing on Berger and Luckmann's (1966)
social constructionism and Gramsci's (1971) notion of common sense.
An attempt is made to explain how usage of the 'underclass' is not
necessarily as problematic as some commentators infer, and that a
structural version of the 'underclass' can be employed in a very different way to the behavioural interpretation.

Social constructionism

The 'underclass' is not just a linguistic construction (i.e. a debate), and
it is also incorporated into and sustains various kinds of social action,
such as policy-making. Luckmann's (1983: 91) contention that 'as a
rhetoric and as a reservoir of justificatory devices, language is a partial
guarantee of socially constructed normal worlds of entire societies,
classes and social groups' is a good starting point for investigating these
themes. The emphasis should be put on *partial*, because there are other
salient factors. It is tempting to treat ideas as if they have a pre-set and
objective reality, existing independent of the social agents who participate in the *creation* and *recreation* of concepts as part of an ongoing process. Indeed 'such is the power of human agency that it can lose its own
authorship of social life to the meaningful constructs it ongoingly
creates and recreates, a process referred to as "reification"' (Berger and
Pullberg, 1966 cited in Henry and Milovanovic, 1996: 24). By claiming
that usage of the 'underclass' is problematic as a matter of course, causal
powers are attributed to the idea, without taking into account that it is
social agents who make the idea meaningful in the first instance. The

idea of an 'underclass' is continually made, and remade, by social actors and the organisational groups to which they belong. A behavioural version of the idea of an 'underclass' may well be better known in wider society, and this may have the effect of distorting counter-arguments and conflicting evidence, but this is not necessarily so because usage of the idea is mediated by a range of different cultural and structural factors. According to Berger and Luckmann (1966: 48) 'social structure is the sum total of typifications . . . of the recurrent patterns of interaction which are established by the means of them. As such, social structure is an element of everyday life' (Berger and Luckmann, 1966: 48). By talking about the 'underclass' in micro-situations police officers generate 'typifications', which may be shared and constitute an objective reality for the individual consciousness of social actors. Furthermore, the idea of an 'underclass' has very a different meaning in the organisational structure of the police service, to that which it has in other organisations such as the media and academia.

While social constructionism has much to offer, particularly its recognition of the significance of the human subject as a creative agent at a micro level, people are bound by certain constraints at a macro level. Social actors add their own nuances to concepts, but these ideas also belong to other individuals and groups, some of whom are in a more powerful and influential position to provide more acceptable and convincing versions than others. The creativity of individuals is thus limited by relatively permanent power structures in wider society which impose restrictions on social action. This occurs at many levels, and one that is particularly relevant here is the ideological.

Common sense

The 'underclass' debate is also built into the 'common sense' views of the world that some police officers hold. According to Gramsci (1971: 323; 404; 419; 423) 'common sense' – diametrically opposed to 'good sense', or practical empirical common sense in accord with the English meaning of the word – is an incoherent, ambiguous and sometimes contradictory set of assumptions, attitudes and beliefs. It is is not characterised by a single, unitary perspective, but is instead 'multiform', hence the proposition that there is 'not just one common sense but that it is a collective noun'. Common sense cannot 'constitute an intellectual order, because it cannot be reduced to unity and coherence within an individual consciousness (1971: 325–6). Gramsci expresses this clearly in the following statement where one's conception of the world is not critical and coherent but disjointed and episodic, one belongs simultaneously to a multiplicity of mass human groups. The personality is strangely composite: it contains Stone Age elements and principles of a more advanced science, prejudices from all past phases of history at the level and intuitions of a future philosophy which will be that of a human race united the world over (1971: 324).

Gramsci takes Marx's examination of the linkages between certain 'popular beliefs' and 'material forces' in the introduction to Marx's *Critique of Hegel's Philosophy of Right* as an example. Here Marx 'is referring not to the validity of the content of these beliefs but rather to their formal solidity and to the consequent imperative character they have when they produce norms of conduct' (Gramsci, 1971: 423–4). In other words, although sets of attitudes, beliefs and perceptions may be incoherent and fragmented, they have the potential to become a force at work in the construction of social reality. The 'underclass' is one example. Although there is a diversity of representations of an 'underclass', which are sometimes at variance with the multiple realities it is constructed to describe, these depictions may sometimes be plausible and persuasive descriptions of various interlocking economic, political and social processes. It is argued that this idea, mediated through various powerful agents and institutions, has an impact on the ideologies deployed in the social construction of notions of public and social order; in this instance, police policy and practice. Gramsci's (1971: 382) reflections on the suitability of particular methodologies for 'study[ing] the birth of a conception of the world' are illuminating on this issue. It is necessary to 'search for the Leitmotiv, for the rhythm of thought as it develops [which] should be more important than that for single causal affirmations and isolated aphorisms' (1971: 383).

From a social constructionist standpoint, inquiry in the social sciences must adhere to certain principles. As Luckmann (1983: 19) put it:

Science that describes and explains the construction of social reality must be able to develop a programme of formalisation (and a theory of measurement) that is appropriate to the constitutive structures of everyday life.

From a social constructionist perspective social actors invest meaning in *the social structure that is an element of everyday life* (Berger and Luckmann, 1966: 48). If this analysis focuses exclusively on extant textual analyses of policing and poverty, many of the diverse and complex issues which surround the policing of the 'underclass' are likely to be overlooked. In particular, the role of individuals who have first hand knowledge and the most insight into these issues would be missing.

In this account the secondary data, official documents and the views of senior police officers and other policy-makers are analysed in a dialectical fashion. This is intended to highlight the main areas where different viewpoints converge and diverge, bearing in mind that this account is more concerned with representations of reality gleaned from various sources of data rather than the 'truth'. The rationale underlying the usage of different data sources is to focus on the dialogue between academic commentary, public debate and police talk. Although increasingly strong mutual relations tie the academy and the police service together, there is a fundamental epistemological difference.

All knowledge is socially constructed, but within the academic community researchers are bound, in principle, by certain methodological rules and practices as well as ethical guide-lines. Similar rules of thumb also apply in the police service, but due to the nature of police-work it is open to the influence of other kinds of thinking, especially common sense (Gramsci, 1971). While such a clear-cut distinction is not always easily maintained, the kind of data obtained from these different institutional settings reflects different bodies of knowledge and practices, which are justified by appealing to their own particular value frameworks, unique histories and traditions. Consequently the discovery and definition of social problems are based on conflicting assumptions about the nature of social reality, what we know and what we can learn about it.

Returning to Gramsci's (1971: 324) definition of common sense, quoted earlier on, a lot of the sociological literature reviewed in previous chapters which critiques the 'underclass' thesis, especially behavioural but also to a certain extent structural versions, is based on the principles of *advanced science* and is intended to be *critical* and *coherent* (Gallie, 1994; Marshall *et al.*, 1996; Morris, 1995; Westergaard, 1992). Regarding police perspectives on the 'underclass', the principles of rigorous empirical evidence *are not appropriate to the constitutive structures of everyday life* (Luckmann, 1983: 19). Police officers' views are necessarily more *disjointed* and *episodic* than academic and journalistic accounts. Due to the nature of police work, the assumptions and rules underscoring sociological inquiry or populist accounts, do not capture the specificity of police officers' unique perceptions.

Some senior police practitoners have used conceptions of the 'underclass' to mobilise their individual and collective opinions to justify particular courses of action and inaction. This has some resonance with regard to two linked yet almost contradictory tendencies within an organisation in England and Wales called the Association of Chief Police Officers (ACPO: see Chapter 6), which have ramifications for understanding the associations standing in the police policy process. At one level of analysis there may be few common patterns in terms of chief officers' views and perceptions on a number of issues, but at the level of ACPO, there is a fairly tight-knit cultural identity, based on a substantial degree of consensus. As a policy-making body, the onus is very much on individual members complying to guide-lines, and there is a working practice which requires dissenters to openly express their disagreement with the party line.

Policing the poor in modern society

The bulk of police research which touches on issues relating to poverty and the 'underclass' concentrates on operational prejudices and stereotypes held by the rank and file, and goes some way towards confirming Murray's (1990: 70) assertion quoted earlier on in this chapter. Such material is generally found in ethnographic research, which gives fieldworkers an opportunity to observe directly front-line policing (Banton, 1964; Cain, 1973; Holdaway, 1983; Policy Studies Institute, 1983; Graef, 1989; Grimshaw and Jefferson, 1987; McConville and Shepherd, 1992; Keith, 1993; Choongh, 1997).

Holdaway (1983) goes one step further in that his research is based on first-hand experiences of policing. Much of this work discusses the police occupational culture which fosters a view of:

> the world as a place that is always on the verge of chaos, held back from devastation by a police presence. People are naive and potentially disorderly in all situations; control, ideally absolute control, is the fundamental police task (Holdaway, 1989: 65).

By watching police officers grapple with the unpredictable nature of their working environment, some of the observers cited above have imputed certain ideas to practitioners. The key issue is how different aspects of policing come to be associated with representations of an 'underclass', and its interplay with the social divisions of class, 'race', ethnicity, sex, gender and age.

Banton's (1964, 1973) work, which has been important in terms of police training, focuses (amongst many topics) on police discretion, or partial law enforcement. Rather than questioning the legitimacy of discretion Banton mulled over the practical uses of this power in everyday police work, and the impact this had on police relations with the wider community. In their interactions with the public, officers make judgements based on their perceptions of the personal, behavioural and cultural traits of the policed. Interpersonal relations are also influenced by the kind of language used in particular situations, and officers communicate with different members of the public 'in their own language' (Cain, 1973: 82; Southgate and Ekblom, 1986: 27; Baldwin and Kinsey, 1982: 47–8). Although contravening official regulations, the compliance of 'lower-class subjects' in general, and 'low-status offenders' in particular, is obtained by using coarse language, instead of imposing legal sanctions (Banton, 1964: 183). Because this depends on the detainee accepting the classification an officer assigns to them, it may result in hardening collective identities into an 'us and them mentality', with the 'possibly serious consequence' of an insurrection (Southgate and Ekblom, 1986: 12).

There is also a spatial dimension to prejudice and the law is enforced more forcibly in 'rougher neighbourhoods' (Banton, 1964: 131). The 'rough/respectable' dichotomy is peculiar to urban policing and other kinds of stereotypes obtain in rural areas (Cain, 1973: 82). In terms of the 'occupational culture', urban policing is made meaningful through the use of a 'fundamental map of the population' (Holdaway, 1983: 81). This enables officers to link the characteristics of an environment with differential police action. One PC observed by Baldwin and Kinsey (1982) described the inhabitants of one housing estate as comprising two kinds of people. On the one hand, there is a 'civilised' majority with whom officers have minimal contact, and on the other hand, the 'priggies' or the 'garbage at the bottom of the bucket' (Baldwin and Kinsey, 1982: 47).

Drawing on American research, Banton assessed social differences in terms of myriad customs and values which differ from one community to another, frequently on the basis of social class (Banton, 1964: 138). The different norms and values held by the residents of some locales explains the polices' selective treatment of particular groups. Such action can be influenced by police officers' past experiences with suspects who have previous contact with the law. Constables may be acquainted with individuals, or alternatively know people as members of a group or class of person, as the inhabitants of particular neighbourhoods and either 'as villains or as law-abiding citizens'. Tying this up with some strands of the discourses on poverty mentioned in previous chapters, Southgate and Ekblom (1986) argued that:

It was certainly clear that, in general, certain classes of person were regarded by officers as 'deserving' or 'non-deserving' according to the previous experiences of the officer – or his colleagues – with that person or with someone seen as similar (Southgate and Ekblom, 1986: 12).

In principle the officer should be unbiased and classless, but in reality there is ample latitude for discriminatory attitudes and practices.

Reiner's (1991) ground-breaking interviews undertaken in the mid-1980s with chief constables in England and Wales show that different perceptions exist at the highest levels of the police. Two-thirds of his interviewees held the view that law enforcement was not related to class, and if there was any bias against the poor, this was not down to the police but to other criminal justice agencies, and the invisibility of white collar crime. Some acknowledged that certain groups would receive disproportionate attention, but this was not because of their class or the 'division between rich and poor' (Reiner, 1991: 204). Police work may deviate from the ideals of due process and sharpen differences between social classes, but it has less to do with the economic structure, and more to do with the 'deeper moralistic discourse' which informs chief constables' social philosophy. The causes of crime and disorder are 'interlinked as symptoms of modernity at an overarching metaphysical level beyond policy control.' In the past, an 'idealised rural haven of a society' was characterised by harmony, stability and a respect for authority, but social changes led to declining deference to the authority of police (Reiner, 1991: 138). This perspective is a more 'conservative' version of former chief constable of Devon and Cornwall police 1973–82, John Alderson's (1981, 1984), and Lord Scarman's (1981: Scarman was given the responsibility, by the government, to conduct an inquiry into the 1981 Brixton riots) 'liberal' philosophies on policing which are analysed in Chapter 7.

There are other ways of distinguishing members of the public, which do not have any class specific connotations, and refer to groups other than the poor. Lee's (1981) notion of 'police property' includes references to sexual orientation, the use of illegal substances, radical political organisations and deviant cultures. Categorisations of 'rough' and 'respectable' are not based solely on class in socio-economic terms, but on whether or not a population is 'a nice class of people' (Cain, 1973: 82). The 'rough' is a broad category, including 'the people living "down at the bottom end" plus a number of others' such as 'criminals and coloured people'. It is generally a negative label but the term is ambivalent and built up of contradictory meanings (1973: 114–5, 228). Despite this the poorest members of society persistently attract most police attention. These and other themes are also evident in the Policy Studies Institute's (PSI, 1983) research which concentrated on police policy and practice in London in terms of relations between police and different members of the public, particularly minority ethnic groups (Smith, 1983a: 1–4). Smith and Gray's volume of the report records the attitudes of both individual and groups of officers and their views about the public. The findings of the report *per se* are not rehearsed here and the main point of interest is the way the population is classified and differentiated into certain categories. The 'underclass' is one idea.

A special conception of social class, mixed with an ideal of conventional or proper behaviour [which] is just as important to the police officers as racial or ethnic groups. In this scale, the 'respectable' working class and the suburban middle class stand highest while the 'underclass' of the poor and rootless, together with groups regarded as deviant, such as homosexuals or hippies stand lowest (Smith and Gray, 1983: 111).

Officers labelled the groups situated in the 'underclass' – as well as prostitutes and pimps – as 'slag' and 'rubbish'. Although only a relatively small population, the police encounter these groups far more than 'ordinary' people, who are property owners and rate payers. There is also an implicit assumption that the 'slag' and 'dross' have less rights than 'respectable' people and should be treated accordingly (Smith and Gray, 1983: 163–5; Choongh, 1997: 43).

Seventy five per cent of chief constables also identified the significance of social divisions for maintaining public order, but more sophisticated and subtle arguments underlay their perceptions (Reiner, 1991: 198). There were a diversity of views about poverty and unemployment in the context of an affluent and materialist society. Production-based conceptions of class were significant, particularly an individual's attachment to the labour market. The 'have nots', although not poor in *absolute* terms, were *relatively* badly off compared to the 'haves'. One officer said that 'the working class has become very, very blurred.' Another commented that there are not the 'distinct financial classes there used to be', adding that 'disharmony is arising not because there is still a broad span of class in society, but because those that are most disadvantaged are more readily identifiable' (1991: 195–6). Thus deprivation is relative and social divisions are far from clear, and the old certainties of class analysis are not relevant to these officers.

The issue of family structure is also mentioned. The breakdown of traditional community controls, the increased number of working mothers – especially single parents – are cited as responsible for rearing 'not youth, but barbarians' (Reiner, 1991: 135). This perspective is, on a number of levels, a weak version of Murray's (1990) thesis, and is congruent with a 'conservative formulation' of the criminological perspective of 'control theory'. Adherents to this perspective hold the view that the erosion of moral and social controls, particularly informal rules at a community level, accounts for crime (Hirschi, 1969 cited in Reiner, 1991: 141). The chief constable quoted above is less explicit in his victim blaming than Murray, but the causal link between family structure and the behaviour of children is still noted.

'Race' and class – policing the city streets

American and British research shows that dividing the population into different sub-groups on the basis of the 'rough/respectable' dichotomy is not just explicable in terms of social class, but also by occupation, education, accent and ethnic group (Cain, 1973; Smith and Gray, 1983; Skolnick, 1966; Bayley and Mendelsohn, 1969). Again there is an assumed connection between 'coloured people' and 'the roughs', and behavioural explanations prevail over structural ones. The view that black people are different, disorganised, unpredictable, unintelligible and violent is consciously perpetuated by police officers, hence the negative and derogatory views police officers have of black people (Holdaway, 1983: 66). Officers sustain these attitudes and beliefs in their descriptions of specific sorts of behaviour, which are disproportionately concentrated amongst particular populations. Although there is no causal relationship between this behaviour and criminality, there is a strong implication that one does.

Later research reiterates the PSI's (1983) findings. According to McConville and Shepherd's (1992) appraisal of Neighbourhood Watch, these schemes are justifed on the grounds that: 'In the world of the rank and file officer, the public contribute little to the need of operational policing; they do not know anything about the criminal classes' (1992: 164). There is the general population and a group composed of 'toe rags', 'scrotes', 'pukes', 'slag' and 'scum'. Communities are divided spatially into 'rough' and 'respectable' areas and 'estates' and 'non estates'. These geographical areas have specific 'race' connotations, which are instrumental in stigmatising 'black' communities in cities such as London and Bristol (1992: 227, 231). These 'special conceptions' of 'race', class and space, which underpin police perspectives amongst the rank and file are also identified at higher levels.

Reiner (1991) did not ask any explicit questions about 'race', but some officers offered their views on the subject of the problems of a fragmented, multi-racial and ethnically diverse society. Despite this omission, it was the most frequently mentioned division. This compromises the belief that stereotypical views are confined to the rank and file, and shows that chief constables also identify minority ethnic groups as being a major source of potential trouble. However, their views are generally more sophisticated and less pejorative (Reiner, 1991: 205–10).

The relative significance of 'race' and class

Some police officers establish a correlation between poverty, the family structures of certain populations, as well as particular geographical areas, with specific kinds of behaviour. A disparate range of activities are lumped together under a single term – an 'underclass'. It has been observed, for example, that an:

> agenda of social problems, which sends coded racial messages without mentioning 'race' (e.g. the underclass), 'crime' and 'riot' have become similarly racially loaded. This is not a universal connection; neither all discussion of criminality nor all discussion of civil unrest necessarily connotes racialised meanings, it is instead the case that such subjects have a propensity to do so (Keith, 1993: 234).

The perennial tension between 'race' and class is a key theme. As argued in the previous chapter there are problems with accounts which accord primacy either to 'race' or class. In his analysis of the American situation, Wilson (1978) argued that class was generally more important than 'race' and ethnicity for understanding structural disadvantage. Miles (1989) has also argued that the material reality of class is the central issue, instead of the ideological construct of 'race'. In relation to policing, Jefferson (1993b) has argued that the reproduction of the 'criminal "Other"' is more about class and structural disadvantage than ethnicity and 'race'. This dispute cannot be resolved here by absorbing 'race' and ethnicity into a 'crudely caricatured' *lumpenproletariat* (Gilroy and Sim, 1987: 99; Kinsey and Young, 1982: 125). The dynamic processes buoying up police prejudice are more convoluted.

Police racism?

Lea (1986) attempts to avoid using a general theory of racism, by referring to 'two polarities, called direct as opposed to indirect racism and

institutional as opposed to individual racism'. More concretely, in relation to policing, either racism is carried into the police service from
wider society or it is an integral element of routine police activity. There
are other interpretations which fit in between these two examples.

Individual racism

The 'bad apple' approach understands police racism to be a manifestation of the psychology of prejudice, which explains discrimination as a
subjective expression of an individual police officer's authoritarian personality structure and their social background (Colman and Gorman,
1982). This hypothesis has been tested in the setting of the 'canteen
culture' where a minority of officers make racist remarks, which is
regarded as mere banter that fulfils the need to maintain a sense of
communality (Lea, 1986: 149–53). The question which immediately
arises is why should racialist talk, rather than allusions to another trait
be so pervasive, if it is only the view of a minority? In Lea's (1986) view
this account of police racism fails to identify a cause of racism because
the suggestion that 'group needs' are determined by the actions of a
'minority' of individuals is unconvincing.

There are several problems with this approach. In his reflections on
his role as chair of the Royal Commission on Criminal Justice (1993),
Runciman (1994: 6) suggests that it is unlikely that people carry their
personal baggage with them in this way, and individual actors conform
to the attitudes and values of wider cultural, ideological and political
collectivities. Thus prejudicial views cannot be attributed solely to the
personalities of human agents but to the institutional and societal contexts in which they work.

Another reviewer argues that in focusing on the police subculture
there is the danger of explaining the behaviour of the rank and file in
terms of 'cultural generalisations of junior police officers which either
provides a rhetorical let-off for their senior colleagues or a convenient
scapegoat for analysis of police/Black antagonism' (Keith, 1993: 14).
These views are not restricted to the lower ranks. One of the chief constables Reiner (1991) interviewed expressed comparable sentiments to
the rank and file, as did a former Commissioner of the Metropolitan
Police, Sir Paul Condon (*The Daily Telegraph*, 7 July 1995) and a former
secretary of ACPO's Race and Community Relations Subcommittee,
Tom Cook (1996). By concentrating on the subjective views of individuals at a micro level, 'institutional practices' at a macro level have
been neglected. The actions of police officers therefore need contextualis-
ing. Other factors such as the 'material institutional practices' which

place indirect/direct individual racist behaviour secondary to state/institutional racism, ought to be considered (Lea, 1986: 153).

Institutional racism

This has figured in many debates in public policy. Lord Scarman (1981: 2.22) acknowledged, but denied, that social policies intentionally discriminate against black people. It is instead necessary to account for the uneven and differentiated impact of supposedly systemic discrimination on different ethnic groups, and also how the pattern of discrimination changes over time and space. However, Scarman conceded that institutionalised discrimination may be unintentional, which raises some questions.

Mason (1982) identified four ways of conceptualising institutional racism. Firstly, the 'conspiracy' version, adhered to by neo-Marxist commentators such as Sivanandan (1982), who suggest that the capitalist system serves the interests of the ruling class, by suppressing those whose interests are antipathetic to the owners of the means of production. Structuralist approaches of this kind, which are either economically reductionist (Sivanandan, 1982) or over-reliant on the concept of ideology (Miles, 1989), cannot explain why a particular social structure is maintained without falling back on a conception of system needs, which, as Holdaway warns, 'tie us to the epiphenomenal form of "race" as a class relation' (1996: 20).

Secondly, there are 'unintentionally' racist effects. Policies may be implemented with the intention of being universally beneficial, but the actual outcomes are inequitable, which in turn disadvantages some groups. This is not an adequate explanation as to why one group rather than another secures benefits, such as the quantitatively and qualitatively different experiences of policing by various subcultural groups within Asian, Black and other minority ethnic communities (Institute of Race Relations, 1987; Stevens and Willis, 1979). This is complicated further if the relationship between these variables and sex and class are introduced. Jefferson (1988, 1993b, Jefferson and Walker, 1992, 1993) addresses some of these issues, and although 'not denying the existence of racial discrimination', argues that the 'production of the criminal Other' is not dependent on 'race' but the divisions of 'age, sex and "rough" working class' (Jefferson, 1993b: 36–9). This view is problematic, though, because the idea of 'race' is treated as if it is real and, moreover, it is used as a resource to structure social action.

Thirdly, the 'colonial approach' argues that the processes through which minority ethnic groups are excluded have been deeply embedded in state institutions, since the building of the empire, which then acquired a dynamic of their own. Pryce (1979) adopts this approach and posits a link between the legacy of colonial oppression and the irrationalities of a malfunctioning capitalist economy in his analysis of the 'lumpenproletarianized' community of St Pauls in Bristol. Pryce's ideas were taken up by Lord Scarman (1981) and John Alderson (1981, 1984) in their respective responses to the Brixton disorders (see Chapter 7).

Finally, there are politically opportunist types of racism. The tightening of immigration legislation, for example, is often justified by the fallacious argument that sound immigration policies are good for 'race' relations. State sanctioned racism of this kind has led some commentators to refer to black civil resistance, and the centrality of 'race' formation in the development of the class structure (Gilroy, 1982, 1987a, 1987b). Following the 1981 riots, Gilroy argued that these conflagrations should be understood as a 'battle for their black civil rights and liberties'. The state failed to appreciate this aspect and 'pathologised' and criminalised such activity. Unfortunately, Gilroy's analysis fails to make an essential distinction between politics and crime. It is difficult to support a view that police suppression of the riots was racist, in the way that Gilroy insists. The hypothesis that society is racist oversimplifies the multifaceted nature of racialised relations, and it is also not a good auspice for the prospects of policy change and social reform.

Recognising the above limitations, Lea (1986: 164) claims that there is:

> a normal interrelation between police work and racism. Necessary generalisations about group involvement in specific types of crime provide an organisational framework in which racist stereotypes, derived from the wider society and reproduced in police occupational culture, can function in particular ways.

The result of the combination of exaggeration, distortion and self-fulfilling prophecies which characterise relations between some members of the 'black' community and the police, has the potential to lead to what Lea and Young (1984) have called 'deviancy amplification'.

Lea's article makes considerable advances on many other analyses of the relationship between the police and 'race', but fails to acknowledge (a) the extent to which 'race' is socially constructed and becomes manifest in many different forms, and (b) how it is *transformed by* and *transforms* other social divisions. For some, to address this problem, it is possible to analytically separate 'race' from 'racism'. This enables one to see racism not inevitably as a product of categorising 'race' in biological terms (i.e. skin colour), but as an outcome of differentiating and subordinating different groups 'according to some essential origin', which has little to do with skin pigmentation (Anthias, 1990: 23). For example, racism is not only experienced by black people, but also white minority groups, like the Irish in the UK and Korean Americans in the US (Cain, 1973: 117; Abelmann and Lie, 1995). If, like Anthias (1990), one accepts that there is no essential and fixed origin, but several origins that are transformed in different socio-historical contexts in response to changing cultural, economic, ideological and political events, there are many racisms which become manifest at specific junctures. Although racism is a product of ideas about race, the interaction of race with the other main social divisions 'within the context of historically produced economic, political and cultural relations' is more important (Anthias, 1990: 24). Although these structural factors are significant Holdaway (1996: 20-1) correctly argues we must not forget the human subject:

A rather more yielding concept, which does not tie us to the epiphenomenal form of 'race' as a class relation, is 'racialised relations' (Smith, 1989). This clearly signals the social construction of 'race' and myriad ways in which relations, ideas and other phenomena become connoted or denoted with the reference of 'race'. The implication is that the world could be constructed in other ways. Racialised relations are not inevitable. Rather than rely on interest-based ideas like ideology, we can direct research to the study of social processes and ideas that in complex and subtle ways construct racialised relations and consequential social exclusion.

In the final analysis the main shortcoming of research into the rank and file is that it does not analyse the relationship between the thinking outlined in the sections above at different policy-making levels, and the complex processes which justify its existence. Below are some examples of senior police officers' views which are markedly different to their subordinates.

From a 'criminal class' to an 'underclass' – connecting academic and police discourse

The 'underclass' is one of many ideas police officers deploy to interpret and formulate a response to urban poverty. According to John Alderson (1984) the concept of an 'underclass' describes very different populations, including 'an inner city "underclass" where crimes of theft and violence [are conceivably] endemic' (1984: 171), and the connection of an 'underclass' with 'industrial disputes and policing of the underclass and ethnic minorities' (1984: 107). In Alderson's own words:

> For my purposes, the underclass was a useful description because if you are considering law and order in a society and behaviour; if you get sufficient numbers of people pushed down and feeling that they are not being dealt with fairly, they may cause criminal problems, they may cause public order problems. But they may just be victims of an unjust society. It is a very difficult situation, but when you are policing this kind of society, your policies have to be such as they may become efficacious.
>
> There are some areas of cities where policemen patrolling the streets are welcomed. There are other areas of cities where the police represent some kind of external force. People just do not relate to them. They represent the affluence in society, and therefore, auto-matically they are the enemies of the underclass. And you have got to know this and understand this, if you are a chief of police, because you order your men to do this, that and the other, and you want to know what sort of people they are policing.
>
> It is a very difficult one, but oddly enough, there are people who live in the underclass, that is as opposed to the middle class and upper class. It is another way of saying lower classes. But they are often the people who need police protection, more than say middle class areas who are quite capable of looking after themselves in many ways (John Alderson, March 1995).

Two themes come out of this quotation. Firstly, the legacy of a black 'underclass' from across the Atlantic is the touchstone. Secondly, the 'underclass' has both behavioural – especially attitudinal – and struc-tural characteristics. In relation to the former, the group identity of this social stratum is based on shared perceptions of injustice and unfairness and a feeling of 'endless pressure' (Pryce, 1979) (Significantly both Alderson and Scarman drew on Pryce's ethnography conducted in the St Paul's district of Bristol a few years before the inner-city riots). These sentiments are expressed against an external force which symbolises the affluence lacking in these people's lives. The 'underclass' consists of people from 'areas of cities' who are opposed to a police presence because of the different sets of values they hold. These attitudes are also divided along class lines inasmuch that the 'underclass' is equivalent to the lower social class. This particular conception of social class does not fit in with conventional sociological analyses of the class structure, lending support to Cain's (1973) and Smith and Gray's (1983) observations. Reiner's (1991) chief constables also highlighted the ambiguity and increased complexity of social divisions. It is not possible to look solely at the class dimensions of the 'underclass' debate as, for example, Jefferson (1993b) has done. Rather than class, 'race' mediated by culture, a social groups' minority status and place of residence are perhaps more important divisions. According to John Alderson:

> In the early 1980s, the urban unrest largely arose out of the conditions and the attitudes which were affecting the minorities, particularly Afro-Caribbean minorities in this country, who tended to have settled in urban centres. That was one factor. In my view, and this is supported by Scarman, policing of the black community, particularly the young males had been at times insensitive. These peoples' culture was difficult for some police officers. You must remember that police officers were almost 100% white, Anglo-Saxon people, policing an almost exclusively Caribbean culture. To start with you have a culture shock between the police on the one hand, and the minority, on the other. That predisposes people to be wary of the others. Furthermore, of course, the culture of the West Indians particularly, is a street culture, where the policemen patrol. Whereas the English, their culture tends to be an indoor culture. They do not often recreate in the streets. Their recreation tends to be indoors.
>
> So you have another factor there. The third factor is of course, that a lot of people felt themselves to be underprivileged. There is a volatile situation really, between on the one hand, the police (and particularly young white police), and on the other hand, the minority culture which is to some extent in conflict. And also a first generation of British born blacks. Their mothers and fathers were born in the Caribbean and regarded coming to this country as some kind of step-up, not to be down. Their sons and their daughters, their sons in particular, were not going to have this.
>
> At the same time, and particularly in London, you had what were known as the sus laws, suspected persons, where you can arrest people merely because you think they may be about to commit a crime. It was an 1824 act and it was used heavily in these areas to arrest people who had not done anything (John Alderson, March 1995).

Thus, the 'underclass' is racialised, arising out of a tension between structural and behavioural factors which are mediated by two cultures, or the culture of young black males and the culture of white police officers. Socio-economic conditions are a factor, but more immediate difficulties arise out of the mutual misunderstanding between different cultural groups, and behavioural and structural factors interact to create a complex mix of social divisions. The division of age also comes into play, and the extent to which culture is structured by age is an issue for police officers working in black communities is recognised. Black youth culture is defined as problematic by constables on patrol, and their response to the behaviour of this group is influenced by their perceptions of cultural differences. Furthermore, such views are sustained and legitimised by more powerful individuals – such as Scarman and Alderson – and, in no simple way, by the organisations which they represent.

It is difficult to attach uppermost importance to any of the social divisions outlined above, but 'race' has been a key theme from to time to time. This category is made meaningful in terms of attitudes and environmental and social conditions. Accounts of the former, typically focus on physical and behavioural differences, and are generally held by the rank and file. Some senior officers have also imputed similar views to their subordinates in the same way that academics have done, while they themselves emphasise cultural and structural dimensions of a racialised 'underclass' instead. There are many exceptions, but as the example of Sir Kenneth Newman (Commissioner of the Metropolitan Police 1982–7) demonstrates, there are also some continuities.

'Symbolic locations'

During the period between the Brixton disorders and the next crop of rioting in English inner cities in 1985, Sir Kenneth Newman had replaced Sir David McNee as Commissioner of the Metropolis. Newman also found the idea of an 'underclass' to be helpful. Like Alderson and Scarman, Newman's views were influenced by academic theories, and some of his views on policing reflect this. As such, Newman's arguments sometimes reproduce the conventional wisdom of sociological and criminological accounts. The statement quoted in the foreword of his final report as Commissioner written in 1986 asserted: 'Crime is a problem for society as a whole, it is too important to be left to the police alone.' Reiterating Alderson and Scarman, he highlighted the significance of social conditions, relative deprivation and poverty, adding that the 'stereotyping, discrimination and exploitation' of minority groups required a solution (Newman, 1985: 18). Despite this, in a talk to the European Atlantic Group in November 1983, Newman constructed a racialised idea of an 'underclass', although some caution must be exercised to avoid over-stating the significance of this statement, because he conveyed similar messages elsewhere without mentioning the 'underclass'. As the Commissioner put it:

> problems arising from ethnic minorities in the UK, USA and in Continental Europe. . . . what many commentators refer to as the "underclass" – a class that is beneath the working class . . . in multi-ethnic areas [youths congregated] in locations associated with the sale and purchase of drugs, the exchange of stolen goods and illegal drinking establishments. The youths take a proprietorial posture in this location: they regard it as their territory. In general they will regard the police as intruders and as a symbol of white society that is responsible for all their grievances. [if a police officer made an arrest] . . . there will be a confrontation which would escalate to a full-blooded riot. A similar situation exists in many ethnically mixed housing estates (Newman, 1983 quoted in Campbell, 1993: 109).

This group was spatially concentrated in particular geographical areas, hence Newman's (1983) conception of 'symbolic locations':

> Throughout London there are locations where unemployed youth – often black youth – congregate; where the sale and purchase of drugs, the exchange of stolen property and illegal drinking and gaming is not uncommon [sic]. The youths regard these locations as their territory. Police are viewed as intruders, the symbol of authority – largely white authority – in a society that is responsible for all their grievances about unemployment, prejudice and discrimination. They equate closely with the criminal rookeries of Dickensian London.

In these places, which included Brixton, mutually antagonistic relationships existed between the police and some black youths, an issue that is investigated in more depth in Chapter 7.

Continuities and discontinuities in 'underclass' discourse

Some police officers have found the 'underclass' to be a useful construct for representing aspects of social order. The empirical veracity of this limited range of examples from police discourse is of course open to question. At the very least, there are three emergent themes. Some senior police officers authenticate and add their own inflexions to the idea of an 'underclass'. Next, despite some strong links between police perspectives on the 'underclass' and academic versions they are simultaneously at odds with each other. Lastly, there is no clear-cut correspondence between the behavioural version of an 'underclass' attributed to the occupational culture by academics, and the structural perspective on the 'underclass' adhered to by more senior practitioners. Chapter 7 will explore the policy implications, but before that the police policy process is discussed.

6
The Police Policy Process in Modern Society

This chapter focuses on three interrelated issues in the context of the 43 constabularies in England and Wales: first, the different definitions of the policy process both *per se* and specifically in police research; secondly, the formal players involved in the determination of policy at different stages of this process; the third task is to evaluate the role of institutionalised power and authority in managing the conflicts and contradictions which characterise relations between policy-makers at different levels.

By concentrating on these three themes the responses of policy-makers to poverty and the corresponding social problems are explored. In the late twentieth century crucial changes occurred in the political culture, and there was a significant change in the way in which social problems were explained. Discussions about these matters have impacted at different points of the police policy process. Although the focus is on policing, it is argued that this activity needs to be located in relation to other service providers in the public, private and voluntary sectors, particularly the welfare state.

Unravelling key themes in policy

The preceding chapters synthesised the respective contributions of social scientists and public commentators towards understanding poverty and crime. How do these issues fit into the context of police policy-making? How do ideas and policy-makers interact to produce change or inertia? What are the policy implications of the processes at work in the police service, which sustain or suppress the everyday 'popular convictions' (Gramsci, 1971: 377) that constitute behavioural and structural interpretations of poverty? Are there any continuities linking élite-type groups at the top of the policy-making machinery with the 'occupational culture' of 'street-level bureaucrats' at lower levels? Such processes cannot be reconstructed in their entirety but some patterns can be identified.

Before outlining the ways in which structural and behavioural perspectives on poverty impact on policy-makers' thinking, the policy process in the police service is examined (Ham and Hill, 1993; Hogwood and Gunn, 1981, 1984). The meaning of police policy has been subjected to some sociological study, but compared to work on other police-related matters this is negligible. Likewise, police-work has been under-researched by those specifically analysing the policy process.

It is demonstrated that there are a diversity of values which are part of a project initially introduced by the neo-liberals, aiming to restructure and reconstitute the state and civil society in modern societies. Since the 1980s this thinking has fundamentally transformed the nature of the public services in British society (Clarke *et al.*, 1994). The macro economic and political ideologies of the New Right and neo-liberals led to a reappraisal of the role of police. One emergent trend is the movement away from the police as a force to a service provider. The impact of these changing values at a macro level on operational ideologies at a micro level, is patchy, largely because government rhetoric is at odds with certain aspects of the police culture, particularly the culture of police chiefs. The ideologies promoting market forces may be used to dispute structural versions of the 'underclass' held by these officers, but sustain the behavioural ones identified amongst the rank and file who are engaged in thief-taking.

Police policy – methodological and theoretical issues

With some notable exceptions (Grimshaw and Jefferson, 1987; Jones *et al.*, 1994; Savage *et al.*, 1996; Savage and Charman, 1996), there is a lamentable lack of writing about policy-making in the police service. This reflects the perennial problem of studying and trying to gain access to élite-type groups in general as well as in the police service (Giddens, 1974; Reiner, 1991). Rock (1990: 2) sheds some light on these problems in his observation that 'Sociology is necessarily a description of the more public features of the social world.' Much of policing is conducted in relatively public domains, but the more politicised aspects are worked out secretly behind the scenes in private arenas. It is useful to compare the non-work settings, where important players engage in resolving disputes and conflicts in order to reach a consensus, to a 'club'.

These ubiquitous informal networks, which are often bound together by unwritten rules, produce a level of social integration amongst élite-type groups required for the task of creating more or less coherent policies.

Other more fundamental empirical and theoretical problems arise when one attempts to come to terms with police policy. The co-authors of one of the few analyses of this topic concludes, 'policy as an authoritative statement signifying a settled practice on any matter relevant to the duties of chief constable' is unimportant, particularly in the case of law enforcement (Grimshaw and Jefferson, 1987: 197). Here we need to be aware that individual chief constables belong to a collective group known as the Association of Chief Police Officers (ACPO) which, as will be shown shortly, is a key policy-making body. For this, and other reasons which will soon be made clear, it is suggested that Grimshaw and Jefferson's (1987) theoretical framework is based more on the requirements of sociological theory than on what actually happens. A review of chief constables' and other senior police officers' written and spoken views on this matter, show that their perceptions are significantly removed from the academics, and that policy is made meaningful in sometimes different ways.

Reiner (1994: 722) has contended that there is a mismatch between what is supposed to happen when policy is determined at the top and what is intended to occur at the bottom. In practice, what the police do is based on a multiplicity of interrelated and overlapping processes which are so complex that the intentions of policy-makers at the top are not always shared, if they are at all recognised, at lower levels. This is part of the 'top-down versus bottom-up debate', which refers to the difference between the expectations of how policy should be made in principle and how policy is in fact made by 'street-level-bureaucrats' (Lipsky, 1980; Hill, 1993: 20). The ideals of an organisation may be at odds with those of the rank and file on the 'front-line', or perhaps more subtly, these officers reinterpret policy made at the top. Due to finite resources, discretion is sometimes exercised and stereotypes are constructed to minimise the feelings of anxiety and uncertainty this creates. However, this may contradict the ideals of the service. This is where the 'occupational culture' literature comes in (Holdaway, 1983). Among the major achievements of this approach is that it investigates the relationship between decisions and plans made at the top, and the translation of these principles into practice. In this sense, it holds precisely to the distinction between policy as it is written and policy in action, and it also indicates that officers at this level act autonomously and independently from senior officers. Holdaway argues that it is imperative that the existence of an 'occupational culture' amongst the rank and file is not ignored if we are to obtain a less distorted image of police policy. Without being sensitive to the often clandestine activities of police officers, it is not practicable to either observe or restrict the level of power they exercise. Thus, any attempts by senior officers to change the occupational culture of their subordinates, is 'the final testing ground of sociological analysis and policy intervention' (Holdaway, 1983: 175).

Almost a decade later a joint project undertaken by the police staff associations in England and Wales, conveyed a similar message. In one force, the rank and file were either unaware of force goals set by chief constables, or they consciously rejected them. Senior officers, on the contrary, thought that constables had knowledge of force goals and objectives (Joint Consultative Committee, 1990). Minimal contact, especially between officers from senior and intermediate levels and the lower ranks, exists as an obstacle to the formulation of policy. In terms of policy-making, there is substantial evidence which suggests that senior officers do not have enough direct contact with officers under their leadership to judge fully the possible effects of policy changes initiated at the top. Therefore, in the research into the 'occupational culture', there is recognition of the importance of process, and the complexity of the patterns of interaction between different policy levels. Jones *et al.* (1994) elaborate on these themes in their definition of policy which refers to changes in the style, organisation and operation of policing and how these interlock with ideas of democracy embodied in other social institutions in wider society. While agreeing with the general thrust of their analyses there are some gaps. An attempt is made to formulate an alternative conceptual framework.

Policy is an amalgam of explicit, implicit, formal and informal statements and practices, which are shaped by ideas such as the 'underclass'. These are underpinned by the 'coherent logic' of ideologies (Hewitt, 1992: 45), which frame a range of different values and resources to justify particular decisions, actions and interventions. In practical terms, the policy process is also shaped by the interaction of a host of influential individuals and groups. Identifying key players is a somewhat arbitrary exercise and there are profound variations across time and space. For example, an officer from Her Majesty's Inspectorate of Constabulary for England and Wales (HMIC) said that the main innovators include:

> Lord Scarman, Sir Kenneth Newman, Margaret Thatcher, Bernie Grant, Justice Popplewell, Lord Justice Taylor. At a local level, those

who are influential range from chief officers to the local community relations officers and Community Beat Officers (CBOs). Constables can influence policy making not just top-down, but also bottom-up. The more that influence comes from the bottom-up, so much the better. The difference between strategy and broad ideas formed at this level, and the views of what people on the ground are experiencing should be bridged. Outside the police organisation, at a local level there are councillors, officers of council, community intervenors.

Amongst these other actors, and not necessarily in order of their importance, are Her Majesty's Inspectorate of Constabulary (HMIC), the Audit Commission (AC), Home Office Police Department (HOPD), the House of Commons Home Affairs, Expenditure and Public Accounts Committees, the Association of County Councils (ACC), the Association of Metropolitan Authorities (AMA); and since the mid-1990s the Confederation of Local Police Authorities (COLPA), various Home Office and independent research units (i.e. HORPU), the Superintendents Association, the Police Federation, members of particular communities and the media. In this chapter the main focus is on individual chief constables, ACPO and the Home Office.

The twin themes of policy in general and police policy are now examined.

The key themes for analysing the policy process

Hogwood (1992; Hogwood and Gunn, 1981, 1984) identifies seven approaches for analysing policy: (i) policy content, (ii) policy process, (iii) policy outputs, (iv) evaluative studies, (v) information for policy-making, (vi) process advocacy and (vii) policy advocacy. Options (iv–vii) are more appropriate for an *analysis for policy* whereas (i–iii) are more clearly suited to the *analysis of policy*. The study of policy outputs can be dispensed with, policy content is significant to some extent, but *policy as a process* is of central importance. Change is also important, particularly *purposive*, and *organisational* change as well as *changes in legislation* and *public expenditure*. In the form of an ideal-type, a dynamic policy process consists of *policy innovation, policy succession, policy maintenance* and *policy termination*. By examining particular examples of policy, some aspects are more important than others, and different approaches are joined together in many ways (Hogwood, 1992: 17–20).

The notion of *policy innovation* describes how governments decide to intervene in a new area for the first time, but such instances are a rarity because innovations are seldom newly created. *Policy succession* refers to a wide range of changes like the substitution of existing policies, the amalgamation of two or more policies, or in some instances the partial completion or ending of a policy, but again these are not new innovations. Policy *maintenance* involves minor adaptations and modifications to keep a particular policy in line with original objectives. Sometimes larger changes than those occurring in the first two categories may be required, notably in terms of the volume of provision. Turning to *policy termination*. As the label indicates this is the 'mirror image of policy innovation'. There are, with a handful of exceptions, few examples of this (Hogwood, 1992: 19–25).

These processes can be situated in the context of a broader debate, namely the difference between 'rational comprehensive' and 'bureau-incrementalist' perspectives on policy (Walker, 1984). The distinction is somewhat artificial and deceptive, because they are in fact two sides of the same coin. The latter, for instance, describes the various ways in which decisions are made in bureaucratic organisations, and the other is used to prescribe how decision making processes should be set up in principle. This leads Walker to claim that 'Both are bureau-orientated' (1984: 85).

The rationalist model – as the name suggests – rests on the assumption that social action follows the laws of rationality, and that there are a set of clearly identifiable and discrete events which are amenable to planning by policy-makers. Initially, an issue is selected and defined. This involves decision making and the selection or rejection of particular strategies for pursuing specific goals and objectives. In other words the means are inextricably bound up with the ends:

1. Faced with a given problem;
2. a rational man first clarifies his goals, values, or objectives, and then ranks or otherwise organises them in his mind;
3. he then lists all important possible ways of – policies for – achieving his goals;
4. and investigates all the important consequences that would follow from each of the alternative policies;
5. at which point he is in a position to compare consequences of each policy with goals;
6. and so choose the policy with consequences most closely matching his goals (Lindblom, 1968: 13 cited in Castles *et al.*, 1971: 28).

The viability of this approach has been questioned by incrementalists (Lindblom, 1959). Instead of viewing the policy-making process as linear and co-ordinated towards realising particular pre-defined goals and objectives, there is often a lack of correspondence between what is intended and the actual outcome. There are also many powerful, unknown, contradictory and conflicting forces which counteract the inexorable logic of the laws of rationality. The rational-comprehensive approach therefore is based on the assumption that it is possible to start from scratch and gradually build a policy from this starting point. Ham and Hill (1993: 84) contrast this 'root method' with the 'branch method', where policy-makers inherit a given situation which they change incrementally, bit-by-bit. This means that there are no major alterations to a policy and that the status quo remains essentially unchanged. In general, incrementalists conceptualise the policy process as 'serial in nature' and one in which 'problem shifting' rather than problem 'solv[ing]' is the defining feature (Finch, 1986).

Walker's (1984) notion of bureau-incrementalism, refers to small scale institutional adaptations based on 'pragmatic' considerations. Changes are minor and concerned with ironing out irregularities and making sure that there are adequate budgetary constraints to ration the usage of available resources. Rather than resolving more fundamental problems, such as inadequate funding, the status quo is maintained without transforming traditional institutional arrangements. By doing this, questions about how a society is organised in terms of who controls and governs it are glossed over. Bureau-incrementalism neglects the existence and effects of power because it rests on a 'pluralist' conception of this resource, which is based on the premise that power is split up amongst many different groups rather than being concentrated in the hands of the few. Consensus and compromise is also overstated at the expense of conflict which may prevent alternative and potentially more radical policies from surfacing onto agendas. In other words, policy determination is constrained by structural barriers. Thirdly, by promoting inertia above change, bureau-incrementalism is essentially conservative (Walker, 1984: 72–83).

Furthermore, incrementalism is not open-ended. It is bound by certain rules, values, principles and 'mission statements' or 'founding goals' which transcend the interests of particular interest groups. Indeed, Lindblom's (1979: 523 quoted in Hill and Ham, 1993: 14; 95–6) later work accepts that the optimism underlying the incrementalist model in the 1950s and 1960s, when the US power structure was interpreted in pluralistic terms, was unwarranted in the decades after. Instead, he described a 'high degree of homogeneity of opinion' that is 'heavily indoctrinated' and which represents the interests of the dominant and powerful groups in society. This compels Ham and Hill (1993: 96) to argue that Lindblom explored the 'operation' of power and ideology (Lukes, 1974). These issues are revisited in due course.

Police research – an absence of policy

Policy is difficult to define, but this is especially so in the police service. In one of their reports into the police service the Audit Commission – a quango set up in 1983 to measure the effectiveness and efficiency of public services and given the responsibility of advising them on how to improve their performance – said that 'Few other public services have staff who are as multi-functional as police officers' (Audit Commission, 1994a: 65). Unlike the provision of health, education and social security where the scale of resources required to respond to social needs can be estimated, police policy-makers often have to react to the unknown. Transition and uncertainty also affect other fields but the nature of these changes is unique for the police. Later on in the chapter it is demonstrated that though the police service possesses these unique characteristics, it has not been immune to the influence of market values and the 'new managerialism' (McLaughlin and Murji, 1997).

The police provide a service which is largely responding to the demands made of them by the capricious public they serve, and particular types of events, such as seasonal, weekly and even daily variations, which cannot realistically be anticipated. This emphasis on 'unplanned drift' ignores three factors (Ham and Hill, 1993: 91). First, although the specific behaviour of an individual or organisation may vary from day to day the rules influencing that behaviour may be approximately identical. Secondly, the extent to which the status quo remains unchallenged requires further analysis. Lastly, certain sections of society, such as an impoverished 'underclass', are regarded as being predisposed towards creating particular kinds of difficulties.

Further unnecessary confusion arises when the inter-connections between policy and operations is discussed. The overused and fundamentally flawed distinction between policy and operations is unhelpful for the analysis of the police policy process. Reiner, for example, has rightly pointed out that:

> Purportedly policy decisions have implications for particular operations, while operational decisions are the individual atoms which constitute what de facto policy is. They may realise or sabotage formal policy. The attempted distinction is ideological rather than logical (Reiner, 1994: 743).

Rather than viewing policy-making and its implementation at an operational level, as separate activities, it is helpful to consider these as different stages in an ongoing process. Policy is re-created as it is implemented, hence the contention that 'street-level-bureaucrats' add their own interpretations to those policies made at the top. This sense of process is sometimes missing from analyses of police policy.

Grimshaw and Jefferson's (1987) study of a provincial force in England, which involved the direct observation of the behaviour of the players involved, is one of the few analyses of different policy-making levels. Their research does not tie up with the concerns of this narrative, but it provides a useful reference point for understanding police policy. Amongst other things, they contextualise policy in relation to three structural determinants of policing, including 'legal', 'work', and 'democratic' dimensions. They examine the inter-relationship between these in several social settings, and ascertain which combination of these structures is the most pre-eminent in determining particular aspects of police policy and practice. Their analysis also focuses on organisational or vertical and occupational or horizontal levels of policy-making, the meanings of policy and practice at different levels, and how these interact with administration and law enforcement. Whilst doing this they 'examine the alleged "gap", not between policy and practice, but rather between particular types of policy and particular types of practice.' Following discussions of policy relevant matters in various institutional sites, clearly defined sets of principles are formulated, and chief constables then disseminate these in the form of 'authoritative statements' to guide practice. 'Unambiguous' policy of this kind, they argue, is non-existent. There is a caveat, however, because in day-to-day administrative work policy is of some relevance, such as the purchasing of cars or computers. It is in the area of law enforcement that policy is less pivotal (Grimshaw and Jefferson, 1987: 17–20).

There are tensions between the organisational statements designated as policy and the extent to which these are incorporated into occupational practices. The general tenor of their argument is that policy is rendered redundant by the legal structure. It is worth quoting them at length to exemplify their hypothesis:

On the one hand, the independence of the office of constable renders problematic the relationship between a chief constable and his officers. It is this problematic relationship – a consequence of the legal structure operating here – which lies behind our finding with respect to policy, namely, that effective operational policy (authoritative statements signifying settled practices of law enforcement) cannot exist. The universality of constabulary independence makes operational policy effectively redundant as we saw (1987: 291).

The essence of their argument is that policy in the form of *an authoritative statement signifying a settled practice on any matter relevant to the duties of the chief constable* is absent. This reflects the reluctance of senior officers to infringe on an integral feature of the ordinary police officer's duties as a 'street level bureaucrat', namely the enforcement of the law by applying discretion (Brogden, 1982: 243–7). Chief constables also exercise discretion in their selection of particular offences, but police officers on the beat have the additional power of virtual invisibility enabling them to act unobserved by their senior colleagues. The rank and file clearly deviate from what senior officers state, but this neglects how policy may be operational, or that the two are, as Reiner's (1994: 737) quotation above registers, inseparable. Discretion is also exercised in various contexts which are framed by rules and ideologies, and the freedom to exercise it is circumscribed by a host of structural constraints. It must be added that these pressures comprise other extra-legal factors associated with police discretion, an issue that is followed up in a few moments.

Grimshaw and Jefferson's restricted definition of policy neglects the multi-faceted nature of this phenomenon and contains two faulty premises. Firstly, their efforts to ground their analysis in a 'concrete' social setting misses out on other factors which are not necessarily intelligible through empirical research. Secondly, social action in general and specifically police policy is not necessarily directed towards explicitly stated goals, and there are implicit, unintended and unanticipated consequences. In contradistinction to Grimshaw and Jefferson's (1987) analysis, what comes out may be policy, even though it is not intended to be, or is not codified as such. The informal is not necessarily antithetical to the formal and the former is not bound to be the 'grey, hazy development underneath' the latter, which conversely, is 'fixed and readily identifiable'. Instead, they are 'continually adapting to each other' (Ham and Hill, 1993: 131).

To reiterate Hogwood and Peters's (1983) thesis summarised previously, policies are rarely conceived out of nothing, but are tagged on to existing arrangements and most policies embellish and succeed older ones. Jones *et al.* (1994) have addressed some of these dilemmas in their assessment of the factors which shape police policy. Primarily, they consider the ways in which those participating in policy-making observe the principles of democracy. Bearing this in mind, they focus on how key players produce organisational changes in the style of 'policing on the ground' in three areas: crime prevention, crime against women and children and civilianisation. They claim that until the 1980s senior police officers regarded their legal independence and autonomy or discretion as inviolable. Consequently discussion or even the identification of policy was rare, and the academic literature tended to focus on legal codes and law enforcement. The authors highlight two problems. Firstly, resources are finite, but the scope for enforcing law is potentially illimitable, and therefore the law is applied with discretion. Secondly, the police perform many tasks that have little to do with law enforcement, such as 'keeping the peace' and crime prevention (Jones *et al.*, 1994: 1–8).

Police policy is made to 'determine the patterns of policing', in behavioural and organisational terms, by recognising the limitations imposed on police work. Thus, 'policy is interpreted as that which is inherent in the actual pattern of policing' (1994: 8). They use the example of officers' tendency to disbelieve women's allegations that they had been raped, particularly before Roger Graef's now notorious BBC 'fly on the wall' documentary about the insensitive interviewing of a rape victim. The authors describe this as a policy, although no explicit or formal statements advocated this practice, which indicates that:

> A policy can be deduced from a pattern of behaviour. Also, where a stated policy is contradicted by the actual pattern of policing, the real policy is likely to be that inherent in behaviour: to the extent that policy is not carried through. It is merely rhetorical (Jones *et al.*, 1994: 7).

This analysis is very much in line with the concerns of this book, but there are three further interrelated themes requiring attention. First, police perceptions and representations of order and their 'typifications' of poverty (Berger and Luckmann, 1966: 48). Second, the different values and socio-political perspectives underpinning their ideas about these phenomena, specifically the main differences between behavioural and structural explanations. Thirdly, the relationship between these two issues and policy-making. The issue of policy is examined below, but it is worth noting that for the purposes of this discussion there are two dimensions: 'policy making as a mental skill and policy making as an institutional process' (Banting, 1979: 4).

Reconceptualising the police policy process

The following definition of policy is eclectic, drawing on a broad range of theoretical frameworks and the views of some of those actually involved in the process. An effort is therefore made to avoid reifying theory above what actually happens.

The police policy process is multi-faceted, consisting of traits which are relatively open-ended and those bound by structural constraints. To understand police policy it is necessary to come to terms with a complicated set of economic, societal, ideological, discursive and political factors, which influence the allocation and distribution of resources. (Resources are defined very broadly, to include values and ideas as well as other more conventional conceptions). Generally speaking, the policy process is characterised by many fluid, competing yet interdependent dynamics, which are mediated by institutionalised power. This process consists of a series of formal and informal decisions whereby competing issues are prioritised above others, leading to the determination of an appropriate course of action in response to a given issue. The necessary resources are then deployed. These processes are at work at macro and micro levels of the policy hierarchy with varying degrees of relevance.

The various types of decisions made and actions taken in the police policy process involve discursive, ideological, material, practical and institutional factors. Firstly, facing uncertainty in their daily work all police officers create meaningful representations of the social world. These representations are constructed on the basis of their personal attitudes and beliefs, which are manifest in the form of discourse. They then acquire solidity in form of values or ideologies which are shared by wider cultural and social groups. Secondly, at a material and institutional level, those exercising effective power unify this plurality of diverse and fragmented viewpoints into more or less coherent identities and outlooks at a macro-level (national) and a range of other more localised cultural identities and perceptions at a micro-level. These representations are sometimes based on explicit statements and practices, but other more implicit factors are also salient. Although the latter are not directly observable, they can sometimes be detected empirically. Before examining some of these issues the formal structure of the police policy process is described.

The main players in police policy-making

The formal roles performed by the main players, including the chief constable, the police authority and the Home Secretary are sketched in Appendix 1. As an outcome of the Police Act of 1964 there are 43 police forces in England and Wales (including the Metropolitan Police and the

City of London Police). Prior to the Police and Magistrates' Courts Act (1994) the police authorities were almost excluded, but more recently their position has, in principle, been strengthened. The contents of these two pieces of legislation cover a wide range of issues that cannot be discussed here.

Chief constables and ACPO – changing priorities

As individual warrant-holders under the Crown, chief constables are non-partisan and impartial law enforcers: the principle of constabulary independence. In reality this axiom is more ambiguous and there have been well documented conflicts between chief constables and police authorities, which do not need to be repeated here (Lustgarten, 1986; Reiner, 1991; Simey, 1988; McLaughlin, 1994).

ACPO was originally set up as a staff association but this body now plays a pivotal role, albeit not necessarily a dominant one, in policy-making both at national and force levels (Reiner, 1991: 362–7; Wall, 1998). The association is made up of a mesh of committees and sub-committees, chaired by chief police officers, who work in different areas of policy: there were over thirty in 1995. These committees have varying degrees of prestige, and their respective impact on policy is dependent on the issues which are at the top of the agenda at a particular moment. Committee members, dates and agendas of meetings are not generally made public, but certain conferences are open to the media (Jones *et al.*, 1994: 292). ACPO is ultimately responsible for determining policy, but decisions to opt for particular courses of action are based on ideas derived from below: policy is formulated not only top-down but bottom-up too. According to a chief constable:

> Policing isn't about political statements. It isn't about political emphasis. It isn't incidentally about police authorities' setting broad frameworks. It isn't about chief constables' giving leadership and direction, setting objectives. Policing is about response to things that are happening in communities by local police offices. That is really what it's about.

However, the most interesting point for our purposes is that ACPO members are bound by rules and a 'corporate identity', and although there is undoubtedly attrition the promotion of consensus is at a premium (ACPO, 1990, 1993). The following four examples given by four chief constables in the mid-1990s make this point:

We organise ourselves nationally into service committees. We are trying collectively to put a voice of the service to central government and the collective representative organisations of local government who still dominate the police authority.

ACPO at a national level is now a much stronger and more influential body than it used to be. We take a much more corporate view about things, and we work on positions that we ought to have in respect to policing issues and policing matters and we come to conclusions and agreements at the chief constable's council, and that becomes national police policy. And this would be observed by chief constables unless he wrote to them and said I cannot agree that that is the right way to do things. Therefore I am indicating that I do not regard that as policy and I don't intend to observe that conclusion. So in other words if you don't agree with it you opt out. That has not happened very often. I think I've done it once. And I'm trying to think now what the issue was. I think the issue resolved itself in the end.

There is a higher level of agreement within the ACPO Council now than there was a decade ago. If a member of the Council disagrees with a particular issue then they are required to sign a written statement indicating their dissent. This is uncommon. The result of this high level of agreement is that the application of policy is more consistent.

The body of forty-three chief constables, called the Chief Constables Council, has quite a lot of difficulty in deciding policy because the chief constables all have slightly different views. So what you are inclined to get is a proliferation of guide-lines. And there is a written axiom that if a chief constable wants to depart from ACPO guide-lines, or ACPO policy, of course he or she should feel free to do so, but ought to commit in writing to ACPO the reason why the chief constable is departing and what grounds he or she would give for that. So you will often find a committee recommending something as policy, taking it up to the Chief Constable's Council. The Chief Constable's Council then doing their best to pull together forty-three different views, and finishing up with something which is called guide-lines, effectively.

The significance of these views for understanding the policy implications of the 'underclass' are revisited in due course.

The Home Office

The Home Secretary and the Home Office are very much in the background, but their values are ever-present. The Home Office disseminates proposed legislation, amendments to existing legislation and other authoritative statements, such as circulars, to ACPO. The latter are 'virtually mandatory' and police chiefs have to give a good reason for disregarding them (Reiner, 1991: 274; Jones *et al.*, 1994: 151–2; Brogden, 1982: 114–5).

As one chief constable has suggested, the Home Office and the Home Secretary are influenced by the ideologies of central government at a macro-level.

> First of all it's beyond the Home Office, it's the government itself, in terms of what the political thrust is on law and order. That's reflected through the Home Secretary and his or her ministers. So they're main players. That means the senior civil servants in the Home Office who work for the Police Department, they are the main players, because they are the ones who convert the political will or obstruct the political will, in some cases, into policy.

Governments and ideologies change over time, but since the late 1970s the ideological standpoint of the New Right had attained 'hegemony' (Gamble, 1988). The revaluation of social values has seen a move away from 'democratic-welfare-capitalism' (Marshall, 1972: 15) underpinned by collectivist values, towards the neo-liberal economics, market principles and individualism of the New Right (Friedman, 1980; Hayek, 1973; 1986). Throughout the 1980s in particular, there is some evidence of 'spontaneous consent' and 'active or passive affiliation to [these] dominant political formations' (Gramsci, 1971: 12) by some police officers (Reiner, 1991). However, there is no simple relationship between the politics of the government and police officers. There are dissenting voices, such as John Alderson, former chief constable of Devon and Cornwall Police (1974–82), but such figures are sometimes silenced and marginalised. However, those views which are repressed beneath the surface on one occasion re-emerge at another time. The relationship between government and police ideologies can therefore change significantly.

Her Majesty's Inspectorate of Constabulary

Although not a member of the tripartite structure, the inspectorate's work is interlaced with that of the Home Office. Since its inauguration, its status has been enhanced. The first Inspectors of Constabulary were appointed in 1856, under the provisions of the County and Borough Police Act, with the purpose of monitoring and ensuring the efficiency of provincial police forces. This role was fairly informal until the Royal Commission on the Police (1962) and section 38 of the Police Act of 1964. Following its enactment the Inspectorate's contribution to policing was formally recognised. In the last quarter of the twentieth century HMI started to address a much wider range of issues than it did in the 1970s.

The role of the HMI changed drastically throughout the 1980s and 1990s (Police and Magistrate Courts Act, 1994), most notably the decision to inspect the Metropolitan Police as well as the other 41 provincial forces in England and Wales. Now the inspectorate is divided into five regions (Home Office, 1995a: 11), and information about overall performance and specialised functions is gathered and rapidly assimilated via centrally determined channels.

The extension of the HMI's 'scope and profile' is arguably bound up with central government and the Home Office, most notably the increased tendency towards rationalisation and control over policing. This has resulted in the HMIC adopting a more interventionist stance, particularly because it is implicated in the Home Office's increasingly centralised position. The inspectorate's refusal to renew Derbyshire Constabularies' certificate of efficiency three times between 1992–4 demonstrates this well.

Police policy – a different approach for framing questions

Policy-making in the police force is stratified and not reducible to the activities of one layer of its organisational structure. At national, corporate, force and more localised levels, policy is based on explicit and formal rules. At lower levels, there are the perceptions of those participating in routine operational activities, such as patrolling constables, who develop their own informal rules and working practices. In other words, different kinds of information are utilised at different levels of the policy machinery. Scarman (1981: 4.15) argues that one aspect of policy is based on various sorts of information:

> Policing decisions are founded not only on statistical analyses but on, among other things, close day-to-day knowledge of the crime in an area, based on reports from junior officers, on contact with offenders and victims, based on perceptions as to community views of important priorities, the whole pervaded by the exercise of professional judgement reflecting years of police experience.

Policy has situationally specific meanings and recognition of context is all important for appreciating how a 'sense of phenomena [must be] grounded in time and place' (Wagner *et al.*, 1991: 9). There are philosophical and practical problems here. With respect to the latter, policy is cumulative, and made up of individual and institutional actions which span the course of a long period of time, and include past events of which policy-makers may lack awareness. Some comments made by a senior official from the Home Office Police Department is a good example of this type of reasoning:

> In the civil service the turnover of staff is very quick, and one does not stay for an especially long time in any particular post or department. Due to these kinds of constraints there is no time to check up on a department's history, and what so and so said about an issue at a particular time.

Rock makes a similar point about the making of victims' policy at the Home Office:

> A large cast of people were responsible for the creation of policy, their contributions were staggered over a number of years, and their views were shaped by a succession of evolving and interacting commitments, stocks of knowledge and social relations. Truths changed over time as accomplishments or failures were noted, new ambitions were formed, and a series of accounts seemed to freeze the past. There was no single, still, independent point where reality was revealed (Rock, 1990: 1).

The philosophical problem, which also has practical implications, is that many meanings are attached to policy, and the task of finding 'Aristotelean essences', is probably inconceivable, but as argued earlier on, there are some universal themes, such as the constraints of organisational authority and power.

This can be illustrated by examining the influence of the 'new managerialism' in the form of the 'Three Es' – economy, effectiveness and efficiency. Beginning with Home Office Circular 114/1983, – but also see Home Office, 1967; House of Commons, 1982; Treasury, 1983 – which aimed to redefine the role of the police. Since then, the influence of managerialism has gathered momentum through the publication of additional Home Office Circulars, the contribution of Her Majesty's Inspectorate of Constabulary (Home Office, 1995a), the Audit Commission and the

Review of Core and Ancillary Tasks (Home Office, 1995b) – the latter was launched in 1993 by the then Chief Secretary to the Treasury, Michael Portillo. The Review set out to determine the service's 'core', 'outer core' and 'ancillary' functions. It is an example of Walker's notion of the 'Treasury brand of bureau-incrementalism', whereby in planning and formulating policy the Treasury imposes limitations on expenditure which affect all of the government departments in Whitehall (Walker, 1984: 117). The Independent Report on the Role and Responsibilities of the Police (Cassels, 1996) supplemented this. Moreover, the White Paper on *Police Reform* (Home Office, 1993b) enabled chief constables to identify those duties which are either 'maximum direct provision' or 'maximum external provision'.

At a macro-level, government officials and senior officers disseminate relatively fixed and codified statements which identify the role and responsibilities of the police. In response to this, ACPO and the Home Office have produced statements regarding 'key operational areas'. The former lists five priorities in the provision of 'key service areas': (i) community relations, (ii) public reassurance and order, (iii) calls for assistance, (iv) crime prevention and detection, and (v) community relations. The Home Office's statement highlights the five main aims of policing (i) to fight and prevent crime; (ii) to uphold the law; (iii) to bring to justice those who break the law; (iv) to protect, help and reassure the community; and (v) to provide good value for money. These appeared in Home Office Circular 27/94 which articulated the five key objectives for policing as being:

(1) to maintain, and if possible increase, the number of detections of violent crime;
(2) to increase the number of detections for domestic burglaries;
(3) to target and prevent crimes which are a particular local problem, in partnership with the public, local authorities and other agencies;
(4) to provide high visibility policing so as to reassure the public;
(5) to respond promptly to emergency calls from the public.

ACPO's (1990) *Statement of Common Purpose and Values* is another example, which was modelled on Sir Peter Imbert's (Commissioner of the Metropolitan Police, 1986–1992) 'mission statement':

The purpose of the Metropolitan Police Service is to uphold the law fairly and firmly; to prevent crime; to pursue and bring to justice those who break the law; to keep the Queen's Peace; to protect, help and reassure people in London; and to do all this with integrity, common sense and sound judgement.

We must be compassionate, courteous and patient, acting without fear or favour or prejudice to the rights of others. We need to be professional, calm and restrained in the face of violence and apply only that force which is necessary to accomplish our lawful duty.

We must strive to reduce the fears of the public and, so far as we can, to reflect their priorities in the action we take. We must respond to well founded criticism with a willingness to change.

Since publication, ACPO's statement has become part of all of English and Welsh constabularies' corporate identities. Significantly, the Home Office's and ACPO's objectives differ in an important respect, inasmuch that keeping the Queen's peace is omitted from the former's 'mission statement' (see Chapter 8).

The salience of these statements is far from clear. Circular 27/94 is an example of a 'mission statement', or what Hewitt (1992: 9) has called a 'founding goal'. These *ad hoc* and *post hoc* justifications are used as rhetorical devices to understate the level of uncertainty the police confront, and to persuade the various audiences to which they are addressed, that the organisation is committed to performing its traditional functions, when in fact new problems mean that it has to change tack and depart from its original aims. The tendency for the service to drift away from its original and traditional aims is an essential feature of policing, though, because it is necessary to continually re-invent the service. In the words of the Audit Commission:

> [t]he complexity of modern policing does not admit the luxury of [such] simple mission statement[s]. The boundaries of police activity have expanded to meet new demands and have shifted from a narrow enforcement perspective to a wider concept of public service. Some argue that to define the services core role too precisely would constrain the flexibility required to police a constantly changing society. But when the increasing demands on the service lead to the police and public being unsure of roles and priorities, clarification becomes vital (Audit Commission, 1993: 11).

By identifying the means through which particular ends are realised, there is the problem of finding the appropriate means to achieve this in practice. The impact these abstract principles have at the micro-level of operational policy is unclear. To overcome this stumbling-block power and ideology are useful concepts.

Power and ideology in the policy process

There are several conceptions of power, or more accurately 'effective power'. Power may be channelled through many outlets and can be exercised diffusely (pluralists) or centrally (élites) (Mills, 1956; Dahl, 1958). In addition to these perspectives, which put social agents at the centre of their analytical frameworks there is also a structural dimension (Lukes, 1974, 1986). It is not feasible to do justice to the literature on power, and only a few issues are examined (for an overview see Clegg, 1989). Power is distributed inequitably amongst various social, economic, political and cultural groups. There are also a multiplicity of power structures which interact under specific ideological and material circumstances. Numerous commentaries imply that power is simply imposed from above, but one must also account for the fact that in the policy process, if anything is to happen at all, some kind of consent and consensus is required from those below.

How is this consensus and consent constructed? Bachrach and Baratz's (1970: 16) 'two-dimensional view of power' (Lukes, 1974; 1986: 9) elaborates on Dahl's (1958) pluralist 'one dimensional view of power. The pluralist conception of power held by the latter focuses on the conduct of decision takers, which entail observable conflicts between the different groups who are each aiming to further their interests. The interests of each of these groups is reflected by the actual route or course of action that they take. In other words, 'where the interests' [of groups] 'are seen as equivalent to revealed preferences' (Lukes, 1986: 9). In their critique of Dahl's (1958) pluralist model, Bachrach and Baratz (1970) introduce the second face of power:

> [i]n conceiving of elite domination exclusively in the form of a conscious cabal exercising the power of decision making and vetoing, he overlooks a more subtle form of domination; one in which those who actually dominate are not conscious of themselves simply because their position of dominance has never seriously been challenged (1970: 16).

The 'overlooked' form of domination in decision making they refer to is:

> non decision-making, that is, the practice of limiting the scope of actual decision making to 'safe' issues by manipulating the dominant

community value, myths and political institutions and procedures. To pass over this is to neglect one whole 'face' of power (Bachrach and Baratz, 1970: 18).

This second face of power describes covert conflicts between actors over actual as well as potential issues. Thus, non-decisions, whereby particular issues are kept off the agenda, are as significant as actual decisions. It reveals the ability of the players involved to determine what is on the agenda so that any of the decisions taken do not threaten the position of the dominant political groups.

Lukes (1974) describes a third face of power which shows that even if a group is unaware of a conflict of interests, this does not deny the existence of a conflict. This disputes the hypothesis that power is only exercised where conflict is observable. This does not dispense with overt and covert conflicts, but illustrates how power may operate to shape and adjust aspirations and beliefs in order that they do not reflect people's interests. This third dimension of power, known as 'latent conflict', is used to question the view that if a consensus exists, power is not being exercised. In Luke's own words there are:

> many ways in which potential issues are kept out of politics, whether through the operation of social forces and institutional practices or through individual's decisions. This, moreover, can occur in the absence of actual, observable conflict, which may have been successfully averted – though there remains here an implicit reference to potential conflict. What one may have here is a latent conflict, which consists of a contradiction between the interests of those exercising power and the real interests of those they exclude (Lukes, 1974: 24–5).

The key issue here is ideology and this brings us back to the Gramscian analysis outlined in Chapter 5.

'Re-inventing the service' – values, policy and practice

Ideology is enmeshed in the policy process, both at a macro-level and a micro-level. The former includes the dominant political and economic values of the day, in this case several types of New Right and neo-liberal thinking, which would still appear to be of relevance for New Labour. According to the 'mission statements' and 'founding goals', the police are now in the business of providing a service in which value for money and consumer sovereignty are revered. These principles are taken up by the tripartite system and are incorporated into corporate and operational ideologies (ACPO, 1990, 1993). This is not necessarily the case in practice. What are the implications for the policing of urban poverty? Hewitt's (1992: 44–5) reference to the 'elasticity of ideologies' is helpful here. He illustrates how different as well as similar values, or 'contrasting but complementary principles', are arranged in such a way that a 'coherent logic' is developed to justify particular kinds of social action or inertia. At a micro-level there are operational ideologies which are sometimes in conflict with those at a macro-level. For example, competing ideological perspectives may be mobilised at different points, between and within these strata. The ideas which acquire 'the solidity of popular beliefs' (Gramsci, 1971: 375) in police discourse are explicitly different from the government's rhetoric, but they are sometimes implicitly bound by the constraints and values underpinning that rhetoric or political ideology. Furthermore, the 'occupational culture' of the lower ranks forms part of an all encompassing police culture which includes other levels, ranging from the intermediate up to the tripartite structure. The diverse range of ideas underscoring representations of poverty, the 'underclass' and social exclusion do not belong exclusively to Lipsky's (1980) 'street level bureaucrats', but also to the more senior street-wise bureaucrats who hob-nob with powerful civil servants and government officials. It is at such points that the ambiguities in talk about the poor, such as the behavioural/structural distinction, come into play.

At a macro-level, police policy and practice is created step-by-step, reacting to changing societal, economic, political and ideological conditions. Two issues arise here. Firstly, the impact of the structural factors mentioned above, and secondly, the ways in which these impinge on actors at a micro-level. If individual Home Secretaries are taken as an example there is little to unify them in terms of the diversity of their individual intellectual standpoints, foibles and idiosyncrasies.

Individuals are undoubtedly relevant but there are other important factors such as the influence of ideology, especially New Right and neo-liberal thinking. Since 1979, their influence has been profound in general terms, but in some specific areas its impact is more uneven and, in others, hardly apparent at all. The all but unconditional support Lady Thatcher gave to her 'boys in blue' was reappraised in the 1990s – remembering that Home Office, Circular 114/83 had set a precedent – and the market values imposed on other public service sectors have been directed at the police. The provision of a service which gives 'value for money' is now a dominant theme in police policy, particularly a high quality of service for the customer (Clarke *et al.*, 1994). Sir John Woodcock, just before retiring from the post of Chief Inspector of HMIC surmised that 'as stewards of a police service which delivers community service . . . [o]ver the course of the next few years, I believe that the service will learn how to develop a passion for the customer' (1993: 15). These developments have a fit with a quasi-market approach:

> while state funding is retained, the way in which services are provided is changed. Decision making is decentralised as the state becomes a purchaser of services which are brought from independent providers competing in an internal or quasi market (Le Grand and Bartlett, 1993). The idea is that internal competition produces more efficient services at a lower price, while affirming consumer sovereignty (McLaughlin and Murji, 1995: 124).

The effects of these changes are not altogether clear. Do all police public encounters take place in the market place? What is the relative status of the poor compared to the non-poor? How do police officers tackle any tensions that may arise between the conflicting requirements of these different groups?

In principle ACPO is immune to political influence, but in practice it is pinned down by the government's ideology and the buzz-words of the market place, enshrined in 'the new managerialism' (McLaughlin and Murji, 1997). Some chief constables show dissent by questioning the government, and on such occasions the Home Office may discipline those who refuse to give their consent. This is unusual, however, and though there are minor conflicts of interest, as Reiner's (1991) interviews with chief constables conducted in the 1980s consistently show, most officers give their consent 'spontaneously'. Although the 'great-man theory of history' (Carr, 1961: 53) has some truth in it, individuals are up against the hidden dimensions of institutional power (Bachrach and Baratz, 1970; Lukes, 1974). In the context of a field in which uncertainty is the main feature there is another general trend, namely the Home Office almost always wins.

The dominance of the Home Office may be maintained in two ways. Firstly, because of the extreme ambivalence and lack of clarity surrounding the status and role of the main players in the tripartite system, the Home Secretary may evade responsibility for a particular policy that they personally devised. This is usually done by blaming the failure of a policy on other levels, or by invoking the ideologically determined distinction between policy and operations, as a way of abnegating responsibility. Secondly, there is the matter of 'delegated discretion'. As Hill (1993: 11) puts it:

> in a sinister way hierarchies may leave discretionary decision making to fall into a specifically biased pattern – for example, involving racism. They leave the responsibility for action they accept, but will not publicly condone, in the hands of subordinates.

This happened in the aftermath of some episodes of serious disorder within poor communities, such as the LA riots in 1992 in the USA and the 1981 Brixton disorders in England. Some specific examples of this are taken as illustrations in the remaining chapters.

Further down the organisational hierarchy, as a consequence of the legal structure and the independence of the office of constable, the codified statements issued by senior officers are not translated into practice. This accounts for the view that there is no policy. This conception of policy is problematic because its multi-faceted nature is glossed over. As Lipsky's 'street-level-bureaucrats' (1980) and the occupational police culture literature shows, this conception ignores the fact that the most crucial difference is between policy as it is written and policy in action. Jones *et al.* (1994) elaborate on this in their definition of policy in terms of the interlocking organisational and behavioural patterns of policy.

The ideological perspectives which characterise the relationship existing between the Home Office and ACPO also impact on relations between other policy-making levels in the force hierarchy. Due to it's 'elasticity', ideology can accommodate conflict, inconsistencies and contradictions, and yet still be bound by a coherent logic (Hewitt, 1992: 44–5). The divergent forces at work at macro- and micro-levels may therefore meet. The government's ideology and rhetoric interacts with the attitudes and popular beliefs which exist in other social organisations and amongst other social groups. If individual views and the perspectives of cultural collectives alone are considered to be important, then there are few continuities. If they are interpreted as the outcome of individuals and groups giving their 'spontaneous consent ... to ... the general direction imposed on social life by the dominant fundamental groups' (Gramsci, 1971: 12), that is an entirely different narrative.

In a 'classless society', the likelihood of the 'underclass' appearing in any mission statement or citizens' charter produced by or for the police service is remote (Jones, 1997). The macro ideologies underpinning these statements become codified in the form of 'founding goals' which then become sedimented into the structure of the tripartite system. The impact of these unambiguous statements on the service as a whole, is far from clear. As Sir John Woodcock has pointed out, the tripartite structure of accountability is 'deliberately diffuse' (1993: 14) and consequently, macro ideologies interact with operational ideologies. This is where the 'occupational culture' (Holdaway, 1983) comes into prominence. Although there is not a single and unified police perspective at this level, a significant part of the work of 'street level bureaucrats' (Lipsky, 1980) is based on minimising uncertainty and creating helpful representations of the environment in which they perform their duties.

It is under these conditions that some of the stereotypes employed by the rank and file sustain ideas that are similar to the behavioural perspectives on poverty (see Chapter 5). Those working in the tripartite system, though closer to the direct influence of the macro-ideologies of the government, also have past experiences of the 'occupational culture' gained when they were members of the rank and file. In addition, there are other elements of the police culture which are unique to the senior ranks. The ambiguity of the 'popular convictions' (Gramsci, 1971: 377) which underscore thinking about poverty are then garnered and woven into the all encompassing police culture. Moreover, as well as police officers' careers changing over time, their views about the poor also alter and become more sophisticated. This shift of emphasis, which is demonstrated in the ensuing chapters, shows that a structural notion of poverty is preferred above a behavioural perspective. In addition to this, the macro-ideologies of the government and the operational ideologies of the police service work dialogically. The result is a powerful cocktail of neo-liberal, managerial and market values which do not formally support certain representations of poverty, such as the idea of an 'underclass', but informally sustain a behavioural version. In contrast to this, there is the existence of 'common sense' thinking amongst senior officers, which emphasises a structural version instead.

7
Policing and the Power of Public Debate

In the UK and the USA alike policing has had to come to terms with the powerful influence of political ideology. This has interacted with academic and public commentaries in the creation of social policies. For example, thinking about poverty, such as the idea of an 'underclass', has been influential in determining the response of some police policy-makers to increased social divisions and exclusion and specifically the problems of crime and disorder which flow out of these (Scarman, 1981: 2.11; Alderson, 1984: 171, 107; Newman, 1983). Since the early 1970s, under the influence of American thinking, the post-war consensus on welfarism in British society came under attack. This coincided with an increase in poverty as well as rising crime, but especially urban unrest. Throughout the 1980s there were outbreaks of public disorder in some of Britain's inner cities which, for some scholars, were a consequence of these changes (Benyon and Solomos, 1987). Some observers regarded these conflagrations to be the British equivalent of the 'race' riots which occurred in the US during the 1960s, and in certain ways the response to the former was conditioned by reactions to the latter.

After the urban riots of 1981 and 1985, the spectre of lawless American ghettos appeared in the British press, and Lord Scarman among others drew heavily on American analyses of racial disorders and anti-discrimination policies because few indigenous sources were at hand (Silver, 1993: 343).

Since then, Scarman's (1981) report has been a key document serving as a guide-line for policy-making in the modern British police service.

This chapter investigates how these events are bound up with the racialisation of poverty in the UK. It also describes how they led to fundamental changes to styles of policing. Firstly, the background and key debates surrounding the 1980s riots are reviewed. Secondly, the cardinal themes in the police policy process at that time are identified. The main concern is with broad brush developments in policy rather than small scale innovations at a local level. Since 1979 neo-liberal governments have introduced the disciplines of the 'new public management' into the police service to make it more efficient, economic and effective and to reduce public expenditure (McLaughlin and Murji, 1995, 1997; Farnham and Horton, 1996; Butcher, 1998). At that time the idea of communitarian or community policing was important. Given that public funds are finite, the police were required to work more closely with various public, voluntary and private agencies to reduce crime and disorder (Alderson, 1981; Scarman, 1981). Thirdly, the particular points at which the ideas about poverty discussed in Chapter 5 may have entered the police policy process are delineated. Some senior officers stress the importance of the structural dimensions of poverty, whereas it would appear that the Home Office and the rank and file tend to favour a behavioural version. Indeed some of the the former have criticised government policy by referring to the complex structural processes which lead to poverty and also unrealistic demands being made of the police.

Poverty, the 'underclass' and racialised disorder

It only takes a cursory glance at the events in Britain's inner cities throughout the 1980s to see that riots have been a significant feature. These were not a new phenomenon, and past incidents had set the tone for police relations with certain sections of the black community at national and local levels in the 1970s and 1980s (Fryer, 1984; Keith, 1992, 1993).

In the aftermath of the 1981 riots, and again following the disorders of 1985 and 1991 and 1992 respectively, the 'underclass' won a place on the agenda of politicians, media commentators and some policymakers. Waddington (1992), Campbell (1993), King and Brearley (1996) and Reiner (1998) provide comprehensive accounts of this unrest, although they do not refer to poverty and the notion of an 'underclass' as such. This chapter is less concerned with the events themselves but more with the public response to them and the various usages of the term 'underclass' at that time.

The key incidents were the inner city riots in Bristol in 1980, and Brixton, Moss Side (Manchester) and Toxteth (L8, Liverpool) in 1981. These events represented a watershed in terms of British policing, and the Brixton disorders led to Lord Scarman's (1981) government commissioned inquiry, which set the agenda for police policy and practice, and legitimated the states response to further urban unrest in Brixton, Broadwater Farm and Handsworth in 1985. It was also the touchstone for interpretations of the community disorders on some 'outer city' estates in the 1990s, even though the circumstances were markedly different (Campbell, 1993).

The National Commission on Civil Disorder (Kerner) (1968) and its analysis of the 1960s American riots, had a profound influence on the contents and recommendations found in Scarman (1981). The Kerner Commission was set up in the aftermath of the riots in Newark, New Jersey, Detroit, Michigan, Wisconsin and the 125 riots in April 1968, which followed the assassination of Martin Luther King (McPhail *et al.*, 1998: 55–6). The thinking about social stratification found in the American literature, particularly the idea of a racialised criminal 'underclass' or 'criminal class', was also a characteristic of Scarman's commentary (1981: 2.11). Another key issue was whether or not the Brixton disorders were 'race riots'. The general consensus in the social sciences is that 'races' as such do not exist but are socially constructed or racialised (Solomos and Back, 1996: 1). The riots in the 1980s were not specifically about 'race', but references to this socially constructed concept are commonplace in discussions of these incidents, regardless of the reality of these events, and as such they were racialised (Keith, 1993; Holdaway, 1996).

These visions of social divisions not only influenced debate but also policy. The academic response to the 1980s riots also alluded to the idea of an 'underclass', but significantly it was not attributed to any particular author. Usage of this representation of poverty was not explicitly based on the behavioural/structural distinction, and as such its meaning was not altogether clear. This had consequences at the time of the arrival of Murray's (1990) behavioural version, because he was able to set the agenda without encountering much in the way of counter-argument and critique.

Public debate and the inner city riots

Solomos's (1986) analysis of the 1980s riots addressed many issues about policing and government policy. A dominant image of the 1980s riots is that the events in some British inner cities were equivalent to the American 'race' riots of the 1960s. The kind of class structure found in some urban communities across the Atlantic was also beginning to emerge in some of Britain's 'symbolic locations', particularly an 'underclass'. This group was excluded from society, primarily by its unemployment, and signified a challenge to order and political stability. Solomos (1986: 7) raised the following questions regarding the riots:

> Were the events a sign that an 'underclass' of black citizens were so marginalised from society that they could only participate by protesting violently? Did existing social conditions and high unemployment create the basis for outbreaks of violence in the future? What role did the police play in the actual course of events, particularly in multiracial areas?

Structural changes to the welfare state and labour market led to increased tension between marginalised groups and the police service, and mounting anxieties regarding the potential for 'no-go areas' to develop in some of the locales populated by these groups. This was more than a concern for the police alone. In wider society, and in terms of public policy, the key issue was the failure of government-led initiatives to tackle the problems of inner cities.

Lea and Young (1982, 1993) mobilised the idea of an 'underclass' in their summary of the different perspectives on law and order policy since the 1981 riots. At that time the structural/behavioural distinction was not an organising principle of the 'underclass' debate. In their evaluation of the diverse range of responses to these events they classify these into three essentially different viewpoints, namely those of 'liberal/social democratic', 'conservative' and 'neo-Marxist'. However, the behavioural and structural perspectives were implicit in these approaches too. For example, a watered-down version of Sir Keith Joseph's 'cycles of deprivation' thesis appeared in 'conservative' accounts. The structural perspective of Giddens (1973) and Rex (1973), referred to in Chapter 4, underpinned 'liberal' and 'neo-Marxist' narratives, although with some significant differences of emphasis between them.

The 'conservative' interpretation emphasised 'race', selfishness, incivility, wickedness, alien cultures and their contribution to decay in the urban infrastructure. This black 'underclass' fell outside the norms and conventions of society as a whole, and the police stood as the last line of defence against 'lawlessness' and social disorder. The proposed solutions to these problems were tougher and more militaristic forms of policing. Conversely, Lea and Young (1982: 6) argue that:

> Liberals point to the palpable connection between Thatcherite monetarism, rising unemployment and urban violence. The riots are

seen . . . as a collective demonstration of despair. The all too frequent violence of the police is the spark that sets the ghettos alight. Black and white youth (emphasis is often laid on the mixed ethnic composition of the rioters) fight together against the arbitrary abuse of police powers.

The main points of the 'liberal' perspective are congruent with most scholarly evaluations of the 1980s riots, particularly the emphasis placed on the strong relationship between exclusion from the labour market, over-dependence on state provided welfare and disorderly behaviour. Thus, social deprivation rather than behaviour was a more significant indicator. Lea and Young (1982) suggest that the 'liberal' version does not see the cause of the unrest exclusively in terms of the actions of minority ethnic cultures but the behaviour of an ethnically mixed group which is alienated from the rest of society. The 'underclass' is therefore not black but a multi-racial group, who take out their frustrations, both with their socio-economic position and against police malpractice, by confronting the police on the streets. To reduce the level of police community conflict, 'liberals' call for the police to be more accountable to the public to ensure that they can win their consent to enforce the law legitimately.

Reflecting more specifically on Scarman's recommendations from a 'neo-Marxist' standpoint, Brake (1983) considers the issue of policing in the inner city and how the Queen's peace can be maintained in this setting. In his view, Scarman's 'liberal report', although identifying an indispensable role for the police and for legal procedure to guarantee that public tranquillity is maintained, kept the issue of the role of central government in the background of the inquiry: 'Scarman highlights the question of specific police practices while at the same time silencing any association between government policies and "their catastrophic effects on the underclass"' (Brake, 1983: 10–11). Further, he adds a different inflexion to the 'underclass' debate, in an attempt to understand how the dynamic process of 'Britain's Metropolitan class polarisation' accounted for the 1981 riots, by describing the structural and cultural forces at work in the creation of a black 'underclass'. This class fraction is defined in terms of the social divisions of 'race'/ethnicity and age.

According to Brake (1983) changes in the labour market caused by the recession, combined with racial discrimination, created a de-skilled, unemployable, poor and state dependant 'underclass'. These structural factors interact with cultural factors, especially 'black' youth culture which is (a) an adaptation to harsh material circumstances and

(b) a way of establishing a strong sense of cultural identity to counter structurally generated forms of social exclusion. This identity is frequently manifest on the streets and in those public spaces which bring them into contact with the police. Black youth view the actions of the police to be connected with their social exclusion from the labour market. They are also perceived to be supporting the 'white' culture that is diametrically opposed to their own. This 'black underclass' has no stake in society and therefore there are few reasons for them to conform. Hence any of the conventional sanctions that can be imposed on the disorderly do not exert much of an influence on the 'underclass'. The police are also seen to represent an authoritarian state, and as such are the target of the resentment of some marginalised populations.

Narratives on the policing of an 'underclass'

A mixture of cultural and structural factors is evident in the above analyses. There is also an historical dimension, specifically in the allusions to the 'dangerous classes'. This theme is addressed squarely by Davis (1989) who makes an explicit link between the twin themes of policing and the 'underclass' in London in the 1860s and 1980s (see Chapter 2). From the former, she examined the Jennings Buildings, a London slum, which was mainly populated by working class Irish people. In the latter, the multi-racial Broadwater Farm Estate is inhabited by an excluded 'underclass'. Both of these places have borne the brunt of selective law enforcement by the police (Davis, 1989).

Although there are some continuities between the two periods, Davis places a greater emphasis on the discontinuities. The main difference is that in the nineteenth century, violent confrontations between the police and immigrant poor were not an issue on the minds of policymakers. Discriminatory policing in the 1860s is therefore profoundly different to that in the 1980s, inasmuch that during the former period the police had the widespread support of the respectable majority in suppressing unruly minority groups. In the 1980s, policing was politicised, and those who were exposed to oppressive police practices mobilised effective oppositional strategies within mainstream politics. The new spatially concentrated 'dangerous classes' that inhabited 'no-go' areas therefore challenged the popular misconception in police history that the police have won the consent of the entire population.

Commenting specifically on the 1985 riots and the conflicting interpretations of these episodes in various narratives, Davis highlights some parallels between 'liberal' and 'conservative' perspectives, especially in media-led commentary. In *The Daily Mail*, for instance, Lynda Lee

Potter stressed the lack of respect for the law in the black community, whereas David Steel (MP) spoke of an unemployed inner city 'underclass'. The distinction between an 'alien culture' and an 'alienated culture' is also implicit in Davis's critical review of these commentaries. The main issues in the 1980s were, first, the intensity and prevalence of disorder which was unprecedented. Secondly, the riots were symptomatic of a crisis in law and order and were an indication that some urban locales had become 'no-go areas' for the police. Thirdly, these developments were the consequence of a disreputable 'black underclass' whose culture was antithetical to the police and the 'respectable' majority.

The police are aware of these trends and have emphasised the dangers a 'criminal underclass' pose for the policing of modern society. The service has detected public anxieties and 'respectable fears' about 'no-go areas', reflected by some police officer's special pleading for more powers to strengthen their 'paramilitarist' capabilities. In part, paramilitarism refers to the equipment and tactics outlined in the Association of Chief Police Officers (ACPO's) Public Order Manual (Jefferson, 1987, 1990, 1993a; Waddington, 1987, 1991, 1993, 1994; Northam, 1988). Davis (1989) argued that these new police tactics and powers signified a further threat to civil liberties. The police's use of these powers during the 1984–5 miners strike is an example of this (Waddington *et al.*, 1989).

Waddington (1993) has claimed that a lot of this writing has held developments in public order policing to be responsible for violent conflicts arising between the police and the 'underclass'. Waddington's scepticism is directed at the authoritarian state thesis which underscores such analyses. However, the view that the police control an 'underclass', and that this is a reflection of the interests of the coercive state, continues to be a convincing and influential argument (Morrison, 1995: 442–3). For this reason it deserves some attention.

Jefferson draws on Cohen's key theoretical arguments and applies these to explain the hegemonic crisis that followed the economic recession of the mid-to-late-1980s. The restructuring of the labour force led to the creation of 'the new *lumpen*'. Police powers were being increased and the service was becoming increasingly unaccountable to the public. Moreover, paramilitarism led the police to exercise their legitimate use of force to maintain public order. Jefferson (1990: 41) has argued that this is especially so in areas:

in which sections of male, especially male, especially black youth and militant dissidents of all kinds – pickets, demonstrators, etc. –

figure prominently with whom the preferred negotiated approach – the 'unwritten system of tacit negotiation' – has never been properly established or has broken down. This breakdown may be fairly temporary, in the case of say a particular industrial dispute, or, in the case of some highly alienated groups – Afro-Caribbean youths, for example – apparently irrevocable.

This work makes some advances because it highlights the complex structural processes at work in the making of an 'underclass', but there is a danger that specific examples of police community conflict can be reduced to the more general requirements of 'neo-Marxist' theory. This type of analysis would seem to have problems because it smacks of a state or ruling-class conspiracy. It should also be added that the police tend to not use of all of their powers, but act in a more restrained way. Waddington (1994: 39), for example, has argued that although the police have had the capacity to erode civil liberties, on the whole, they have decided not to do so. Thus law in writing is of less importance than law in practice. Also, Keith (1993: 81) has rightly argued that the 'neo-Marxist' perspective tends to treat all challenges to civil order as if they are the same, without acknowledging significant contextually specific differences. For example, in the above quotation, Jefferson conflates industrial disputes with alienated youth, without mentioning the different social and political conditions experienced by these groups. More crucially, Keith (1993: 253) refers to the extent to which the nature of mobilization of the different groups involved in disorder changes over time and space.

In their synthesis of the work completed in the 1970s and 1980s, Brake and Hale (1992) argue that policing was oriented towards an 'underclass' of young people who are excluded from social citizenship. This impoverished and disenfranchised element – including minority ethnic groups, 'urban deviants such as gay people, hippies and the *lumpenproletariat* of the city' – stands in stark contrast to the 'respectable', 'working' and 'suburban middle classes'. The police sub-culture maintains these distinctions in practice in their work as agents of social control.

Reflecting on Dahrendorf's account of the 'underclass', mentioned in Chapter 4, Reiner (1994: 756) argues that this group is a de-incorporated section of the working class, and a direct consequence of the free-market economic policies of the New Right. Moreover, the prospects of this group being re-integrated into society are negligible. Their exclusion from citizenship leads to alienation from society's universal moral values. These interlocking themes are explored in further detail by Lea and Young (1993) who take on board the tension between structure, culture and behaviour. They claim that:

> American developments are paralleled by those in the UK, indeed in many major capitalist countries in the west. The economic forces at work are the same – Los Angeles, London, and all other cities are all the same part of the world capitalist economy (Lea and Young, 1993: xxvii).

They focus on the ongoing dialogue between Murray's (New Right) and Wilson's (1987) structural interpretation of an 'underclass', particularly the notion of 'social isolation'. The debate between Murray and Wilson also corresponds with the debate in criminology between 'right realism' and 'left realism'. Since the mid-1980s Lea and Young (1984) have demanded that the political left should recognise the scale of problems in deprived inner city communities and the reality of high crime rates affecting them. Reflecting on the 1980s they add that the reluctance of the left to tackle these issues meant that the New Right seized the initiative instead. They argue that 'left realist' criminology should address the same reality but from a different political standpoint. Rather than drawing on Murray's ideas they direct their attention towards Wilson's structural analysis. Indeed the following quotation indicates that this is a major element of their analysis, particularly their allusion to:

> the way in which subcultures are shaped by material circumstances. In the case of the ghetto underclass the material predicament that presents itself in isolation: the collapse of economic opportunity and, as Wilson points out, not 'welfare dependency' but rather cuts in levels of welfare support both in the form of social security and unemployment benefits and support for the family and community structures which over the last two decades have been systematically undermined (Lea and Young, 1993: xxvi).

Referring to an article printed in *The Financial Times* (5 May 1992), they contextualise this theoretical perspective in relation to unemployment, decline in the inner cities and the spatial concentration of minority ethnic groups and riots.

Police policy – structural and cultural changes

At the time of the 1981 riots, police policy was not an explicit item on the agenda of sociological inquiry into these areas. Likewise some senior police officers at that time held to the unwritten assumption that there was no such thing as policy. This was justified on the grounds that the principle of constabulary independence, especially in operational matters, was sacrosanct. Policing was a very complicated job which lay beyond the comprehension of those outside the profession, and in terms of public order policing those below the level of the senior ranks (ACPO, 1985). Examples of disagreement, particularly over the issue of the democratic accountability of the police between some chief constables and police authorities in some force areas illustrate this (Kinsey, 1985; Simey, 1988; McLaughlin, 1990). The denial of the existence of policy is artificial and mirrors ideological concerns rather than social reality.

These issues pose some descriptive and analytical problems, but expanding on the definition of policy outlined in Chapter 6, this appraisal is interrogated in more detail, concentrating on two key government endorsed documents. Lord Scarman's (1981) inquiry into the Brixton disorders and Home Office Circular 114 (Home Office, 1983a). The former introduced a communitarian model of policing, combined with elements of paramilitarism; and the latter injected the managerial principles of neo-liberalism into the police service.

Dominant themes in police policy in the 1980s

Although context is of primary importance in understanding the policy process, Scarman (1981) claimed that some overarching principles circumscribe police work at all times and in all places. Sir Richard Mayne's instructions issued to the 'New Police of the Metropolis' in 1829 are taken as an example. In Scarman's (1981: 4.56) words:

> The function of our police has been authoritatively defined as:- 'The prevention of crime . . . the protection of life and property, the preservation of public tranquillity'.
> This threefold function requires 'consent and balance', words which I take to mean that, if the police are to secure assent of the community which they need to secure their operations, they must strike an acceptable balance between the three elements of their function.

The failure to strike such a balance was almost universally considered to be key issue at the time of the Brixton disorders.

Scarmanism

Scarman's (1981) inquiry into the Brixton disorders focused on policing and the wider social context in which it is performed, including the welfare state and the labour market. In terms of policing the main problems are as follows. There was a deterioration of police relations with some members of the community of Brixton, because of the overreliance on 'hard' policing, such as the activities of the Special Control Group (SPG), like 'Operation Swamp, 81'. Through extensive surveillance, this operation was implemented to flood the area of Brixton to detect and arrest burglars, by stopping and arresting supposedly suspicious people on the streets and then taking them to the police station for interrogation. The above factors, combined with the insensitive use of the 'sus' laws, or the charge of being a suspected person under section 4 of the Vagrancy Act of 1824 (see Chapter 2), antagonised some of the policed. 'Swamp 81' was one of the triggers, or flashpoints, precipitating the Brixton riots. Scarman summed up the quandary of policing a multi-racial community in terms of the difficulty of reconciling two potentially incompatible aims and objectives:

> how to cope with a rising level of crime – and particularly of street robbery (in the colloquial phrase 'mugging') – while retaining the confidence of all sections of the community, especially the ethnic minority groups (1981: 4.11).

Other matters included individual racially prejudiced police officers – institutional racism was denied – and distrust of the police, especially of their role in investigating complaints made against officers. Centrally important to this was the collapse of police liaison committees and the lack of police consultation of communities concerning policing in Brixton.

Scarman recommended that changes in recruitment were necessary to increase the intake of members of different minority ethnic groups, improved training, amendments of the Public Order Act (1936) and changes to the arrangements for the investigation of complaints made against the police. A significant innovation was the development of an institutional apparatus necessary for police community consultation, and Scarman (1981) suggested that a statutory framework be set up to facilitate local consultation between the Metropolitan Police and the community at borough or police district level. An institutional framework of this type could set up a forum in which the police and public could engage in dialogue to discuss their mutual expectations of their respective roles. Scarman's call for community consultation was accepted by Lord Whitelaw, the then Conservative Home Secretary, albeit with some reservations, and it was only a matter of weeks before Scarman's proposals were added to an already existing thread of informal police discourse. It took a while for this to become a formal element of the police policy process (Keith, 1988; Morgan, 1992), and it was not until three years later that these principles were embodied in section 106 of the Police and Criminal Evidence Act (PACE, 1984).

> Arrangements shall be made in each police area for obtaining the views of people in that area about matters concerning the policing of the area and for obtaining their co-operation with the police in preventing crime in the area (1984, section 106: 1).

Since then, police consultative committees (PCCs) have been established at a sub-divisional level in most force areas.

Lord Scarman's 'basic thinking remains as expressed in the Brixton report' (Personal communication, 20 February 1995). Most crucially, community consultation has become a statutory requirement (section 106, PACE). One aim of these consultative committees was to institutionalise conflict by talking about policy rather than by fighting on the streets.

The 'Three Es'

Simultaneously, Home Office Circular 114 (Home Office, 1983a), which embodied the 'Three Es', *economy, effectiveness* and *efficiency*, was disseminated. This mirrored the concerns of the Financial Management Initiative (FMI) set up in 1981 by Baroness Thatcher (Conservative Prime Minister 1979–90), which was intended to cut government expenditure, especially in the civil service. Sir Derek Rayner, then Managing Director of the British retailers, Marks and Spencer, was appointed as 'efficiency adviser' and set up the Efficiency Unit, located at Central Office. Under Rayner's leadership the FMI introduced business values and market disciplines into the public services, requiring them to make cuts in spending and to run government more efficiently. At the beginning of the 1980s the police service, described by Thatcher as her 'boys in blue', avoided any contact with the FMI but by 1982 they directed their attention towards the police. These and several other market values are now enshrined, albeit in a modified form, in the highly influential work of the Audit Commission; also set up under the first Thatcher administration (Butcher, 1998: 25). Its primary objectives are the quest for economy (reducing expenditure), efficiency (performing the right tasks), effectiveness (doing the right thing) and good practice.

In tandem with the emergence of the Audit Commission, certain aspects of Circular 114 were a precursor to the ethos of 'new public management' which took off in the 1990s. Some of the micro developments and the points at which these intersect with broader developments in policy are discussed when the policy implications of the poverty of the 'underclass' are examined.

Circular 114 addressed several other issues, especially the policy implications of finite resources which have to be distributed in response to ever-changing pressures, demands and priorities. The main difficulty is in identifying where human resources are most needed at a particular time. As well as covering the issue of effectiveness and efficiency the circular also includes advice and guidance on community consultation and multi-agency approaches. Increases in crime and disorder and the establishment of bodies responsible for community relations, required a substantial increase in police funding, but this was no longer economically viable. The Home Secretary had to consider applications for an increase in police establishments by taking four criteria into account. First, the Secretary would have to be satisfied that the available resources would be used to maximum utility and that their use would be in accord with pre-determined priorities and objectives. Secondly, applications must be specific and not general. Thirdly, if additional posts are required the police authority must be able to provide the necessary funding. Fourthly, because the government only reviewed expenditure plans annually, increases will be granted for a year ahead. This is because:

> The Home Secretary [therefore] attaches importance to the determination of objectives and priorities in the police service, and to the allocation of resources and deployment of police and civilians manpower in a way that will most effectively and efficiently secure those objectives and priorities (Home Office, 1983a: para. 6).

Although planning is an indispensable requirement, the exceptional is also taken into account, because unanticipated events will occur from time to time, and resources will need to be reallocated periodically to respond to more immediate problems requiring urgent action.

As well as restating the general principles sketched by the Tripartite Working Party on the Police Act of 1964, another significant point made in the circular was that policy objectives should be clear to all ranks. To counter some of the arguments underpinning Grimshaw and Jefferson's (1987) one-dimensional definition of policy (discussed in Chapter 6) the following point, contained in Circular 114, is illuminating:

the views and experiences of more junior officers can make an important contribution towards the formulation of policy, and should be valuable resource to the Chief Officer or the local commander who is considering or reviewing his aims and objectives (Home Office, 1983a: para. 9).

Police policy is therefore multidimensional and is not just dependent on those authoritative statements issued by chief constables and the Home Office.

Policing poverty – the policy implications

In the words of John Alderson:

> The idea of an underclass can cause the police policy makers to react in one of two ways. One is to regard them as a constant source of trouble, and pass laws like the sus laws were passed in the nineteenth century, to control them. Or you can take a more welfare approach and say, 'well these people have big problems', therefore, we have to address the problems that are causing any criminality that may arise.
>
> I have heard people say, for example, when being interviewed, that the reason they deal in drugs is because they can make more in a day than they can in a month if they are working, because they do not get paid well, or if they are on the dole. And so they turn to criminality for economic reasons. And all of these things have to be understood by the police. Policies have to be suited to fit it. That is where if you have a good community policing policy, you will have officers working amongst these underclass, who understand them and do collaborate with social workers, probation officers, teachers, and others to keep people out of juvenile delinquency, delinquent behaviour. Here police work becomes very close to social work, as well as being criminal work too. So it is important to the everyday thinking of ordinary police officers, which should be adjusted in this way, and they should not just see themselves as avengers going into depressed areas merely as some kind of external threat. But they should try to get into the fabric of these areas to understand them and try to prevent victimisation of old people, and young people who are victimised by crime in these areas. The less well off people have to be policed in a much more sympathetic way, but always at the same time, having the capacity to react firmly and strongly to maintain order.

The question is does this have any bearing on policy making. It did up to a point inasmuch that the idea of community policing is now being established and these people are being observed by the police in maybe a more sympathetic and understanding, but firm way (John Alderson, March 1995).

The policy implications of the 'underclass' are twofold. First, there is the *firm* and *strong* approach. Second the communitarian or *welfare* approach. For the purposes of this chapter the former refers to paramilitarism and changes in public order policing. Jefferson (1993a) and Waddington (1993) have discussed this matter and nothing is added here. The second perspective is a major component of Scarmanism, and this *welfarist* dimension implicitly underpins the modern police service in the US and the UK (Mawby, 1990: 30). The slippery concept of community is an integral part of this perspective. Scarman, Alderson and Newman added a new impetus, albeit as a philosophy rather than an institutional mechanism, to this aspect of police work.

Communitarianism – the welfare approach

Throughout history the concept of community has lacked a fixed meaning, and has been defined in many ways. It is beyond the scope of this book to focus on this topic in any detail, but there are important themes. Firstly, we all live in communities, but the boundaries of each of these are rarely clearly demarcated. The size or scale of communities range from the global, national, regional, urban/rural to more localised communities such as neighbourhoods, estates and families. These are differentiated and fragmented along the lines of the social divisions of 'race', ethnicity, class, age, sex and gender. All of these criteria intersect in various ways across time and space.

Secondly, ideologies are mobilised by institutional agencies who define and shape communities. Lacey and Zedner's (1995) work on the relationship between community and contemporary criminal justice provides a helpful starting point, and is used to scrutinise Alderson's philosophy of community policing. This is important because some of this thinking was taken up by Scarman, and although the precision and utility of their ideas about community policing can be contested, these figures brought the issue to the top of the police service's agenda in the aftermath of the Brixton disorders.

According to Lacey and Zedner's (1995) account of community, the term is rarely clearly defined in discussions about policy. As well as spatial, temporal, organisational and many other socio-economic and cultural bench-marks, it has an ideological dimension. In their own words, community:

> evokes a cluster of values – solidarity, reciprocity, mutuality, connection, care, sharing. Significantly, political discourses of community are generally characterised by a slippage between ideological and institutional reference points; and the slippage significantly affects the meaning of these discourses (1995: 302).

These different meanings in the context of public policy discourse can be split up into to three categories. First, notions of community may be embodied by the public, quasi-private and voluntary organisations responsible for the determination of policy. Second, a community is a designated geographical area where policies are made to tackle a specific set of problems in that locality. Third, a community in the 'role of beneficiary' where policies are made to regenerate feelings of attachment to a place. In this book, the usage of community in police talk is a concern, specifically those 'ideas of community . . . [which] have been invoked for both "diagnostic" and "therapeutic" purposes' (Lacey and Zedner, 1995: 301).

'Policing the plural, multiracial and participatory society'

In the evidence he submitted to Lord Scarman, Alderson (1981) outlined the main principles of his philosophy of communitarian or community policing. Alderson described the general thrust of his ideas in terms of three interrelated themes:

> I began in the early 1970s, during the recession, to consider my position about policing this area of Devon and Cornwall, where I had 3000 officers and 500 civilians. I wrote a piece called 'From Resources to Ideas'. What do you do if you cannot get any more policemen and you cannot get any more power or you do not want any more power? And you just cannot get any more equipment. What do you do? Do you just bemoan it and sit down, or do you think of different ways of achieving your objectives? The objectives were the prevention of crime and the maintenance of public order. It was out of that, that community policing, in my terms, and this is very important, in my terms, grew.
>
> I must at this stage say some chief constables would say when I was campaigning nationally and internationally for community policing,

'What is John Alderson talking about? I have being doing it for years.'

Well they were talking about something different.

The first thing to remember is that when I was talking about community policing, it was a model of community policing whereas some chief constables, and in their ignorance I may say, of what I was saying; they obviously had not read what I had written. Community policing was merely putting a policeman on the beat in a particular area. That was not community policing à la mode. Community policing meant that the police surrendered some of their autonomy to the community in return for the community's active assistance. And that meant consultation. So there had to be a consultative committee in a community, set up by invitation purposefully for this scheme of community policing. So one, community policing meant consultation. And it was only out of the Brixton riots that we got it through Scarman. That consultation should be part of police administration. It was a very, very important and significant policy move. That is the first part of community policing in the sense that I described it and developed it. There must be consultation.

Point two, there must be inter-agency co-operation, that is co-operation between the police, the social services, the probation service, the welfare services and the educational services. Because all these people's work impinges one on the other, in a community, either because families are in desperate straits, or because they are not doing well at school or because they are getting into bad company. And nobody knows all of the information, but if you pool this knowledge of all the services you have got an immense understanding. But the rivalry between the organisations, and the lack of a will to understand each others role was quite profound.

There was a woeful lack of co-operation throughout the country. So the second leg of community policing, after you have established your consultative committee, which you ask the public what they think about what you are doing and what you would like to do. Secondly, and of paramount importance is collaboration between the agencies, or inter-agency co-operation, which means joint training between them at some level. And certainly out of that I set up what I called a *Joint Services Youth Support Team* – social workers, policeman, aided by probation officers, and teachers – working together on problem families. To try and diminish criminality.

The third point was allocating a police officer or officers to a particular community, so that they would know this community. Those are the three dimensions of community policing as I developed it in the 1970s. One, there must be consultation. That is why it was so controversial in Scarman because the chief constables did not collectively like it. Secondly, there was positive collaboration between other agencies. Thirdly, there was the allocation of police to particular communities so that they would get to know them, understand them and be known by them (John Alderson, March 1995).

The first strand of Alderson's ideas were discussed in the previous section, and became a formal component of the police policy-making apparatus. The other elements were also significant, and although they are not a formal part of policy and practice they have exerted an informal influence via Scarman's report.

Scarman's usage of the term community includes some of the elements that Lacey and Zedner (1995) outlined above. Scarman was sensitive to its complexity, but he failed to spell out in any detail the practical consequences of this complexity for policy-making. Scarman described the multi-racial community of Brixton in terms of its ethnic diversity, in the context of the various communities which are served by the Metropolitan Police, and further afield, in the context of a multi-racial society. In other words, there is a national as well as a self-contained local community which are both *racially* and *ethnically* divided. Scarman paid most attention to the racial characteristics of local communities, namely the 'black' community and ethnic minority community. These racialised categories were also subdivided into different sections. There was a generational divide consisting of older members, young black people and young people as a wider group. Community leaders, the local authority and the police made up the other community groups. The provision of a framework for maintaining good relations between the police and the community is a 'central' police function. Also, by recognising the conflicting expectations of different sections of the community, concerted efforts were made to reduce the level of suspicion and enmity within local communities. This was the responsibility of all officers in the Metropolitan Police but there were also specialised personnel called Community Liaison Officers (CLOs) at a divisional level, as well as Community Relations or Community Involvement Branches. These officers were in touch with all groups within the community, and sought to involve the educational sector by establishing contact with children and teachers through school visits. This was a specific police priority for the ethnic minorities and vulnerable juveniles.

What were the main conflicts between the police and the community they policed? How could the police avoid their becoming by reason of their professionalism, a 'corps d'élite' set apart from the rest of the community? The main consideration, then as it is now, is to enforce the law, but in doing so, avoiding causing friction and accentuating divisions within a community. The police's position in relation to the community is defined in the following terms:

> The police must exercise independent judgement: but they are also servants of the community. They enforce the law on behalf of the community: indeed they cannot effectively enforce it without the support of the community. The community pays them and provides them with their resources. So there has to be some way in which to secure that the independent judgement of the police can not only operate within the law but with the support of the community (1981: 4.60).

The key difficulty for Scarman is that there is not necessarily a correlation between theory and practice, and there may be a mismatch between ideas about community and the reality which the word is intended to represent. The principle cannot be applied in any simple way in the face of an *ethnically diverse community* in the context of a *multi-racial society*.

Scarman focused on the confusion generated by different notions of community policing. He rejected the view that *soft* or community policing is diametrically opposed to *hard* or more specialised operations, such as the actions of the SPG during 'Swamp 81'. Categorisations of this kind cannot be maintained because the police perform a plurality of overlapping tasks. To rebut the criticisms of some senior officers, he said that the argument that community policing is only workable in rural areas and inappropriate in urban settings is based on a misunderstanding of its actual meaning. Those who claimed that it was simply a case of putting more officers out on foot-patrol failed to realise that this was only one element of his model of communitarian or community policing (Alderson, 1981: iv). The assumption that Home Beat Officers (HBOs) – the nearest the police service has to the near-mythical 'bobby-on-the-beat' – are not an integral part of the mainstream of operational policing was questioned (Scarman, 1981: 5.48). According to Scarman, community policing is 'policing with the active consent and support of the community' (1981: 5.46). The community can also be involved in police policy and operations, except on those occasions when secrecy is required.

If chief officers, with the encouragement of the Home Office and HMIC, do not communicate with the community to win its support and consent, then a potential outcome is the erosion of its efficiency. Scarman's (1981) description of what should constitute community policing is as follows:

> I have emphasised in Part V of the report the importance of involving the community in aspects of policing: but there must also be effective police involvement in the community. Provision must be made for the police to be involved, like other important social agencies, in community re-development and planning. The social functions of the police – in handling the problems of the elderly, domestic disputes and juveniles for example – are important to the social health of the community. The police derive from these functions a wealth of experience which can be of great value to those involved in planning and determining social provision. It is vital that the law and order implications of environmental and social planning should be taken into account at the earliest stage. . . . There is also, I suggest, scope for much closer liaison between the police, the other local services – the probation service, social services and housing departments – and the voluntary sector – such as the churches. . . . Law and order is a community problem and the police are not the only service which has a function in this area, although they carry, admittedly, the leading responsibility (1981: 6.9).

This echoes Alderson's definition, submitted as evidence to Scarman, particularly the emphasis on inter-agency co-operation. What were the practical consequences?

Scarman's inquiry led to a profound and long lasting reappraisal of police policy and practice. A commitment towards area and community based initiatives, tied up with a co-ordinated multi-agency approach, emerged as a significant strand in discussions about the future direction of police policy and practice. In 1984, the publication of an interdepartmental Circular (8/84) was sent to chief constables and local authority chief executives. This kind of thinking was embodied in the then Commissioner of the Metropolitan Police, Sir Kenneth Newman's style of policing, who encouraged inter-agency co-operation and made a strong case for increasing the role of quasi-voluntary agencies. In his 1983 report Newman referred to liberal notions of citizenship and an unwritten 'notional social contract' to instil a sense of personal responsibility into individuals, because the easy availability and convenience of centrally organised facilities – whether it be the police, health service or education – [is] encouraging a readiness to relinquish grasp on elements of personal responsibility which should properly remain discharged by ourselves (Newman, 1984: 9).

This decline of autonomous self-government explained the failure of some communities to address their own problems.

To remedy the problems caused by an over paternalistic welfare state, area and community based initiatives were recommended, such as 'Neighbourhood Watch' which had been imported from the US (Bennett, 1987 cited in Mawby, 1990: 11; Johnston, 1992; McConville and Shepherd, 1992). These localised strategies were implemented to accommodate the complexity of a 'pluriform' society. As Newman put it, 'Neighbourhood policing – now firmly established at Notting Hill and Hackney – is a recognition of the fact that it is a feeling for locality of London which should determine the level and nature of policing' (1984: 14). The language used implied that the cultural diversity of specific locations is characterised by mutual recognition and tolerance of otherness. However, London's rich and multi-ethnic character has negative connotations because cultural differences can lead to misunderstanding, ignorance, fear and racial prejudice (Newman, 1985: 64). For example, Sampson *et al.* (1988) take Neighbourhood Watch as one element of the multi-agency approach adopted in the 1980s to show that a feeling for locality may be partly based on prejudice. They observed that Neighbourhood Watch:

> can reinforce class distinctions between the respectable middle classes, who will co-operate with the police on this basis, and the unrespectable working classes, who will not. Who is to be defined as 'respectable' or 'unrespectable', moreover, will tend to derive from police categorisations of the local population (Sampson *et al.*, 1988: 486).

However, as shown in Chapter 5, in Newman's view the distinctions were racialised more than they were grounded in class.

This emphasis on the shared responsibility for policing was a reaction to Newman's concern that centrally organised facilities could undermine individual self-responsibility. As in other areas of social policy throughout the 1980s, inter-agency co-operation, community consultation and self-help coexisted with the enhancement of the means of 'social control'. Newman was quite enthusiastic about this tendency without being concerned about the contradictions and tensions:

> Policing is merely a sub-system of the total system of social control. The Departments of Education, Health and Social Services, Environment and Manpower Services are the most obvious agencies capable of making an impact on the quality of social control.... Perhaps we should use the expression 'Social Control' in a benign sense, to provide a unifying concept within which the activities of police and other agencies can be co-ordinated. Each component of the social control system should examine its policies and operations and order it priorities towards a unified strategy for addressing the worst aspects of social disorganisation, particularly those associated with crime and the fear of crime (Newman, 1983: 108).

Attempts to put these forms of policing into practice have come up against some obstacles which are examined in the following chapters, although some elements have been built into New Labour's Crime and Disorder Act 1998, particularly the statutory partnerships between the police and local government.

Police policy and the construction of the 'underclass'

Among the processes shaping and sustaining social divisions such as the 'underclass' is the work of the police service. At the beginning of this chapter, two questions cried out for some answers. First, what were the main developments at a macro-level and micro-level in police policy throughout the 1980s? Secondly, to what extent did structural and behavioural versions of a racialised idea of an 'underclass' have an impact on the organisational culture, policies and practices of the modern police service?

At the turn of the 1980s policing was, as it is now, ever-changing, but some general tendencies can be discerned. The service was reformed, but without any fundamental transformation of the tripartite system. The pace at which these alterations were made was variable and some changes are more noticeable than others. At the turn of the 1980s, at a macro-level, the ideologically driven neo-liberal project of the Conservative government materialised. The disciplines of the market and the FMI's quest for efficiency, effectiveness and economy in the management and running of the public services was introduced into the culture of the police *service*. There were two other trends: first, the police as a law-enforcing and quasi-paramilitarist force, which invested resources in providing training and equipment for public order operations, and secondly, the police as a quasi-social service. This two-pronged communitarian approach, included (1) formal arrangements for police community consultative committees under section 106 (PACE) and (2) informal welfare approaches, consisting of inter-agency co-operation and multi-agency strategies. The former policy is statutory and has been implemented at a national level. The latter allows considerable scope for discretion at a local level, and the introduction of these strategies has been patchy and implemented in a piecemeal fashion. The extent to which this philosophy has informed policy and practice is explored in the ensuing chapters, particularly some of the barriers that have surfaced.

These developments in policy were based on many different contributory factors, including the popular beliefs and convictions that were propped up by political ideology. Public commentator's and policymaker's understanding of the actions of individuals and families in riotous *imagined communities* also rested on similar assumptions. A *racialised criminal underclass* is one example. This was not mentioned in formal discussions at Whitehall, but neither was class for that matter. This division was not at home in the Thatcherite discourse on families and individuals. The relationship between 'race, riots and policing' in the metropolis was closely monitored by the Home Office, however (1983b; 1984; 1989). As shown in Chapter 5, at a micro-level, the idea of an 'underclass' with strong racial connotations was attributed to police officers by some academics (Smith and Gray, 1983). The 'underclass' also became manifest at the higher levels of the police policy machinery itself, particularly at the level of ACPO. In contrast to their subordinates, senior officers referred to a structural version of poverty, the 'underclass' and social exclusion.

Scarman's 'criminal class' was, in part, perceived to be the outcome of 'relative' rather than 'absolute' deprivation and structurally generated decline in the inner city (1981: 6.28). This stratum was not necessarily associated with ethnic minority groups *per se*, because not all members of this group are concentrated in deprived inner city areas or participate in disorderly behaviour. However, racially coded messages are given off by Scarman's explanation of the policing of social problems. The riots were not specifically an issue of 'race', but other references to this ideologically constructed division were made about other aspects of the disorders. Although the meaning of 'race' is ever-changing and not always a feature of police discourse and police practice, some aspects of police work have historically been imbued with race specific connotations (Keith, 1993; Holdaway, 1996). Although commenting on the American debate, Katz's (1993: 100) observation also rings true about the issues discussed in this chapter: 'In popular impressions (although not in fact), the colour of the underclass is black.'

Attempts to resolve the uncertainties and conflicts that arise in interpreting and constructing social reality are context bound. The notion of community is one example. The provision of an efficient and effective police force at a community level is in part based on perceptions about societal, economic, cultural and behavioural characteristics of a community, however it is defined. As Alderson (1981: xi) put it when he wrote about policing by consent:

> Policing has to go with many cultures (if legal, of course) not against some and with others. That is one reason why policing has to be community-based to be effective. It must be sensitive to religious, racial, class and other differences and be prepared to compromise with the monolithic characteristics of a large bureaucracy such as the modern police force, and to learn to serve the people not the organisation.

In other words, ideas about the poor and the 'underclass' are woven into different elements of the police culture, as a representation of certain kinds of behaviour in particular communities. This sort of thinking is one of many ideas which guide policy-makers. The beliefs and attitudes which constitute the idea of an 'underclass' are created out of contextually specific ideological and material conditions. For example, the demands that can be made on the police are potentially infinite but are constrained by finite material resources, hence the '3 Es'. As well as the disciplines of the market introduced at a macro level, there are communitarian values at a micro-level. The quest for economy, effectiveness and efficiency, undertaken in national and local communities, necessarily takes contextually specific factors into consideration. In this case the relationship between riots and criminality is one of these relevant concerns. As the quotation above from Alderson indicates recognition of social differences and divisions are important guide-lines for the formulation of a response to such events. Due to a combination of fiscal constraints and ideological values, representations of complex social differences and the processes which shape them, are necessarily partial. For instance, the ideological project of Thatcherism placed individual and personal responsibility at the top of its list of priorities, to attack the principle of collectivism and minimise state expenditure. Communitarian accounts recognised the dimunition of the role of centralised authorities and suggest that local organisations should be made more democratically accountable, and that families and individuals should be strengthened. Although the ideological justifications of these approaches were different, there was some scope for convergence. It was at such moments that the concept of an 'underclass' could be put to use, either to justify more forceful strategies of social control or a more benign quasi-social service function. The following split is not always as clear-cut as this, but the former has more in common with behavioural perspectives on the 'underclass', and the latter a structural version, of this often confusing idea. At that time the latter was starting to become increasingly popular amongst senior police officers.

8
Policing Poor Communities

Drawing on concrete empirical analyses and the personal views of some practitioners, this chapter explores the practical consequences of some of the developments outlined in Chapter 7. Ideas of community continue to be important in police policy-making circles, and this part of the book concentrates on the variety of ways these notions have been employed to rationalise the policing of poverty. A major outgrowth is the view that different public, private and voluntary agencies need to co-operate and work together to ameliorate social problems. This chapter examines the complex relationship between policy-making at a national level and how it is put into practice within some local communities. A key issue is the link between the rhetoric underlying ideas of community and their utility for responding to the real problems of poverty and crime. Throughout the forces of England and Wales various styles of communitarian policing (Alderson, 1981; 1984; Scarman, 1981) underpinned police policy-making, but in the mid-1990s there were intimations of a departure from some of these principles. It is necessary to consider four factors: first, the ongoing influence of the values and philosophy underlying community policing, taking the Metropolitan Police as an example. Secondly, has there been a significant revaluation of the police's role in these areas? Thirdly, what are the policy implications? Finally, have these changes had any bearing on the 'underclass' debate?

Responding to local communities

Elaborating on Sir Kenneth Newman's 'Force Goal', his successor in 1986, Sir Peter Imbert (1988: 13, 21), restated two objectives: (i) the decentralisation of decision-making and (ii) the importance of developing policing plans and policy via community consultation and public co-operation. The strengthening of relations between the police and community was a prerequisite for maintaining public tranquillity. He proposed to achieve this by improving communication between the police and policed, so that the latter had sufficient and adequate information to understand the operational objectives of the former (Imbert, 1988: 18–9). Imbert embraced community consultation as a way of avoiding further deterioration of relations between the police and some sections of the public, and as a means to reduce tension. As well as drawing attention to the formal apparatus in place for community consultation (section 106, PACE, 1984), informal strategies were mentioned too. This refutes some of the criticisms levelled at formal provisions by the left realist criminologists, for example, who contend that the police fail to understand the complexity of communities (Crawford, 1995; Kinsey, Lea and Young, 1986). At least as far as Imbert's rhetoric goes, this criticism is misplaced. Likewise Loader's (1996: 19–20) claim that the police 'proceeds as if the … "community" were coherent entities existing without conflict and capable of expressing a single voice', down-plays some police officers' sensitivity to the conflictual conditions under which police work is done. By stressing the role of informal procedures Imbert's conception of community rests on a set of assumptions that are more insightful than ideas assigned to police in some critiques of community policing. For example:

> We can think of a community in the sense of people who live in a particular place, such as a village or housing estate, or in the sense of people defined by some common interest or characteristic. Clearly one person can belong to several communities, one geographical, one racial, one professional, each having a different relationship with the police. Police officers deal with individuals but the force as a whole, in policy and administration, relates very much to communities. The differences are vast. Policing an amiable, affluent and leafy suburb and policing an inner London council estate where drugs are a problem represent quite different challenges (Imbert, 1989: 11).

Imbert alludes to an array of social divisions and the realities in which they are embedded. Communities are conceptualised along the lines of 'race', space, occupational status – though not class. On the one hand, the nuanced relationships connecting individual and collective characteristics are recognised, and such perceptions are more in touch with how individuals and groups belong to a multiplicity of communities than some criminologists sometimes suggest. On the other hand, the minutiae of these differences are polarised into two groups, one affluent and the other criminogenic.

In terms of policy the primary objective was peace-keeping, and wherever possible the prevention of crime, without damaging the quality of the relationship between police and community. The force was restructured to facilitate better communication to avoid the creation of mistrust and suspicion. Operational command at a district level was abolished and authority and control was devolved to local commanders, thus giving them greater autonomy (Imbert, 1988: 19). Moreover it gave them more scope to respond to the demands of an assortment of fragmented communities. This new form of 'geographic policing' enabled divisional and area commanders to ascertain the views of their communities and tailor policy according to their needs (Imbert, 1988: 22). The general trend is a movement away from policing of communities towards policing with communities.

Representing community change

In Chapter 7 perceptions of a racialised criminal 'underclass' were current in police circles, but in the immediate period after that, discussions about 'race' became more subdued. However, the Metropolitan Police did submit crime figures to the Home Office for the purpose of analysing different categories of crime by ethnic group (Home Office, 1983b, 1984, 1989). References to other social divisions such as class were also discussed less openly by senior police officers than they had been in the first half of the 1980s. This may in part reflect the then Prime Minister, Margaret Thatcher's rejection of the idea of society and social class, and its substitution by individuals and families. Following the unrest in Handsworth, Birmingham, in 1985, the then Home Secretary, Douglas Hurd, said that this and the other events at that time 'were not social phenomena, but crimes' (quoted in Rose, 1996: 92). This demonstrates the 'hidden face of power' at work in determining which issues are overlooked by the 'mobilisation of bias' (Bachrach and Baratz (1970: 44). In other words:

> non-decision making, that is the practice of limiting the scope of actual decision making to safe issues by manipulating the dominant community values, myths and political institutions and procedures (Bachrach and Baratz, 1970: 18).

The values of the Home Office, Home Secretary and the government's ideology limit the scope of debate to a limited range of issues:

Political systems and sub-systems develop a 'mobilisation of bias', a set of predominant values, beliefs, rituals, and institutional proced- ures ('rules of the game') that operate systematically and contributes to the benefit of certain persons at the expense of others. Those who benefit are placed in a preferred position to defend and promote their vested interests. More often than not, the 'status quo defenders' are a minority or elite group within the population in question (Bachrach and Baratz, 1970: 44).

The government steered debate away from structural factors, such as the patterns of socio-economic inequality, that Scarman (1981) had highlighted, because talk of this kind would have been in contradistinc- tion to the ideological project of the New Right.

The macro constraints of this mobilisation of bias were met with a creative response by some police officers, and there was growing dis- quiet in the Metropolitan Police towards government policy. The Scot- land Yard policy unit produced 'confidential annual Metropolitan Police internal appraisal documents' which focused on social condi- tions in the 'two Londons' (Metropolitan Police Force Appraisal, September 1986, part II, cited in Rose, 1996: 95). The year after 'Polari- sation and Development' in the police district (Metropolitan Police Force Appraisal, 1987) was published.

Imbert also wrote in his annual reports of 'deprived inner city areas' (Imbert, 1988: 70), 'the disadvantaged', 'social deprivation', and 'mar- ginalisation' (Imbert, 1992: xvi), and 'inner city divisions where urban deprivation, crime, fear of crime and community creates considerable policing problems' (1988: 19). The 'haves and the have-nots' was the term used in the 1989 Metropolitan Police Force Appraisal (Rose, 1996: 97). At the Metropolitan Police Commissioners Conference in 1991, Imbert said that the poor:

will be the last to benefit from any recovery. This will serve only to emphasise the economic polarisation that has been taking place over the last decade. Whatever means of measurement are used, the top 20 percent has been getting richer, and the bottom 20 per cent poorer (Imbert quoted in Rose, 1996: 97).

What is the relationship between these views and Lord Scarman's contribution to the 'underclass' debate? Imbert's (1991: xii) review of the Scarman report demonstrates a close relationship:

But what of conditions in our inner cities? Have the factors which were said to 'underlay' the disorders been addressed? Housing, education and employment were identified as key areas in 1981. It is not for me to evaluate the changes that have taken place since then. However, the crime map fits all too closely over the map of disadvantage. The socially deprived, homeless and the young are all especially vulnerable, and can too easily fall prey to crime itself, or to the illusory opportunities presented by it.

Thus there are implicit continuities with Scarman's thinking. Concerning the 'underclass', on his retirement in 1992 Imbert said that:

> society ignores at its peril the importance of the deprived and disadvantaged underclass in the growth of crime [and going on to say that] in the years to come, the idea of better service delivery would have more impact on policing than rigid law enforcement (*The Times*, 30 July 1992).

What about the policy implications?

Imbert certainly had developed a service ethic, underscored by the rhetoric of the 'Plus Programme' (launched in 1989) which embodied the Metropolitan police's corporate identity and signalled a call for change in the police culture, particularly the transition from a force to a service. This was a precursor to ACPO's *Statement of Our Common Purpose and Values* (see Chapter 6). The stress on police professionalism and quality of service 'pre-empt[ed] certain aspects of the "new consumerism" contained in the Citizens Charter' (Savage and Charman, 1996: 49). Following his retirement, Imbert's call for better service delivery would eventually be challenged by a government committed to rigid law enforcement. It is here that the values of corporacy and consumerism can be seen to be bound up with descriptions of poverty and the 'underclass'. The reference to the 'underclass' serves as a critique of government policy, whereas the service ethic is at home in the government's discourse on the '3 Es' and the incremental growth of the 'new public management' (McLaughlin and Murji, 1997).

Sir John Woodcock (1992: 1932), the then Chief Inspector of HMIC, in a speech he gave to IPEC in London (as part of joint presentation with Sir Peter Imbert) also made similar connections. On that occasion Sir Kenneth Newman's historically informed views were more significant.

> What is happening to the police is that a 19th century institution is being dragged into the 21st century. Despite all the later mythology

of Dixon, the police never really were the police of the whole people but a mechanism set up to protect the affluent from what the Victorians described as the dangerous classes (Woodcock, 1992: 1932).

Rethinking police policy and the 'underclass'

Two distinctive strands of police policy can be discerned. On one hand, the development of the formal and informal policies based on the philosophy of community policing. On the other there was not a monolithic, clear working ideology for the police but one consisting of traces of neo-liberalism and communitarian policing.

Also, by refining the arguments outlined in previous chapters, it is argued that in police discourse, 'underclass' narratives cannot be reduced to 'race', class or any other conventional social divisions. There are various clusters of social divisions, which are not based on traditional divisions, but are a specific property of the police service's organisational culture. For example, a police superintendent remarked that the issues addressed in this chapter are interconnected, but not:

> in any kind of pure academic sense. The connection is part of the social tapestry within which we work, and it is a very complex tapestry. And it is only when you work in the field, and you see it day-in-day-out, that you can actually see the kind of connections, and the connections are oblique, they are confused and there is not a lot of clarity. It is not a clear picture. But it is that uncertainty which almost defines the picture. And it is one of the things, you have to be fairly sophisticated in policing terms, you have to kind of get a handle on all the various facets of that picture, and you have to keep them all in mind and manage them all.

However, the powerful structures and agencies at work in articulating these divisions are more or less permanent fixtures. The opinions and values of those nearest to the apex of the police policy hierarchy, namely central government, carry most weight, and it is at this level that the complex social tapestry is often simplified. Moreover, it is the over-simplification of these issues at the top which makes the task of policing on the front line more difficult, because the rhetoric often does not match the reality.

Police narratives and the 'underclass'

Sir John Woodcock, the Chief Inspector of HMIC (1990–3) wrote that

> Utilisation of tension indicators in relation to potential inner city disorder has improved the ability of police to respond to disturbances in such areas. 1992 did not see a major repetition of the inner city disturbances which occurred in 1991 and in a number of previous years. However, the difficulties of policing inner cities remain acute. There remains a debate among criminologists and social commentators about the link between social deprivation and crime. It is not for the inspectorate to enter that argument, however, it is probably fair to say that, while crime reaches across all milieux (and many people from the most deprived backgrounds live exemplary lives), police officers in many inner city localities fear that a substantial number of young people in these areas are becoming detached from social norms. It was interesting that Andrew Neil, the editor of *The Sunday Times*, spoke in the prestigious James Smart Lecture about the breakdown of the nuclear family as being a crucial issue in the development of an 'underclass' in Britain. It is police officers who have to see most directly and acutely the impact of that underclass on the victims of the crimes they commit. The Police Service fully endorses any moves to give support to those struggling to bring up children in the current adverse economic circumstances which affect such localities (Home Office, 1993a: 29–30).

The main concern here is the Chief Inspector's appropriation of Neil's 'underclass', which draws exclusively on Murray's many contributions to *The Sunday Times*.

Murray's arguments were explored in Chapters 3 and 4, and there is no need to rehearse the core criticisms again. The point here is that Woodcock, in part, based his argument on Murray's contribution. The identification of a group in the process of becoming detached from social norms was derived straight from Murray, but significantly, Woodcock's assessment of the policy implications of changes to the family structure are quite different. Murray's frequent calls for maximal self-government and minimal central government involvement are reversed by the Chief Inspector. Woodcock's definition therefore recognises the ambivalent relationship between the poverty of the 'underclass' and its involvement in crime and disorder. Although he is drawing on an overtly behavioural analysis of these social problems his own views have much more in common with a structural perspective, and there are overlaps with Alderson's communitarian thinking (1984). As shown in Chapter 7, Alderson also argued that the 'underclass' included the vulnerable. To reiterate the retired official's words, these 'are often the people who need police protection, more than say middle-class areas who are quite capable of looking after themselves in many ways' (John Alderson, March 1995). Although some of the former Chief Inspector's ideas echo some of Alderson's claims, Woodcock's description includes further ambiguities. Persisting with Murray's thesis, the Chief Inspector asserted that criminal and delinquent behaviour is the result of the breakdown of the nuclear family which contributes to crime and disorder. However, due to adverse economic circumstances family units headed by lone parents are also perceived to be vulnerable and in need of support. Thus the relative significance of offender and victim based perspectives is not fixed but continually changing. Moreover, the emphasis shifts from Murray's behavioural version of the 'underclass' to one which focuses on the political economy and structural factors instead. How have some policy-makers responded to Woodcock's claims?

A senior officer from HMIC recognised the notion of an 'underclass' but questioned its relevance:

> We could discuss this all day. It is an idea that constantly changes. The underclass is not necessarily involved in disorder and riots. There is no connection. If you go down the road of saying underclass and disorder or the underclass and crime, that is a very dangerous generalisation. Scarman's criminal class. It may be, but an underclass does not necessarily imply criminality. An underclass is low privileged, the underprivileged.

This officer mentions the ever-changing status of the 'underclass', which has less to do with its conceptual history and more to do with the complex relationship between crime and social class. Instead of using the language of class analysis, society is divided up into the privileged and the underprivileged. These terms are rarely used in public and academic commentaries on the 'underclass', and therefore the officer adds a unique police perspective. The 'underclass' does not figure in this officer's description of the work of the inspectorate, and this practitioner was keen to distance the inspectorate from this notion. He even resorted to saying that it was Murray's and not Woodcock's idea, a view which failed to appreciate that Woodcock made a conscious decision to use the term. Furthermore, the officer put forward a definition (the underprivileged) which, like Woodcock's (social deprivation), has more in common with a structural perspective. This indicates that both of their familiarity with the concept extends beyond Murray's explication. However, the officer from the Inspectorate did warm towards the familist aspect of Woodcock's description, which is more closely related to a behavioural perspective.

In terms of policy the Home Secretary and the inspectorate does not play a major part:

> Well, it may be discussed in very general terms, but in the previous year I have not received any correspondence from the Home Secretary asking how are the underclass. It is too simplistic. If an officer is involved in the provision of a police service in an area it is necessary to identify characteristics of a particular area. If there is an underclass, that is necessarily taken into account. It may have an impact on policy making but only among other things. It is given due cognisance.

A senior official from the Home Office Police Department was also quite dismissive of the 'underclass':

> It does not inform us. It is not crucial to our thinking. It is a debate that goes on. It is not particularly mentioned in discussions. No one is saying that an underclass is the key to it all. If it were a disaffected slab of society that would be very worrying. It is not significant in terms of decisions made at the Home Office, and it is not reflected in policy. It is discussed elsewhere, particularly in the media. It is more likely to be discussed when we take time off from doing our day to day work.

Although the 'underclass' is acknowledged it is not an issue. This official's understanding of the 'underclass' rests on the assumption that it is a disaffected group. Again this term is not common currency in debates on the 'underclass'. Consistent with the government's position on disorder and crime, disaffection implies an attitudinal difference rather than a socio-economic difference.

It would appear, therefore, that the 'underclass' is not a matter for concern at the macro-level of government policy. In this setting the distinction made between formal and informal discussions is not particularly helpful, because by arguing that something is not discussed formally but informally glosses the overlaps between the two. In Chapter 6 it was argued that policies are formulated out of many interpenetrating material and ideological forces, and that many of the decisions taken in the policy process at the highest levels occur in informal settings. Important political speeches are drafted at home at weekends. The same applies at other levels of the policy hierarchy. Thus Woodcock's choice to use the word 'underclass' did fit in with at least one strand of Home Office thinking. The relationship between language and reality, theory and practice is undoubtedly complicated, and it is true that the significance of this word should not be overstated, but neither should it be underestimated.

Policing the 'underclass': at the interface of policy and practice

A year before the 1997 General Election a chief constable identified some of the issues that arise when the relationship between policy and the 'underclass' is examined:

> Now the policy-making I'm talking about when it comes to the underclass, is a much wider sort of policy-making, not within the police service, but the policy-making that should inform central government thinking across the board. That's rather a 'have you stopped beating your wife question', because you are making the assumption that central government acts rationally. Well they don't.
>
> Local government acts in partnership with all the other players, and there is a pretty good partnership with all the other players, and there is a pretty good partnership between the different departments and at local government as well as between local government and other parts of the public sector and the private sector and the voluntary sector. The departments of state don't understand the meaning of the word partnership when it comes to themselves, and you therefore don't have the sort of across the board thinking that would prevent the growing underclass.
>
> I don't like the idea of a criminal class. The growing idea of an underclass, the people that are excluded. When you look at, for example, the lack of co-operation between the Department of Health and Department of Social Security and local government over care in the community, the amount of money available. . . . You could look at the cross between education and health, and education or criminal justice.

There are a whole host of things nationally, and if you look at the lack of connection between income, Inland Revenue policy and DSS policy over the poverty trap. All the things that make life difficult for people who are nearly always where there is a failure to communicate at central government level. So, there was a lot of people, I would suggest, like me around, in local government and there are individuals in departments at the centre, who recognise this problem, but I haven't noticed any change.

The 'underclass' has entered into the police policy process at various junctures but connects most concretely in inter-agency work, a branch of community policing. Two perspectives on this issue are addressed. Firstly, these police-led strategies have been criticised by some writers because they are 'designed to take over other agencies and use them for its own ends of "total policing"' (Lee, 1995: 315). Furthermore, although 'it appears to offer an alternative to repressive police practices and strategies, it is but one aspect of a disciplinary regime aimed at reinforcing social discipline along a continuum of coerciveness and engineering consent and support for the police' (1995: 315). Secondly, Campbell (1993: 97) has argued that by the 1990s communities had been, in stark contrast to the 1980s, abandoned:

The prelude to the 1981 riots saw 'flooding' saturation which overwhelmed and criminalised communities; but the 1991 riots were preceded by the absence of police from the neighbourhoods that erupted. In fact, these neighbourhoods were abandoned by crime managers: they had been given little or no police service. Crisis in public order erupted in the absence of effective investigation and intervention.

The views of some chief constables suggests something more complicated than either of these scenarios.

Taking stock of community policing

According to Koch and Bennett (1993: 38) the term community policing is 'rarely used by the police in Britain' but, echoing Alderson, it has been 'incorporated into police thinking' as a philosophy. There are also some ideas about what community policing is, what it is not, and the kind of obstacles which obstruct translating this philosophy into practice. One chief constable has expressed views which are in accord with Alderson's:

I've always thought [community policing] was a good idea. The main principles are that we should police by consent, that we should be seen as the police of the people rather than the police of the state. That we should be keeping the peace first, and that we should be bearing in mind that the word policing comes from the same root as politics. What we are talking about in policing is the art of the possible just as politics is the art of the possible. Because you can't do everything with 50 odd million people with 130 000 odd police officers, you clearly can't control if all 52 million people decided to do something we could not stop, and therefore we have to bear this in mind. Now it never gets to that point, but it should be in our thinking that we should be doing things that are welcome to the community.

In other words 'total policing' is not feasible because of the constraints of finite resources. Furthermore the police are not simply an extension of, in Althusser's (1971) terms, the ideological and repressive state apparatus. There are other dilemmas which limit these approaches. Another chief constable referred to the following difficulty:

But what you then really have to be careful about is that you make sure that you are in the right part of the community, because you could have for example, in a suburb of the town, a place like Moss Side, Manchester, Collyhurst or Chapeltown, Leeds. You could have a small group of people in that community who are sufficiently violent and powerful to cause the law abiding majority to keep quiet, or even to say things that they don't really believe in out of fear. Now that's a very difficult point to get round.

Restoring and maintaining the Queen's Peace is much more complex than the critics of community policing would allow us to imagine. Police intervention in community affairs is partly responsive to public demands and not only determined by a wish to expand the mechanisms of social control, or in Cohen's (1985) words of 'net widening'. As well as those aspects of police policy based on legislation, formal statements and advisory guide-lines there are other more informal dimensions to communitarian styles of policing. Police officers – at both national and local levels – work with a multiplicity of vague definitions of community. Indeed the conflict and tension concentrated within communities, however roughly community is defined, is interpenetrated by discussions taking place both at national and more localised levels.

Likewise the 'underclass' sometimes makes certain aspects of police policy meaningful at both force and constabulary levels.

The profound influence of Scarman is frequently noted, especially the section 106 committees and the enhanced co-operation with other organisations. Community policing is not only about working with other powerful organisations, whether they be governmental, voluntary or private agencies. It is also about co-operating with the people living in the communities in which they work.

From peace-keepers to crime-fighters

Since its inception the police service has performed three inter-related tasks: the prevention/detection of crime, the preservation of life and property and the preservation of public tranquillity. After Scarman, the conventional wisdom has been that the preservation of public tranquillity should be a priority, realised through various styles of community policing, but since the mid-1990s the detection of crime, cast as 'crime-fighting', has come to the forefront (Home Office, 1993b; Police and Magistrate Courts Act, 1994; Cassels, 1996; Home Office, 1995b). Indeed, 'keeping the Queen's peace is not mentioned', which signifies a departure from one of the core principles underpinning the modern police service (Newburn and Morgan, 1994: 144). This is taken as a starting point to address the three issues mentioned at the beginning of this chapter. First, has there been a significant revaluation of the police's role in these areas? Second, what are the policy implications? Third, have these changes had any bearing on the 'underclass' debate?

A new conventional wisdom?

One of the chief constables who was directly involved in putting Scarman's recommendations into practice in the MPD in the 1980s has said:

When I worked in London I was responsible for introducing all the recommendations of the Scarman's report, in the Metropolitan Police. And I was at a number of public meetings where Lord Scarman was present. And he took the view that the preservation of public tranquillity meant that the police should sometimes not enforce the law in order to ensure that public tranquillity was preserved. And he thought this in terms of Brixton and Toxteth. Things should have been handled better. That was not a situation which I entirely agreed with because in the areas that we were talking about, public tranquillity had already dissipated, if you like. If you look at places like Railton

Road, Brixton and All Saints Road, Notting Hill, as they were in those days. I don't know what they're like now. And if you looked at Moss Side and parts of Toxteth. And in fact if you look at Moss Side and parts of Toxteth today, public tranquillity does not exist. It may be necessary to enforce the law to restore public tranquillity. A very delicate balance. You might need, in a sense to almost say well we are going to go in and deal with this and it might mean there is a tremendous ... it might mean that there's quite a strong opposition and reaction to us. But in order to get back to a normal state of affairs, as it were, you have got to do that.

I think that is an area where Leslie Scarman was not actually following his argument through to the extent that he should have done. Public tranquillity, the normal state of affairs, quality of life is the bottom line for everybody. What people want is a decent quality of life. And I actually believe that one of the main functions of the police service is to try to secure that, in those areas where policing can secure quality of life. That means in terms of dealing with public disorder, public nuisance, crime, traffic matters because, funnily enough, in some respects they are as important.

The White Paper and the PMCA does quite clearly make the point that fighting crime should be the priority ... but peace keeping is also a priority.

Another chief constable shared a similar view:

There has been a real tension as to what is the role of the police since the police were first created in 1829. And the tension has been, what are the police? Are they a law enforcement agency or are they a peace keeping agency? And the overwhelming weight of history and law is that we are a peace keeping agency, primarily. The prime role of the police is the preservation of public peace, the Queen's Peace.

This government is the first one to try and change this, overtly. And there is a real tension because there are times when, if one looks at policing as a continuum, with on the one hand, peace keeping, and on the other hand, law enforcement, it actually moves along that continuum. And at different times and on different occasions law enforcement has primacy and at others peace keeping. But the balance overall is that peace keeping is the key role and has been the key determinant as to how the police have achieved public acceptability.

Change that and you potentially change the whole relationship of police with society and therefore you fundamentally change policy making. Because it stems from the definition, the model that you actually use. And it is important to see that that model is very clearly understood, because sometimes to enforce law you have to initiate a breach of the peace. Other times, to preserve the peace you actually deliberately do not enforce the law. And so I think – if you go to the White Paper and Core and Ancillary Tasks – there is a change of emphasis at government level.

What are the policy implications?

In terms of policy-making in my force, I think the policing plan for the force will indicate the wide area that's in there. Right at the heart of it, of course, are the key policing objectives that are set out by the Home Office. And they are aimed specifically at dealing with certain crimes. But those aims would have been there in any case. I personally don't believe that they should have been posed by the Home Secretary. We should have developed our own law enforcing initiatives or crime fighting initiatives at a local level, and we would have come up, I suspect, with very similar objectives to those national objectives. But it is the question of how much the imposition of those at a national level interferes with, what is, I think the local responsibility of a police authority and a police force, of identifying what the local problems are and then dealing with those local problems.

So again I think the local environment is more important and I think of those national objectives unless they are were something quite outrageous, where there is an insistence that under those national objectives that we should deal with some sort of crime that was not a major concern to local communities. Then I really don't think they really effect the way in which we identify these important priorities, which dictate what our policing policies are.

One of the above chief constable's colleagues made the following remark:

Nothing has changed in ——. Keeping the Queen's Peace is the prime task of the police service as far as I'm concerned. And I continue to say that, and shall continue to say that.

It does represent a change in the direction of policing where its acceded to. I'm not sure that you have actually got many forces that are changing it significantly because the effect of putting crime to the top would be lose the Queen's Peace, and in any case keeping the Queen's Peace has to be the priority.

If you like, the impact on policy making that it has had, has been to emphasise the need for the Queen's Peace – it probably wouldn't have been so concerned with it if people hadn't got ideas into their heads that fighting crime is the most important. As a result of that, I've been saying very forcibly, and in our plan last year and this years, say this very forcibly, that keeping the Queen's Peace comes first. The preservation of public tranquillity.

Yet another chief claimed that the police had not oriented themselves to crime-fighting:

The broad response I would have to say is, in the short term, no, but great concern that over time it could. If that same philosophy were to be maintained, and the delivery of funding were determined on following certain principles.

If however they switched police funding – and the Home Secretary could – to what proportion of your forces is in the CID as opposed to on traffic or whatever, what proportion of success you have in dealing with burglars, or this that and the other, and ignoring a whole number of other things, then it could skew it very, very considerably. That is my personal and our collective concern for the future. I can say, hand on heart, that no particular comment of any Home Secretary in the four and a half years that I have been chief constable has caused me to change my mind on anything in policy terms, but I listen very carefully.

The general consensus is that in the context of the tripartite system, power has been shifted further to the centre, and that the Home Secretary has enhanced influence over policy formation, particularly in terms of setting objectives. However the Home Secretary's attempt to make 'crime-fighting' a priority was not accepted by the individual chief constables mentioned above, and one can safely assume that this is the case nationally, because ACPO collectively only very rarely publicly disagree on any issue. Whilst there have been no discernible conflicts or changes thus far, there is potential for a clash of interests. The ramifications of these issues for the 'underclass' debate are explored by connecting them with another dimension of central government activity and its influence on policing at local levels. Loveday's (1996: 99–100) assertion is the reference point: 'Targeting the "underclass", the undeserving or a "criminal class" is clearly designed as a primary police task by a government which exhibits an almost pathological commitment to that which is measurable.'

The above comment is related to the 1990s reforms and the increased government control over policing, especially the birth of the 'new public management'. The policy implications of the 'underclass' are also different in this context. In contrast to the 1980s and early 1990s where the idea symbolised disorderly communities the new 'underclass' is more criminal than disorderly. During the 1990s the government's 'respectable fears' and anxieties were transposed from riotous communities onto criminals. Although crimes are committed in these settings, the government's rhetorical usage of the word crime tends to focus on criminal offences that are committed by individuals. Consistent with neo-liberal thinking, both in political and public discourse, these offences and offenders are divorced from a wider social context (see the comments of Hurd and Thatcher above). Despite this, the criteria used to predict the workload of police forces undermines the credibility of this view. The formula for funding the police, of which the two main elements were a 'crime management index' and 'the disorder index', were based on the demographic characteristics of geographical areas:

> The factors taken into account in the crime index were the number of single parent families, the number of people living in council estates, the proportion of people in rented accommodation, and, with heaviest weighting, the numbers of unemployed and long-term unemployed. The factors in the disorder index were identical, with the addition of the number of people who lived alone in terraced housing (Rose, 1996: 100).

These indices of social conditions are similar to some senior police officer's conceptions of a structurally generated 'underclass', but in the view of one chief constable, this connection is only partially valid:

> I don't think it is set from the point of view that there is an underclass. You could actually almost define who are going to be potential members of that underclass from those statistics but I think that is a by-product rather than a causal factor for using that analysis.
> And so it's starting on the people issue again. And it is an implicit recognition that social conditions have an impact on police activity. Although politically that won't be said. But it is a recognition of that, otherwise why do you include unemployment statistics? Why do you include one parent families? Why do you include population density, rather than sparsity? Why do you look at all the derivatives of what they call strivers and different formulae?

Although it is not possible to dispute this officer's assessment of the precise relationship linking the 'underclass' and the index included in the funding formula, the description of these broad categorisations and indices of social conditions are similar to the perceptions of other chief constables. There are also some connections, albeit oblique, to the structural school of the 'underclass' debate. This is an example of the most direct and explicit references to some of the main social divisions which constitute the 'underclass', with the notable exception of 'race'. This further complicates the issue of identifying the relative significance of particular groupings of social divisions in different versions of the 'underclass'.

In the *Front-line Britain* documentary (ITV, 27 February 1996: mentioned above) two chief constable's descriptions shared commonalities. Jim Sharples, then Chief Constable of Merseyside Police and President of ACPO said:

> We know that a significant proportion of crime is committed by young males about the ages of fifteen to twenty-five. Often out of work, aimless, time on their hands, and so what you have got is, in a sense, a witches' brew. You have got unemployment, young males, that category of the population where we know that crime is committed anyway. They have no money and the temptations must be great. Now it does not excuse the behaviour, the behaviour is completely and utterly unacceptable. The criminal needs to be dealt with, I'm just merely saying that in those circumstances you have got a real mix of the factors that can lead to some of the problems we see.

Similarly Sir Ron Hadfield, then Chief Constable of West Midlands Police remarked that:

> It's very hard to join society. The things that they seek to acquire, they can't get unless they do it unlawfully. And the rules that you and I live by are meaningless, they literally don't exist. And there are a number of reasons for that, parental influence and so on. I could give you six or seven of them and I'm sure I don't need to. Now do they commit a disproportionate amount of the crime? I don't think they do but what they do do is live in an environment where a disproportionate amount of crime is committed. They are exposed to it far more than anyone else. They are themselves victims of it more than others, and they probably haven't had the constraints that you and I have on them not to commit crime. There are no rules.

Significantly Hadfield made other comments, quoted in *The Observer* (18 February 1996): 'Our rules mean nothing to the underclass.' Before considering the junctures at which these different descriptions coalesce, some chief constables perceptions on the 'underclass' and its policy implications are acknowledged.

One chief defined the 'underclass' in quasi-sociological terms, specifically the structural version, with quite specific policy implications.

> I'm not sure yet whether an underclass has emerged. I'm worried that it might. My concern is very much that we are seeing what may be a sea-change in our society in the recognition, not only by the rest of society, but by those who form part of it. There is a separate underclass. It's what Marx defined as the changing consciousness from a class in itself for a class for itself. And it is of concern to me that there is a significant number of the population in my police area who feel they have no stake in existing society and therefore have nothing to lose. And if they take that to its logical conclusion then one would have to adopt different means of policing in order to counter it. Because if they have no stake and are not threatened by any of the normal sanctions, then your normal means of doing things lose all significance and you change your policing from much more of an issue of trying to keep the balance between, maybe different groups of social mores or whatever, may be to be more of a paramilitary, in which you are acting in a clear repressive matter in relation to a sub-group or sub-section. And that is extremely worrying indeed. And that is linked very clearly to unemployment and social deprivation and the sense of alienation, that in some areas, may be ethnically articulated. In areas like this it isn't, but it's just there. It's actually within the white working class on the estates of — manifesting the same kind of things that you see in Chapeltown in Leeds, in Brixton, St Pauls, Handsworth. So that to me is perhaps the most critical area.

This officer draws attention to an 'underclass' which consists of behavioural and structural dimensions. The latter include references to exclusion from the labour market and the concomitant social deprivation. The former is explained in terms of different social mores and alienation from mainstream values. This account shares common themes with other senior police officers in terms of these near universal characteristics. One link is that the locales selected as examples to understand the present are those racialised communities which acquired a reputation in the 1980s. The notorious and predominantly 'dangerous places' of the 1990s are also noted, but only in as far as that they form part of a bigger picture. Unlike some of the perceptions about the unrest in the latter, the continuities rather than unique and novel dimensions are stressed. Instead of pointing out differences in the scale of the problems and the alternative policing styles in these different times and places, the 'underclass' has not undergone any transformation.

Consistent with a Marxist conception of the class structure the 'underclass' is viewed in rather static terms in the context of a capitalist economy, rather than as a process. Different sub-groups and sub-sections are incorporated into an unchanging class structure without any re-configuration with other divisions taking place. Having said that, the constable does take on board ethnicity to describe the situation in his own force. This does not fundamentally alter this interpretation and ethnic differences are not especially significant because they are collapsed into class.

In terms of policy, policing the 'underclass' is not just about communitarian strategies oriented towards maintaining order, but by the re-imposition of order through the legitimate use of force. When there is no balance between order maintenance and crime control, normal policing becomes difficult. It is under such circumstances that the 'underclass' comes into being, where it has an impact on the police policy process. It is a sign that the potential for communication, consultation and co-operation has gone.

Another chief constable offers a very different perspective on this issue which has less to do with any of the 'core' police functions. The peace-keeping-crime-fighting continuum is not the main concern in this officer's view:

We see an underclass being created by perceptions of poverty, low self-esteem, under-employment, low achievement and we believe as a force, as we do that self-esteem is absolutely critical to the individual's armoury in allowing him to say no to drugs, violence, crime. Then one of our big drives is towards making sure that the underclass does not grow by investing effort, through partnerships, into pre-school and junior school education. So in that sense, I think it is effecting policy. There is genuine enlightenment that sometimes works against the Home Secretary's wishes about cautioning. If we sense that somebody is part of a really desperately underprivileged group in society we might feel disposed to caution more than if somebody came from a very privileged background, and re-offended multiply. And it is not terribly logical because of course deprivation can occur when there's lots of physical possessions in the home. It can simply be a very cold mother and father. So judgements like that are difficult to call.

Apart from that I can't think of obvious examples, where we have deliberately changed policy, modified policy, or implemented policy because of a perception of an underclass. It is not something that has impacted strongly on our strategic thinking. It is a matter of social concern for us, but the only way in which it has emerged is in our determination to do something through schools programmes to try and help the up and coming generation.

In contrast to the previous chief constable the 'underclass' is perceived to be a stratum in the making rather than an already excluded and alienated layer of the class structure. More energy is placed on diverting young individuals away from the criminal justice process. Prevention through inter-agency co-operation is the name of the game. It is a community approach, focusing on potential offenders, based on a predictive model of factors which contribute towards criminal and delinquent behaviour. Although structural variables such as under-employment are relevant, their impact can be minimised by the police co-ordinating their activities with other organisations to target particular individuals. Poverty – defined loosely in terms of the privileged and the underprivileged – and the individual's attachment to the labour market are mentioned, but the young and the family are the divisions which are at the top of this officer's agenda. The conceptualisation of these divisions is more fluid than in any of the other versions, but structural phenomena are more significant than behavioural traits.

Policing crime, disorder and poverty

'Underclass' narratives, based on a structural version, have filtered into some senior police officers' thinking, with varying degrees of impact. The following points are the most relevant. Firstly, it is one of many ideas used to make certain aspects of police work meaningful, and there is leverage for the concept to be articulated with other concepts. The 'underclass' may surface in relation to other social divisions or particular kinds of behaviour. Secondly, there is a lack of unanimity among officers in relation to the details of their individual perceptions, but overall a structural conception of the 'underclass' is considered to have some impact on the police policy process. The extent to which structural or behavioural factors are of over-ruling importance is significant for the analysis of the police policy process.

Senior officers refer to structural factors by conceptualising the 'underclass' as an individual and sub-cultural group reaction to austere socio-economic conditions. The predicament of the 'underclass' is therefore not the responsibility of the police, and as such is not a policy-relevant issue. The behavioural perspective also interpenetrates certain points of the police policy process. These characterological assessments focus on unchanging personality structures. The latter are observed most at the macro level of the Home Office and central government, where structural accounts are dismissed. Although it is said that socio-economic conditions have no bearing on crime and disorder, the Home Office take these factors into account in determining the allocation of funding to police forces. Many senior police officers see a connection between socio-economic exclusion and crime, and although they have the power to promote such perceptions, the Home Office has the power to discredit and cancel out these views.

Those police officers that note the impact of a structurally excluded 'underclass' on police policy and practice address the issue in two ways. First, the prevention of crime and keeping the Queen's Peace amongst the 'underclass' depends on a communitarian approach. This includes primarily police-led initiatives or different strategies led by other government as well as private and voluntary agencies; but into which the police have some input. Secondly, in those locations where there is no public tranquillity and high rates of crime, 'normal' policing is not possible, and the police apply their legitimate use of force to restore law and order.

Policing the boundaries of social divisions

There are continuities and discontinuities in terms of the police policy process and the underclass debate which link the 1980s and 1990s. In the 1980s the 'underclass' was used by some senior police officers, who did not attribute the idea to a particular author or perspective, but shared a set of common reference points to this sociologically defined concept. By 1989 the 'underclass' had become a familiar idea in many walks of life. It is possible to ground it more if the differences between structural and behavioural usages are noted. Combined with neo-liberal ideology, the behavioural version legitimated the efforts of central government to deny that there are any links between crime, poverty and the nature of social order. In short, there is a 'criminal class' unconditioned by the economy. Some senior police officers criticised this politically motivated and partial account, and instead talked of the adaptations of groups excluded from economic, political and social citizenship: a structurally generated 'underclass' surplus to the requirements of the economy.

Despite the changing nature of perspectives on the 'underclass', some police perceptions of this idea in the 1980s were similar a decade on. Although Murray's ideas have informed police thinking (the then Chief Inspector of Her Majesty's Inspectorate of Constabulary, for example), Woodcock and the other senior officers mentioned above, paradoxically drew on a combination of structural and behavioural factors. The latter are frequently watered-down by the inclusion of culture in their accounts. The main social divisions, although articulated in different ways, are persistent. 'Race' was at the centre of the 'underclass' debate in the 1980s but in the 1990s it was not, in police terms, an issue. However, this overlooks the more subtle ways in which crime and disorder were racialised inasmuch that these phenomena were interpreted by reinterpreting the 1980s, thus corroborating Keith's (1993: 234) contention that there is a 'propensity' for riots to 'send racial messages' and 'connote racialised meanings' even though the issues at stake are totally different. Sir Paul Condon's remarks about African-Caribbean youth and street crime (see Chapter 5) and the police's failure to arrest and prosecute the killers of a young black man, Stephen Lawrence, in a London street, contradict this view, but these issues are bracketed-off from this book.

The dominant themes in policy which were set into motion by Scarman have been enduring, particularly Alderson's communitarian model of community policing. The idea of community is still in circulation, embodied in the formal arrangements made under section 106 of PACE (1984). The informal principles of community policing have also been taken up in many constabularies, although there is much scope for discretion at the different levels of the policy process within each force. These patterns in policy have also interlocked with changes in the style of public order policing. Although the latter is generally considered to be a tactical and operational concern, the consultative side of police policy has been built into some of the practices of those working at the interface of scenes of disorder. The police as a *service* and as a *force* are therefore two sides of the same coin.

Two criticisms are often levelled at these two developments in policing. Firstly, there is the risk that if the police are more 'tooled up' to respond to violence, then the policed are also prepared to go that bit further. According to the logic of this argument the level of violence intensifies, increases and spirals uncontrollably. To paraphrase Weber's maxim, the use of force inevitably leads to more force. Secondly, the benign term community policing conceals other trends such as the dispersal of disciplinary mechanisms (Foucault, 1977) and the expansion of social control (Cohen, 1985), facilitating the management and regulation of problem populations, hence the discourse of 'actuarial justice' (Feeley and Simon, 1994; Gardiner, 1995; Lee, 1995). It has also been argued, by implication, that the over-involvement of the police in communities is the main problem (Gilroy and Sim, 1987). Both of these approaches are ideal-typical and do not describe the complexity of policing and the continually changing social order in which police work is performed. Take the first argument. Reliance on force has been residualised and in many community disorders in the 1990s, force has only been employed as a last resort (Waddington, 1994). Policing has been more concerned with the policing of public order than of public disorder. The second argument is also problematic. The police and the other agencies with whom they have co-operated have not occupied public and private spaces in an undifferentiated and uniform way. Policing is not that effective or efficient. Furthermore, Campbell's (1993: 97) claim that communities have been abandoned is unfounded as policing is not that ineffective or inefficient.

Police policy-making, based in part on communitarian principles, has become more sensitive to the specific localities in which services are provided, but government policies made at a national level, do not recognise any strong links between poverty and crime, and therefore impose constraints on the work of the police service in poor communities. The concept of an 'underclass' framed at a national level by commentators such as Murray, is regarded as too simplistic by some senior officers for addressing the complexity of local and national issues. Despite this mismatch, some officers have taken the idea on board, tailoring it to represent the locales where they work. These accounts, rooted in a structural approach, rest on the premise that a lot of crime and disorder is the adaptation of distinctive sub-cultural groups to structurally generated forms of social exclusion. Police officers express these views in the same committee rooms and corridors as Home Office ministers and the Home Secretary. The latter have the power to turn the views of the former upside-down, and by implication lend support to Murray's version of the 'underclass'. Senior police officers have questioned this version of events by employing a critique that is founded in the structural version of the 'underclass' debate.

9
The Changing Nature of Crime and the Workless Society

In this chapter it is argued that debates about the policing of poverty are potentially entering a new era: the workless society. This epoch is characterised by four distinct developments. The view that full employment is no longer a feasible option – epitomised by Dahrendorf (1985) in the UK and William Julius Wilson (1996a) in the USA – is gradually being accepted by some police policy-makers. Secondly, despite recognition of this problem British and American governments are struggling to produce a creative response to this scenario. Thirdly, discussions about poverty, crime and disorder continue to be based on the behavioural/structural distinction. However, there is a tendency for senior politicians to hold the possibly mistaken assumption that a change in the character and behaviour of the poor – rather than socialised public policy – is the main solution to these problems. Finally, if this is the case, it is unlikely that policy-makers will be able to respond suitably and judiciously to this predicament.

The chapter is split up into three sections, beginning with the hypothesis that in the context of contemporary trends in the labour market, full employment is conceivably no longer a realistic objective. Secondly, drawing on concrete empirical examples, police perceptions of poverty and social divisions in British society prior to the 1997 General Election are surveyed. Lastly the discussion focuses on 'the Atlanticist drift towards a system of "work-welfare"' in social policy, which attempts to confront the problem of social exclusion by creating an inclusive society that incorporates citizens into the work force, thus reducing their dependency on state benefits (Mizen, 1998: 44; Mead and Deacon, 1997). The British government has also turned to the United States for ideas to assist its campaigns against crime and disorder, by importing 'zero tolerance' policing styles (Hopkins-Burke, 1998;

Dennis, 1997). In the context of these two tendencies, it is necessary to investigate the consequences of structurally generated unemployment on the behaviour of socially excluded communities.

A 'work society that is running out of work'

Dahrendorf (1985: 119) borrowed the above phrase from Hannah Arendt, to describe globally generated structural changes affecting the British economy in the mid-1980s, pin-pointing his analysis on the impact of these metamorphoses on the behaviour of young people leaving full-time education. As in the rest of the world, amongst the consequences of these changes were unemployment, non-employment and inactivity, increased poverty, social exclusion and crime and disorder. In the twenty-first century it would appear that Arendt's maxim contains an element of truth, and it accurately describes the experiences of some individuals and groups within the American and British labour markets. For many people, work remains central to their personal and social identities, although fluctuations in the global economy and the flexibility of labour markets, create conditions of uncertainty and insecurity. Joblessness is profoundly affected by spatial and temporal factors, and it is necessary to be aware of the differential impact of these developments at macro and micro levels on regional, national and international economies, and on individuals, households and neighbourhoods. At all times the interplay of structure and human agency, or of political and moral economies should be considered. Race, ethnicity, sex, gender, age and disability are integral parts of this equation too. The issue is further complicated by the Byzantine-like nature of the relationship between employment in the formal and informal sectors, unemployment, non-employment, joblessness, worklessness and inactivity; and the phenomena of poverty, crime and disorder.

Empirical work which examines the transformation of labour markets attests to the growing problem of worklessness, but draws attention to its uneven distribution in different geographical areas, where there may be poverty in the midst of affluence, as in *A Tale of Two Cities* (Taylor, Evans and Fraser, 1996; Fainstein, Gordon and Harloe, 1992; Wilson, 1996; Buck, 1996). Despite the complexity of these trends there is an emergent common theme. Throughout the world the processes of de-industrialisation and the re-structuring and re-orientation of economies towards services, instead of manufacturing, has had profound repercussions. In the US, cities such as Detroit, Los Angeles and New York have been affected particularly badly (Wilson, 1996a; Davis, 1990).

In the UK relatively higher levels of joblessness are concentrated in the inner cities and in what were traditionally mining and industrial areas (Green and Owen, 1998). For some these changes are a consequence of post-Fordism.

In sum, post-Fordism refers to the restructuring of the linkages between labour and capital in the industrial sector, brought about by changes in the global economy, and their impact on international and regional economies. Due to the emergence of new technologies, production line mass manufacturing (Fordism) has been weakened and replaced by a more flexible system of production. As labour has become increasingly separated from capital there has been a rapid expansion of information technology and the service sector. Of course this brief summary is an over-simplification of thinking about post-Fordism, but in Hoggett's view these changes are related to a particular pattern of social polarisation (for a detailed commentary on post-Fordism see Amin, 1994).

The police and the workless society

One of the leading authorities in the sociology of policing has described some of these changes and their effects on the police.

> Economic changes have transformed the economic and social framework, dispersing the centralised 'Fordist' production systems of modern times (Hall and Jacques, 1989) and polarising the class structure into what is often referred to as the 'two thirds, one third society' (Therborn, 1989). While the majority participate, albeit very unevenly and insecurely, in unprecedented levels of consumption, a substantial and growing 'underclass' is permanently and hopelessly excluded [Dahrendorf, 1985, ch. 3; Galbraith, 1992] (Reiner, 1997: 1038–9).

Following on from this observation there are two different kinds of policing. On the one hand there will be a '"service"-style organisation in stable suburban areas', and on the other hand, '"watchman" bodies with the rump duties of the present police, keeping the lid on underclass symbolic locations' (Reiner, 1997: 1039). These global trends are augmented in some North American cities where private policing has taken off:

> The well-heeled shelter in security bubbles shielded by space, architecture, technology and private guards, while the underclass are consigned to the dreadful enclosures of the urban ghettos. The public

police inherit the residual role of patrolling the frontiers between these. In this role they also act as sandwich boards for society's values of fragmentation and division (Reiner, 1995b).

Hoggett's (1994) analysis of policing and the 'underclass' makes a similar point about British society. Social polarisation, including exclusion from the labour market, housing and education have been brought about by post-Fordism and the changing structure of the labour market (Hoggett, 1994: 46). Acknowledging the justifiable worries about the pejorative connotations attached to the 'underclass', particularly its usage by the political right, Hoggett implies that there is a 'socially excluded layer' requiring an analytical category. In the 1960s and 1970s attempts were made to reincorporate the casualties of capitalism through cultural, political and administrative systems of control. By the close of the twentieth century, disenchantment was so rife that inclusion is no longer the objective. The task now is to identify, isolate and manage groups, hence Davis's (1990) notion of 'spatial apartheid'.

> Clearly, in Britain the underclass is less racialised and the drugs economy does not yet play the role that it does in many USA cities. Nevertheless, the spatial isolation and exclusion of the underclass in Britain is quite striking. In a city like Bristol, for example, the 'cordon sanitaire' around the inner area of St Paul's is even stronger today than it has ever been, whilst the outer city estates of Hartcliffe and Lawrence Weston are literally physically decoupled from the rest of the city. Such places are out of sight and therefore out of mind; there is virtually no social or physical mobility here, people are 'locked-in' to such spatial communities. My hypothesis is that rioting and lawlessness in such areas is seen less and less as a social problem requiring policy action. It may soon be useful to think in terms of collapsed communities (Hoggett, 1994: 47).

How do senior police officers define and conceptualise these changes?

Policing the neo-liberal legacy

Towards the end of the twentieth century one chief constable said:

> I think a number of my colleagues and I agree that we do have an underclass and a developing and growing underclass. The concern with people who are unemployed, and those who are unemployed

for a long time, or people who leave school and can't get employment, is what do they do with themselves? What hope have they got for the future? And if the employment market is constricted, not growing, then the prospects for those people become increasingly difficult. People from the lower social classes who leave and do not have the skills perhaps that they need to get jobs where there are jobs to be had. It must be an awful prospect for them, and perhaps, I'm sure quite a few of them turn to crime as a way of earning a living.

The 'underclass' is synonymous with the lower social classes. People from this stratum have an unstable relationship with the labour market, which under some circumstances may lead them into crime. The police target individual criminals but these are placed in the context of a larger group: *a developing and growing economic underclass*.
  In a deputy chief constable's words:

In places like —— where the mines have closed there is an underclass. It is not large but is new and shows potential that it may grow. It is like venturing into a criminal area. For those who leave school now, and unlike the generations before them who went down into the pits there is nothing to do. Some people from these communities have started to go to Amsterdam and buy drugs. After entering the drugs world they then return, importing the drugs to sell them for profit. The direct importation of drugs such as amphetamines, forms the basis of a criminal underclass. The are clear areas in —— and —— where there is the emergence of a drugs underclass. The drugs trade is lucrative at the top end of the market. In some instances the user is also the supplier. These entrepreneurs buy drugs, use what they want for themselves. They then adulterate the remainder of the drugs and sell it to make profit.
  The underclass is small. There are only some people from a criminal class. There are also a few families of third generation criminals. Much of the crime in these areas is drug related. It is focused in the inner cities and run down areas. A member of the police authority in —— said that drugs perpetuates an areas bad name. The problem with this is that drug related crime is real and does need to be addressed. Scarman's criminal class and the drugs culture is burgeoning. Drug related problems used to be concentrated in the inner cities but now they are evident in areas where they had traditionally not been. A drugs factory was recently discovered in ——. Amphetamines

were manufactured in this place, not by blacks, but by white lads on an industrial estate. This was not heard of at the time of Scarman but now it is commonplace.

Here the focus is on drugs and the changing reality of drug related crime. There are some continuities with the 1980s – the inner cities and the issue of drugs – as well as discontinuities. Unlike Scarman's criminal class, in the 1990s the 'underclass' is populated by 'white' rather than 'black' males who inhabit run down urban areas. There are other more persistent trends, though, such as the intergenerational transmission of criminogenic tendencies. This forms the basis of a small, *growing underclass, criminal class, criminal underclass* or the *emergence of a drugs underclass*. As well as cycles of delinquency the officer quoted above talks about industrial decline in the area policed by his force. The closure of many mines and manufacturing industries has led to high unemployment. In coming to terms with the prospect of long term unemployment some school-leavers have become involved in illegal activities. A new manufacturing base has been set up on some industrial estates by an entrepreneurial criminal class.

Unlike the sociological writing on the 'underclass' – and even though attention is drawn to structural factors and the accompanying social divisions which fit in with this work – these divisions are concatenated in a novel form. Class is not only understood in terms of one's relationship to the forces of production, but also in terms of individuals, families and communities relationship with crime and disorder. The adaptation of sub-cultural groups to structural decline is described in terms of criminality. Again, senior police officers' perceptions of the many social divisions which enter into the 'underclass' debate are at odds with academic perspectives. Police perceptions are much more sensitive to local and particular circumstances, although the extent to which it can be said that these mirror the national debate is unclear. The only certainty is that the 'underclass' is socially constructed and re-created constantly, and that the specific configuration of social divisions in a particular definition are unlikely to remain fixed for long.

The 'underclass' therefore exists in the back of officers' minds, and from time to time, comes to occupy a more central position in their thinking. The concept is therefore not totally at odds with the ways in which officers think and act while performing their everyday tasks. However, this concept is not always helpful because accounts such as Murray's are too simplistic for understanding the complexities of the world in which police officers work.

A superintendent, an area commander who had direct experience of what Waddington (1994: 192) calls the '"community disorders" that have intermittently rocked the inner-cities and "dump estates" of Britain' said:

There is an underclass. Almost fifty per cent of young people are unemployed on some estates. There is a second and third generation of young men who have not seen work. It affects males in particular and in a different way to females. Many females can find some work, even if it is only as part-time check-out operators in super-markets.

In general there is widespread social deprivation. Many kids are drawn into crime as a result of boredom. Added to these problems is the fact that social security benefit for sixteen-year-old school leavers has been stopped. Some of these young people are a drain on their poor families. On one of the estates, there is an old bridge near an old Ear, Nose and Throat (ENT) site at the hospital, where some of the kids who have been chucked out of home go and sleep rough. These groups of young people shop-lift alcohol from a nearby off-license, and steal property from nearby residents. In general they do not cause many problems, and unless they have been drinking, one can walk past them without one's safety being threatened. They are a socially deprived group, an underclass, with no real hope in life. They have no jobs. A few of them may do some moonlighting but not many of them. There are those amongst these disaffected youth who are drawn into crime. Some of these people have families and they may experience similar problems.

There is an element of truth in Charles Murray's thinking and there is not much evidence to argue against what he says. In the United States, for example, there are those who have dropped out of society, and the necessary steps should be taken to avoid the same happening here. Having said that, though, there are also some who disagree with Murray's arguments.

In weighing up of the relative merits and demerits of Murray's thinking, this officer did not uncritically adopt Murray's description. Unemployment, crime and family structure are all registered, but there are more points on which Murray's and the police officer's respective descriptions diverge rather than converge. Indeed the superintendent's appraisal is closer to Wilson's (1987) thesis. The description included references to unemployment, but this is not considered to be an outcome of a rational choice made voluntarily by young males. Instead there is a long history of unemployment. The closure of manufacturing industries and the expansion of the service sector has resulted in two trends. Manufacturing is no longer the dominant form of production, and the traditional labour intensive occupations performed by unskilled, semi-skilled and skilled manual labourers have disappeared. Secondly, the jobs remaining in the service sector, such as retailing, are generally open to females. The crime and low level disorder on the estate is due to young school leavers and other young people; some of whom are homeless. These individuals are there largely as a result of unstable families. For the most part their presence is not regarded as serious and in general the place this officer is charged with policing is quiet and peaceful.

In comparison to Chapter 7, 'race' is not an issue, but this does not signal a shift to a class-based analysis. Instead, the 'underclass' debate is broadened to cover other issues that go beyond the matter of the relative significance of 'race' and class. Although the individual's class, or their relationship to the economic organisation of society is important, this is subordinated to other divisions. The main division is sex and the extent to which the individual's position in the labour market is gendered. However, this does not support Campbell's (1993) argument that a crisis in masculinity somehow leads to the kind of scenario outlined in *Goliath*. Male unemployment is also experienced differently across the generations. Age as well as sex is therefore significant; economic inactivity and its impact on males and females is also contingent on age. The conventional wisdom that male unemployment and crime is the main issue is challenged by this officer who reduces the problem to youth unemployment, deprivation, disaffection and sometimes criminality, rather than sex alone. Among this group, which falls outside of the labour market, age and attitudes are more important than sex and gender.

Two inspectors from the policy unit of the same force offered views about the whole force area. The first one said:

> There is an 'underclass' in some of the more deprived areas in the force. Many young people in these areas have no work. They go to bed in the early hours and get up late. They have nothing to do and have no real stake in society.

Again age is the most important division, mediated by structural (non-employment) and behavioural (the hours they keep) factors. The other one said:

The underclass is largely a consequence of planning. Many attempts have been made to rehouse problem families but these have not resulted in the desired effect. It was hoped that by introducing these vulnerable families into established residential areas that this would provide a solution for many of the difficulties they were experiencing.

According to this officer the 'underclass' is a spatially segregated section of the population. In a similar vein to Wilson (1987, 1989), the negative effects of 'social isolation' are mentioned. Both of these inspectors' accounts do not place the 'underclass' specifically in the context of policing, however.

A chief superintendent from another force, who was responsible for policing one of the other estates mentioned in some of the journalistic and more scholarly discussions (Campbell, 1993), and police talk about the 'underclass', said:

> In ——, the underclass is not relevant. On some other estates and from my memories of other areas there may be a danger of one emerging. In some of these places, there are those who have never been employed or who have only a slim chance of finding employment and some who have been unsuccessful at school, who may be in danger of becoming a criminal underclass. That is not to say that the long term unemployed automatically become a member of a criminal underclass. That is one of the difficulties with the idea. These difficulties and problems affect some areas but not that location. It is more of an issue where there are rampant drugs sales and addiction, and the kind of problems they represent.

The relationship of the individual to the labour market is the main reference point used to identify the existence or emergence of an 'underclass'. Unlike other historical periods and the debates that have surfaced at these different times, the association of criminality and the 'underclass' are not, as Gattrell (1990: 251) insisted, 'axiomatic'. Despite this, crime and concomitant behaviour are by implication never far away from the 'underclass'.

Tough on crime and tough on the causes of crime

We will be investing an additional £250 million over the next three years to help ensure that all our policies work together to reduce crime.

We will target resources on the areas which are effective and cost-effective. This will make sure we have the greatest impact on crime within the resources available.

But our policies are not just to focus on crime itself but also on the underlying causes of crime. Social exclusion, under performance at school, peer group pressure, family background are all contributory factors which are being addressed by the Government.

Through all these efforts and by working together we can succeed in cutting crime and making a radical difference to the quality of people's lives (Michael, 1998a).

On 2 May 1997 New Labour was elected to govern Britain, after eighteen years of Conservative rule. In a speech given on a London council estate, the Prime Minister, Tony Blair, said that the government would address the problem of 'an underclass of people cut off from society's mainstream'. In the autumn of that year, a Cabinet Committee on Social Exclusion (Social Exclusion Unit, SEU) was set up under the leadership of the PM. The Unit was not given any additional resources and it accepted the Tories' spending limits for the first two years in power. This was backed up by the belief that: 'the people we are concerned about, those dropping off the end of the ladder of opportunity and becoming disengaged from society, will not have their long term problems addressed by an extra pound a week on their benefits' (Mandelson, 1997: 7). Moreover, the SEU would only be able to deal with poverty under the right social and fiscal conditions, and when the required resources were available (*The Guardian*, 15 August 1997). For New Labour, employment is the best method of tackling poverty and creating an inclusive rather than an exclusive society.

The reformed New Labour Party stated clearly that it no longer shared the preoccupations of Old Labour: equality and the redistribution of income underpinned by social rights for individual citizens. The new objectives were equality of opportunity, combined with personal responsibility and social obligations. At the 1997 Labour conference Blair said: 'a decent society is not based on rights. It is based on duty. Our duty to each other. To all should be given opportunity, from all responsibility demanded'. The emphasis would be on social exclusion rather than poverty *per se*, and social inclusion could only be achieved through the redistribution of opportunities in schools and in the labour market instead of just income (Lister, 1998: 217). The New Deal and Welfare-to-Work were set out to realise these objectives in practice.

The Unit's original remit was to encourage co-operation between government departments, local authorities, voluntary agencies and the business community, to develop anti-poverty policies. The Unit targeted:

> groups who are in poverty, lacking the means to participate in the economic, social, cultural and political life of Britain:... the five million people in workless homes; the three million on the nation's 1300 worst council estates; the 150000 homeless families and the 100 000 children not attending school (MacGregor, 1998: 262).

Expectations of what the New Labour government will achieve in the long term are mixed. It may be that there have been marked shifts in government policy and ideology; and at a rhetorical level – and, some would argue, in reality – the government has advocated tackling social exclusion, in parallel with the development of anti-crime and disorder strategies which mean the deployment of neo-liberal and behavioural perspectives on poverty and crime no longer have a place. For example, New Labour's election manifesto pledged 'to be tough on crime and tough on the causes of crime', by 'tackl[ing] the causes of crime in key areas like youth unemployment and training, school truancy and exclusion, parenting and youth cultures' (Labour Party, 1997: 26). 'Zero-tolerance' and calls 'to take tough action against anti-social neighbours, including new powers for police and local authorities to impose new community safety orders' would appear to indicate something else (Labour Party, 1996a, 1997: 26). In this sense, the behaviour of poor families is at the heart of the government's anxieties in this area of social life, which are not unlike the 'respectable fears' which undergirded the Tories' criminal justice policies.

Given the above, one may therefore be less sanguine, and conclude that there are some continuities between the Conservative and New Labour administrations (Murray, 1994). Indeed New Labour have expressed that they wish to 'move forward from where Margaret Thatcher left off, rather than dismantle every single thing she did' (Mandelson and Liddle, 1996: 1). Since then New Labour have talked of the 'Third Way' which combines neo-liberal and social democratic principles. It is based on the view that Keynesian economics are no longer relevant in the global market place. Although *laissez faire* economics require regulation to reduce their deleterious impact on communities, New Labour would appear to be only willing to intervene when it is absolutely necessary (Elliott, 1998).

What are the relative merits and demerits of these disparate standpoints in relation New Labour's commitment to tackle social exclusion, and how do its crime policies – through the Crime and Disorder Act and so-called 'zero-tolerance' policing strategies – impact on the poor? Although it is far too early to arrive at any sensible conclusions, on the basis of the historical evidence amassed in this book, it is argued that future explanations of poverty and crime are likely to be characterised by elements of both structural and behavioural perspectives. The emphasis on employment as part of the solution to social exclusion and the problems which flow out of this, has a fit with a structural perspective on poverty. Simultaneously, 'zero tolerance' of anti-social behaviour is oriented towards families and 'reinforcing responsibility' on children and their parents to tackle youth crime (Family Policy Studies Centre, 1998: 1). The above should be put into the context of New Labour's political philosophy, which is preoccupied with 'the irresponsible who fall down on their obligation to their families and therefore to their community' (Mandelson and Liddle, 1996: 20). This advocates balancing rights with personal responsibility and social obligations; hard work, the Victorian value of self-help, morality and family life. This confirms Gilroy's (1987: 5) worries about the 'legacy of Victorian moralism expressed in socialist writings' (referred to in Chapter 1). This is a curious admixture of Murrayism, neo-liberal values, Etzioni's communitarianism and Christian/ethical socialism (Deacon and Mann, 1997; Etzioni, 1993, 1997; Murray, 1994; Dennis and Erdos, 1992). Blair and his protégés accept that individuals and families may find themselves in unpropitious circumstances, but in the last analysis, their moral responsibility should stop them from adopting deviant lifestyles. In exchange for being given opportunities, citizens should be dutiful and recognise their mutual obligations to the wider community. In doing so, they will be integrated and included in society. Those who do not perform their duties, face the prospect of being marginalised and stigmatised or reintegrated through shaming (Etzioni, 1993; Braithwaite, 1989).

In the domain of social security – or the Americanised notion of welfare – and its policies set up in response to unemployment, New Labour has in certain respects not deviated significantly from their Conservative predecessors; primarily in their refusal to make any commitment to increase expenditure, and also because it has 'enlarge[d] the workfare framework established by the Tories' (Gray, 1998: 4). Drawing on King's (1995) contribution, one commentator has rightly characterised this as an 'Atlanticist drift towards a system of "work-welfare"' (Mizen, 1998: 44; see also Mead and Deacon, 1997). This entails policies which try to find job-seekers employment through work placements, training schemes which make job seekers more employable, and workfare, which requires job seekers to work as a condition of receiving benefit. For example, during the Thatcher and Major years means-tested benefits were used more frequently than benefits derived from social insurance. The eligibility criteria and availability for work tests were much stricter. There were also tougher sanctions, including the withdrawal of benefit for those who refused 'approved training schemes', and compulsory courses were introduced to offer counselling and to motivate job seekers (Mizen, 1998: 44).

Frank Field, Labour MP and former Chair of the Social Security Select Committee and Government Minister, was an influential figure in rethinking New Labour's welfare policy and in drafting the Green Paper, entitled New Ambitions for Our Country: A New Contract for Welfare, published in March 1998 (Department of Social Security, 1998; Field, 1995; 1997). Field's ideas are multi-faceted and it is not possible to examine them at any length here; several authors have already done so (Oppenheim, 1998b; Deacon and Mann, 1997). A more modest aim is to extract the main themes. Field is less concerned with traditional divisions between the rich and poor, based on differential income levels, than with the distinction between the 'work rich' (households with two-earners) and the 'work-poor' (households with no earners). The panacea for poverty is being 'active' by participating in paid work, instead of being 'passive' and dependent on welfare. This reflects a clear commitment to ending the Labour Party's association with the principles of egalitarianism and the redistribution of income and wealth: 'If a welfare reform programme is to be successfully enacted it must be seen as relevant to the majority of our society, not just the poor' (Field, 1995: 21).

The organising argument of Field's contribution is that people are more strongly motivated by self-interest than altruism. Self-interest is not necessarily a problem in itself, but individual advancement must be married with the common good. He argues that means-tested welfare benefits do not stigmatise claimants in the way they did in the 1930s, but have given claimants perverse incentives. They have failed to encourage thrift, honesty and independence, and 'are steadily recruiting a nation of cheats and liars', especially amongst lone parents (Field, 1996: 11). In some ways this echoes Murray's arguments (outlined in Chapters 3 and 4) which focus on the attitudes and behaviour of the 'underclass'. Instead of encouraging the 'underclass' to enter into or re-enter the labour market they have, unintentionally, been encouraged to be dependent on welfare and, in some instances, to fraudulently obtain social security payments. Field is building on developments in welfare policy found in the USA (outlined in Chapter 3), where tax credits were introduced to replace in-work means-tested benefits, because involvement in the tax system (employment) is far better than dependence on benefits.

Tony Blair's government persisted with Peter Lilley's – Conservative Secretary of State for the Department of Social Security until 1 May 1997 – Jobseeker's Allowance and the project of tightening eligibility conditions; increasing the number of 'options' for training; introducing more punitive sanctions for those who refuse to co-operate; and a general 'hardening of the work discipline to be imposed upon the unemployed' (Gray, 1998: 1; Bryson and Jacobs, 1992). In common with Clinton in the US, Blair's Welfare to Work and the New Deal introduced the 'work ethic', in order to replace welfare with work for all able bodied individuals of an employable age, including lone parents and the disabled (Finn, 1998; McKay and Oppenheim, 1997; Cook, 1998). By promoting equality of opportunity, the 'emphasis [was] on education, training and paid work rather than the redistribution of income through the tax-benefit system' (Lister, 1998: 219).

At the outset, the New Deal was funded by a one-off windfall tax on the privatised utilities which raised £3.2 billion (*The Sunday Telegraph*, 4 January 1998). The schemes operating under the New Deal were intended to integrate paid work with benefits and to target four specific groups: the young who had been unemployed for more than 6 months; adults who had been unemployed for two years or more; lone parents and the disabled. The bulk of assistance in the first instance was directed towards young people. In May 1998, the 122 000 young people under the age of twenty-five, who had been unemployed for more than six months, were offered an initial 'gateway' training programme and personal advice lasting up to four months. If this did not secure them employment after that, they would be more or less compelled to take up one of five options, each lasting between six and twelve months: employment in the private-sector subsidised at £60 per week; work experience in the voluntary sector; participation in an Environmental Task Force which included a benefit top-up; approved full time education and training; and self-employment. Those who refuse the above choices face having their benefits cut by up to 40 per cent. A further £350 million was set aside for the long term employed. In July 1998 employers were given £75 per week to subsidise the employment of the long term unemployed aged between 25 and 35 years. In the autumn of that year, non-mandatory New Deals were introduced for lone parents and the disabled, which aimed to offer advice, find suitable training schemes and eventually work (MacGregor, 1998: 253; Lister, 1998: 220; *The Sunday Telegraph*, 4 January 1998; *The Guardian*, 5 January 1988). However, as part of its goal of moving away from tax and spend policies the government did propose to cut benefits to lone parents (*The Guardian*, 9 December 1997). Only the future will tell us whether or not these policies achieved their objectives. Lister's (1998) cautious overview identifies the potential stumbling blocks:

> Thus, while we have a government committed to promoting social inclusion, it appears to have abandoned the goal of promoting greater equality. The question has to be whether, in the context of entrenched structural inequalities, genuine social inclusion, including the eradication of poverty, is possible without greater equality (Lister, 1998: 224).

The above reforms also fit in with the government's anti-crime strategies which were also based on addressing various forms of exclusion:

> The causes of crime are being addressed across government, and reforms to youth justice will help to nip offending in the bud.
> The welfare-to-work programme to get young people off benefit and into work will help divert young people from crime. The New Deal is now operating in the Prison Service, enabling offenders to join the scheme two months prior to release, to facilitate their reintegration into society. The Social Exclusion Unit is dealing with the interlinked problems of truancy, school exclusions, homelessness and high crime estates (Labour Party, 1998: 13).

On being elected, the Labour government prioritised youth crime and justice (Labour Party, 1996b). This was a reaction to the Audit Commission (1996c) report, Misspent Youth, which pointed out that 65 per cent of school-age offenders had also been excluded from school or were persistent truants, and that each year, on average, 7 million or a third of all crimes are committed by young offenders under 18. The then Home Secretary, Jack Straw, argued that this signalled a need to 'break the excuse culture' by increasing parental responsibility (*The Guardian*, 26 September 1997). The Crime and Disorder Act (1998) passed into law reparation orders, faster justice, increased prevention and support for parents and children in families under stress. There were also curfews for children and a reduction in the use of cautions. Most significantly, the Crime and Disorder Act (1998) outlined a statutory framework to underpin the formulation of crime and disorder partnerships. Alun Michael, Home Office Minister said:

> What we will do is place a new joint responsibility on the police services and local authorities to develop statutory partnerships to prevent crime and enhance community safety by means of Community Safety Orders. We recognise how plagued many neighbourhoods are by continual anti-social behaviour by individuals or groups of individuals (Michael, 1997).

These national guide-lines would be used by local authorities to tailor anti-crime and disorder strategies which are responsive to the particular needs of local areas. These partnerships require chief police officers and local authorities (councils and districts) to co-operate with police authorities, probation committees, health authorities and a variety of other players, to devise strategies to prevent crime and disorder in specific localities. This formalised many of the informal relationships described in Chapters 7 and 8 which were incorporated into communitarian and community policing.

This discussion focuses on 'zero tolerance' policing. Although the introduction of this policy preceded the 1997 General Election there are thematic continuities. It would appear that the role of the police is to be essentially the same as it was envisaged by the last Conservative government of the twentieth century:

> For 150 years the police have been at the forefront of the fight against crime. To be effective the police and other law enforcement agencies require sufficient powers to do their job and the support of the public, and effectiveness is also linked with efficiency (Labour Party, 1998: 4).

The case for 'zero tolerance'

'Zero tolerance' is the latest in a long line of strategies introduced by the police to control an 'underclass' (Crowther, 1998). It is shown in previous chapters that the perception that the police *police* an 'underclass' has been a key aspect of several authors' accounts of the social control of poor communities (as contained in Jefferson, 1990; Reiner, 1994; Morrison, 1995, for example). This work refers to a 'criminal underclass' in the aftermath of various episodes of urban unrest, claiming that the disorderly behaviour of an excluded population surplus to the requirements of the capitalist economy has led to changes in the direction of police policy and practice. In the final decade of the twentieth century, 'zero tolerance' policing focused on the involvement of the 'underclass' in street crime and low level disorder. Morgan (1997) made the most explicit connection by asserting that '"Zero tolerance" is all about sweeping clean those inner city junctions where tourists and professional commuters briefly encounter the dispossessed underclass – the mad and the sad, as well as the bad'. In a similar vein, Ellis (1996) remarked that in 'King's Cross, one of London's best known red light districts, infested by prostitutes, pimps and drug pushers, the problems of underclass criminality are acute and costly.' This contention and other related debates are contested from an historical perspective, primarily by reflecting on the trends apparent in 'zero tolerance' policing.

The launch of 'Operation Zero Tolerance' by the Metropolitan Police, in collaboration with the City of London Police and the British Transport Police, in King's Cross on 18 November 1996 was a six week experiment. This built on 'Operation Welwyn' which was also initiated by the Metropolitan Police in co-operation with Islington and Camden councils in 1992. The rationale underlying these and other operations was outlined in the Metropolitan Police's 1995/6 'Policing Plan' which called for a partnership between the police, the public sector, private and voluntary agencies as well as the general public: 'to target and prevent crimes which are a particular local problem, including drug-related criminality' (Metropolitan Police, 1995).

The notion of 'zero tolerance' was popularised by New York's Republican Mayor, Rudolph Giuliani, and the then Police Commissioner, William J. Bratton, who are both indebted to the 'right realist' criminology of Wilson and Kelling (1982) and their appropriation of Zombardo's 'broken windows' hypothesis. In accord with this, the practice of 'zero tolerance' policing entails a crack-down on all offences and offenders. By targeting less serious crimes such as aggressive begging, graffiti, dropping litter and low level disorder, the police come into contact with more serious offenders (Bratton, 1996; Bowling, 1996). This part briefly reviews the impact this strategy has had in New York Police Department (NYPD), particularly the claim that it has been of some success. Since the introduction of 'zero tolerance' policing in the summer of 1994 the number of homicides were reduced from 1582 to 1182 in 1995 and 983 in 1996. In 1990 the figure was 2245, which indicated that the rate was falling anyway. For robbery, in 1993 there were 85 892 recorded offences compared to 59 721 a year after the operation was launched.

These statistics must be treated with caution, though, because there are other possible determining factors for this reduction including: a displacement effect; demographic changes, particularly a decline in the youth population; increased job opportunities following the end of an especially bad period of recession; and the introduction of more mandatory and longer prison sentences which resulted in 'criminals' being kept off the streets for longer periods. It is therefore difficult to isolate the impact of 'zero tolerance' policing on crime and disorder (Chaudhary and Walker, 1996; Johnston, 1997; Letts, 1997; Read, 1997).

The importation of 'zero tolerance' policing

In the UK the notion of 'zero tolerance' policing gained the support of both political parties in debates on law and order in the run up to the 1997 election, particularly in speeches highlighting the threat that beggars and the homeless pose to public order. However, some senior police officers have expressed their scepticism (Pollard, 1997). In Waddington's (1997: 27) view, 'zero tolerance' 'undercut the liberal sentimentality that dominated the 1980s. It legitimised "getting tough" with criminals'. Michael Howard was the first government minister to refer to the idea, but for the purposes of this chapter, Tony Blair's (1997) notorious comments in the *Big Issue* interview in January 1997, where he backed police action that targeted beggars, is a more significant example of an influential politician alluding to the idea. Blair's statements corroborated Jack Straw's earlier references to 'street beggars, winos, addicts and squeegee merchants' and his calls to tackle vandalism and nuisance neighbours. Significantly, Straw was impressed with 'zero tolerance' following his visit to New York in the summer of 1996 (Travis, 1996). Morgan (1997) has argued that even more crucially Blair 'endorsed "zero tolerance" policing [as] just the latest attempt by New Labour to distance itself from the "soft on crime" skeletons in its Old Labour law and order cupboard'.

It should be noted that the police operation in King's Cross is significantly different to both the reality of 'zero tolerance' in the USA and the rhetoric of politicians in the UK. Primarily, the pattern of crime in these respective societies is very different. According to Superintendent Smith, the local police commander in King's Cross in 1997, the intended usage of the notion was as a 'sound-bite'. In the UK 'Operation Zero Tolerance' was to a certain extent an intensified version of 'Operation Welwyn' introduced in 1992 by the Metropolitan Police. Both were intended to tackle drug dealing and prostitution. However, since the introduction of 'Operation Zero Tolerance', politicians and police have targeted beggars and the homeless. This reflects the rationale outlined in a Home Office team's report submitted to Ministers in 1996 which stated that 'anti-social behaviour can stimulate criminality by creating an environment that attracts the more criminally inclined and implies that their conduct will not be subjected to effective controls' (cited in Johnston, 1997). Thus 'Operation Zero Tolerance' includes elements of Bratton's (1996) approach. These are tailored to the specific problems found in some locales in London and combined with communitarian initiatives such as 'partnership policing' and 'problem oriented policing' (Goldstein, 1990; Pollard, 1997). Such developments add to the confusion and complexity of talk about 'zero tolerance' policing and its relevance to controlling an 'underclass'. What about the effectiveness of these models?

As I have previously pointed out, evaluations of 'Operation Welwyn' show that there was a reduction in drug dealing. Since 1992, 425 drug dealers were convicted, and it was estimated that the number of street drug dealers operating in this area had also fallen. It may be that some displacement had occurred (Campbell, 1996), but other assessments of the impact of these operations suggested that there was an improvement in the quality of life of residents and workers in the targeted areas (Crowther, 1998: 73; Dennis and Mallon, 1997ab; Romeanes, 1998; Johnston, 1997).

At a cursory glance 'zero tolerance' policing would seem to have made few inroads into everyday policing outside of London, and Hartlepool and Middlesbrough, both in Cleveland, were two of the few places where a police force explicitly based some of its activities on this style of policing (*The Times*, 1996). Since DCI Mallon adopted 'zero tolerance' policing in Hartlepool the number of recorded offences were halved. In Middlesbrough reported crime was reduced by a fifth within six weeks. Before Christmas 1996 an average of 75 crimes (20 of these were burglaries) were committed each day. By February 1997 the comparable figures were 60 and 12 respectively (Chesshyre, 1997: 22). A similar scheme was piloted by Strathclyde Police in Glasgow, the Spotlight Initiative, which began on 1 October 1996 (Orr, 1997). After consulting the public the police found that people were less frightened of murder and rape but more anxious about the security of their property and their personal safety in public places. In partnership with Customs and Excise and local authorities the police devoted a significant proportion of their operational resources to target all crimes, involving 20 000 stops and searches in the first month. Overall, the number of recorded offences fell by 9 per cent. Drug related arrests rose by 1300. Serious assaults declined by 12 per cent, robberies by 5 per cent, common assaults by 4 per cent and break-ins by 9 per cent. Arson fell by 10 per cent, vandalism by 4 per cent and there were 1687 fewer crimes against motor vehicles (Crowther, 1998: 74; Ellis, 1996).

Although 'zero-tolerance' is far from being an homogeneous style of policing there are some themes common to each of the above schemes, and there are some striking parallels between these and Alderson's model of community policing. First, they all rely heavily on a visible presence of police officers. Second, all the schemes have been introduced in response to public anxiety about high levels of crime and disorder and more general concerns about community safety. Third, there is an emphasis on the police consulting different public, private and voluntary agencies (Crowther, 1998: 74). Indeed, as shown above, the Crime and Disorder Act (1998) placed a statutory responsibility on local authorities to work with the police to tackle crime and disorder and to set local targets for reducing the scale and prevalence of these social problems. Home Office Minister Alun Michael announced:

> Over recent years, many communities have been devastated by petty disorder and anti-social behaviour. We want to ensure that this intolerable situation does not continue.
>
> For the first time our Crime and Disorder Act sets out a framework for local people to work with the police and local authorities to solve local problems – together.
>
> It also gives the police and courts new powers to prevent the behaviour of individuals intent on causing harm and distress.
>
> In turn this will help to rebuild the foundations of our communities and at the same time assist in cutting crime (Michael, 1998b).

The long term effects the Crime and Disorder Act (1998) will no doubt be evaluated in the early years of the twenty-first century.

It seems certain that 'zero-tolerance' policing, as cited in the above examples, has had some kind of effect on crime rates, especially in the short term. However, there has been considerable resistance to the concept from senior police officers in other constabularies. The main concern is that the prioritisation of 'crime-fighting' criteria may create problems. Charles Pollard (1997), Chief Constable of Thames Valley Police, argued that its implementation may actually instigate further social problems. Rather than 'nipping crime in the bud' we might see disorder on the scale of that which erupted in the inner city riots of the 1980s and on some of Britain's lonely and forgotten 'outer-city' or 'peripheral' estates in the 1990s (Crowther, 1998: 74).

Punishing the workless

If the rhetoric of politicians and some public commentators is taken seriously, police policy and practice is oriented towards a workless and excluded 'underclass' which – in the case of 'zero tolerance' – is primarily made up of the workless, homeless and beggars. In the late twentieth and early twenty-first centuries the 'underclass' was not involved in inner city and 'outer city' riots or community disorders, but low level disorder, and therefore there are differences between the 1980s, the early 1990s and the mid-1990s. Despite this, it has been argued that 'zero-tolerance' policing is targeting groups in 'underclass'-type positions. Having said that, analyses of this style of policing are ongoing and its long-term impact remains to be seen. In the meantime there is likely to be much speculation, but the view that if 'what happens in the United States will happen in the UK' holds, then one possible development is that described by Jerome Miller of the National Centre of Institutions and Alternatives, namely:

> There is a danger that zero tolerance can intensify the criminalisation of an entire class. The way things are going now, nearly 75 per cent of African-Americans and millions of Hispanics will have criminal records – having being booked and charged – by the time they reach 35. We have cities where one young black male in three is either in prison, on probation or awaiting trial (Miller, 1996 cited in Chaudhary and Walker, 1996).

The new consensus on law and order has been demonstrated by the high level of agreement over the issue of 'zero tolerance' policing. The 'underclass' is also a feature of debate about this approach to policing. Chesshyre (1997: 24) suggests that the police need little encouragement to engage in 'zero tolerance' policing and that, 'They have a lexicon of terms for low life: "toe rags", "bunch of crap", "shite", "scumbags".' There are run-down areas where such people – the underclass – live, and day-to-day policing is concentrated on these areas. In contrast to previous occasions when a relationship between policing and the 'underclass' has been identified, scant attention has been given to the influence of structural factors on 'underclass' formation. The arguments of 'right realism' are prevailing over those associated with 'left realism'.

For example, the 'mad, sad and bad' – consisting of the homeless and beggars – are partly in that situation because of personal choice; individual inadequacies and bad behaviour rather than wider structural factors are said to be the main causes of their social exclusion and poverty. It is imperative that further work is done to make the distinction between behavioural and structural versions of the 'underclass' more explicit. Failure to do this is likely to result in explanations of social problems and social divisions that emphasise the immorality or innate deficiencies of individuals, without taking into consideration the effects of structural constraints.

10
Conclusion

The narrative concludes by arguing that our understanding of poverty needs to be based on making more explicit the distinction between the behavioural and the structural variants. Some critics have questioned usage of the former because it tends to caricature the poor and blame them for their own social position. However, some key policy-makers as individuals and in groups do not necessarily engage in the sort of 'victim blaming' associated with the behavioural perspective. They hold the view that crime and poverty are a result of complex structural processes, mediated by the culture of individuals and communities that are attempting to cope with adverse material conditions. By emphasising a structural perspective on these phenomena, policy-makers highlight the extent to which they cannot address the problems of the excluded society without more help from central government.

The main body of this account analysed the relationship between discourses on crime and poverty and the police policy process in modern British society. This dynamic interrelationship was examined by considering its place in a broader cultural and structural context, including a critical analysis of the influence of American thinking. A central issue is the relative significance of behavioural and structural perspectives on these problems and their relevance at different levels of the police policy machinery. A principal concern was the relationship between those policies and practices devised to construct order in divided communities through communitarian strategies, which are sometimes backed-up by the police service's legitimate use of force. Some criminogenic and disorderly 'symbolic locations' and 'riotous communities' were taken as examples to illustrate these processes. This concluding chapter brings together the main strands. Time is taken to reflect on some of the key issues and to identify the main themes: (a) debates about crime and poverty contained in academic, public commentary, journalistic and public policy discourses; (b) the police policy process; and (c) the points at which ideas about poverty have been a useful guide-line for the intellectual and practical tasks involved in the social construction of police policy and practice. These issues are situated in their relevant socio-political context, taking into the account the interaction of macro-level and micro-level factors at global, international, national and local levels, particularly political power.

Some themes in debates about poverty and crime

Wilson's observation about the American situation is a useful signpost to describe ongoing trends in modern Britain:

> The term ghetto underclass, rarely invoked during the past two decades, is now frequently used by both social scientists and journalists in descriptions of the growing social problems – joblessness, family disruption, teenage pregnancy, failing schools, crime and drugs – that involve many of those who live in the inner city (Wilson, 1996b: 223).

Chapters 2, 3 and 4 explored the significance of this disputation from an historical perspective in the context of discourses on poverty and the policing of the underclass in the US and the UK. While not pretending to cover everything, it provided a critical overview of the different usages of these concepts in journalistic, public policy and academic discourses. This part identified a problem, namely the diversity of representations of poverty and crime and the various puzzles these represent. The lack of clarity found in these commentaries is an outcome of three quandaries: (i) the wide-ranging subject matter; (ii) conceptual issues and (iii) the values underpinning these concepts. This sets the tone for the rest of the chapter which examines the distinction between behavioural and structural interpretations of poverty and crime.

The problem of representing poverty

Much of the confusion at the core of conceptions of poverty is a reflection of the complexity of the subject matter they describe. There are a multiplicity of reference points, including shared spatial location and social isolation, welfare dependency, families headed by a lone parent, low educational attainment, a lack of marketable skills, unemployment and economic inactivity, and involvement in criminal, delinquent and disorderly behaviour. These are not always linked in the same way and certain issues are more important than others at specific temporal and spatial junctures. For instance, the poor are featured in numerous accounts of crises in housing, education, health and income maintenance or social security policy. With regard to these areas, crime and disorder – with the notable exception of social security fraud – have not been central issues. This commentary has focused on these missing topics, and the work of the police is, not surprisingly, centre-stage.

Conceptualising poverty

The conceptual make-up of different ideas about poverty are extremely complex because they are shaped by their articulation with other social divisions: class, 'race'/ethnicity, sex/gender and age. The controversies and ambiguities of theories on these divisions are further complicated when they are tagged onto the 'underclass'. It was shown that the old certainties about these social divisions are becoming increasingly blurred and more ambivalent than ever before (Anthias, 1998). The 'underclass', in a sense, symbolises this uncertainty. This is demonstrated by some senior police officers' representations of the policing of the 'underclass', particularly those grounded within a structural perspective.

Social values and the 'underclass'

The particular set of values which inform different perspectives on poverty also leads to difficulties. It was argued in Chapter 5 that values are an important part of all areas of social life and determine the ways in which human beings perceive the world and how they conduct themselves:

> values and theory shape our understanding of [the world]. In social science there are no important facts independent of the theories that organise them. Hence, we must take account of the conflicting frames that organise thought and action (Rein, 1983: xi).

The values underpinning theories are a powerful impetus underlying the construction of ideas, systems of thought and human action (Berger and Luckmann, 1966). The conflicting frames used to organise these different practices may produce outcomes that are far from clear-cut and the values underpinning a commentator's understanding of a particular topic may lead to distortion. By mobilising a particular set of values, certain kinds of countervailing evidence or arguments, which are underscored by different value frameworks, may be rejected or obfuscated.

This is a political issue. Conflict and disagreement is inevitable because everyone has their own values but it is necessary to be alert to the pitfalls of adopting an absolutely relativistic perspective on this matter. It is also necessary to take stock of the degree to which some values are imposed on social groups, or that some people consent to certain value frameworks because contradictory evidence and values are hidden from them. If they were aware of counter-arguments they may have markedly different views.

In late modern society there are a plurality of values woven throughout the complex social tapestry in which human beings think and act. However, some values have more clout than others, especially those promoted by social actors and agencies in society who are able to exercise effective power. Such individuals and groups are able to iron-out conflicting or contradictory values and principles, although they may meet various kinds of resistance.

Many values impinge on discussions about crime and poverty, especially in relation to the identification of the dynamic economic, ideological, political and social forces and processes which cause them. These values not only underpin descriptions of these social facts but are also used in policy-making. For the purposes of clarity, these were split up into two perspectives: the behavioural and the structural. This distinction is of central importance for interpreting the relevance of these disputes and their place in police discourse and in the police policy process.

Behavioural and structural approaches in their social and political context

The values which inform thinking about poverty and crime are of critical importance, because the diagnosis of the social problems is associated with any action taken to remedy these problems.

The behavioural perspective is epitomised by Murray (1990, 1994) who holds to the view that the concept of an 'underclass' does not describe the condition of poverty *per se* but explains a certain type of behavioural adaptation to it. Young men's involvement in crime and disorder, for example, is caused by poor parenting on the part of young unmarried women or the 'dismembered family' (Dennis, 1993). Other contributory factors are the voluntary idleness of men, whose rationally made choice not to participate in the labour market, in tandem with their unwillingness to contemplate the tall order of parenthood, leads them into crime. These individuals are labelled as 'barbarians', who

exploit the rights of social citizenship without fulfilling their obligations and duties to wider society.

Although popular in media and political discourses various academics
have questioned Murray's (1990) assumption that poverty and the mixture of behavioural responses to it are rooted in the individual, and
exist as an expression of unmediated rational choice (Morris, 1994).
Despite this, Murray's ideas have won support at all levels of society,
particularly among neo-liberals: the Republicans in the United States
and the Conservative Party in Britain. Recent changes in the political
culture of these countries has indicated that the Democrats and New
Labour are also giving their support to the general thrust of Murray's
thesis, albeit with some minor reservations.

Partly because it is reminiscent of many other historical debates
reviewed in Chapters 2, 3 and 4, Murray's 'underclass' is often categorised as a novel variation on an old theme. However, it has a novel
dimension. Before acknowledging this difference, several issues concerning the reasonableness of Murray's arguments need to be clarified.
Primarily, Murray's response to men behaving badly is understandable
for two reasons. First, care should be taken not to fall into the trap of
exonerating those responsible for committing crime or behaving in an
anti-social manner. Such behaviour, even if it is described as a form of
protest, rebellion or uprising, deserves to be challenged. Second, Murray's views may not be that different from the majority of people and
their anxieties about crime and punitive attitudes towards criminals. Of
course, this is problematic because some people's expressed wishes on how
certain criminals should be treated, would constitute a criminal offence
if their ideas were actually put into practice. Nevertheless, the power of
public opinion cannot be ignored, however disagreeable it may be.

The minority of individuals who engage in criminal behaviour are
not twenty-first century Robin Hoods. Those who attack ethnic minority shopkeepers and the premises of big businesses are undeserving of
the support of apologists. Those who throw bricks at police officers or
missiles at their vehicles should, arguably, to paraphrase the former
Conservative Prime Minister of the UK (1990–7) John Major, be *con-
demned* rather than *understood*.

However there are more problematic responses to such actions. For
example, some claim the disproportionate over concentration of such
crimes amongst the poorer members of our society is a reflection of the
status of an 'underclass' – in Gans's (1993) words – as a 'caste' or a 'race
apart', classified in terms of its inherited behaviour. Such explanations
are deficient because they ignore how poverty, and other structurally

generated forms of social and political exclusion, may have an impact too (Westergaard, 1995: 117). This kind of thinking therefore signals a profound change from the kind of analyses that were promulgated by academics in post-war British society before the 1980s.

Since the 1970s structural accounts have consistently suggested that an 'underclass' – a sub-stratum beneath the working class – incorporates the casualties of socio-economic changes in a post-industrial capitalist society. Instead of behaviour in isolation from other variables, changes in the labour market and the exclusion of citizens from welfare and the world of work are the key causal factors. There is social polarisation and increased poverty, but no concrete evidence of a separate group which is permanently detached from mainstream society exclusively in terms of its behaviour or because its members have a different 'mind-set' characterised by different norms and values. Perhaps, with the exception of a small minority of individuals, participants in criminal and disorderly acts actually share some, if not all, of the values held by other people in wider society. Even those who do not observe certain rules and regulations, in all probability hold to others. Instead of there being a distinctive 'caste' or 'race apart', certain marginal groups within structurally excluded sections of the population may form sub-cultural groups, which though situated in an 'underclass'-type position, act not in accordance with individual pathologies but in response to external (social) pressures, combined with a degree of circumscribed choice. It is necessary therefore to put such behaviour into a structural context. Social divisions are thus shaped by structural and cultural factors rather than simply by behavioural forces (Lea and Young, 1993; Matza, 1964).

Since the late 1970s the major institutions in America and Britain have been subjected to many important changes, most notably the redefined role of central and local government, and the review of the part that they should play in the allocation and distribution of resources. Given the volume of changes that occurred it is only possible to highlight broad tendencies. Gamble's (1988) phrase, 'free economy, strong state' is a useful reference point. Perhaps one of the most notable trends is that, in Walker's words (1991), 'a strategy of inequality' has been deliberately pursued. The bearing these changes have had on the formation of an 'underclass', in a structural location rather than as a result of its behaviour, are well documented in the main body and only a brief summary is outlined here.

At a macro level the *laissez faire* economic policies of successive neo-liberal governments have created the necessary conditions for a free market economy to replace an inefficient and ineffective state-run economy. Neo-liberal ideology, in various guises, has played a crucial part in making this possible, and the ideological project of the New Right, particularly of the Republicans in the USA and the Conservatives in the UK, has been realised in three principal ways. The election of the Democrats in the US and New Labour in Britain has not significantly changed the political culture, and despite shifts in rhetoric, both are following a broadly neo-liberal agenda in economic and social policy as well as crime policy.

First, the prioritisation of individualism above notions of collectivism and public welfare have eroded the notion of 'society'. It has been argued, for instance, that in the UK, T.H. Marshall's (1972) model of citizenship, in the context of 'democratic-welfare-capitalism', is becoming increasingly less relevant, coming under attack across the political spectrum from neo-liberals on the right and communitarians and ethical socialists on the centre-left (Deacon and Mann, 1997; Driver and Martell, 1997; Hughes, 1996). The word citizen is still in circulation but it has very different connotations, with the shift away from a rights based conception of citizenship towards one that is based on duties and obligations. The new trend is to set store by the sovereignty of the individual consumer. These changes can be seen as part of an attack on government intervention in economic affairs in general and the welfare state in particular. According to the neo-liberal argument, government involvement in the economy weakens individual enterprise and initiative. The institutional provision of welfare for broaching essentially private and individual matters undermines personal responsibility and fosters dependency on the state.

Secondly, the individual agent is *free to choose*, and can act by exercising choice, so long as the actions of a particular citizen do not interfere with the individual liberty of other citizens. Choice is defined in terms of the individual's relationship to the mechanisms of the market. Thirdly, and closely related to individual choice, is the emphasis on personal responsibility, specifically the obligation placed on individuals to provide for themselves and the other members of their family. For example, in a speech given in September 1997 Frank Field summed up New Labour's ethos:

our reform agenda is dominated by a new emphasis on responsibility as well as rights: the responsibility of parents, absent and present, to care emotionally and materially for their children; the responsibility of adults of working age to work; the responsibility of welfare recipients to escape from dependency (Field cited in Lister, 1998: 222).

It is each individual's duty to avoid dependency on the 'nanny state', and if they fail to perform these duties then they are, in the final instance, responsible for their situation. What are the ramifications of these structural and cultural changes for understanding these discourses on social problems? What influences have these macro economic, structural and cultural forces had on the concepts' many referents and the values underpinning them?

Taking the first issue, all of the main criteria associated with the 'underclass' include poverty, non-participation in and exclusion from the world of work, single parent families, crime and disorder, social isolation and the spatial concentration of these factors, are all real social phenomena. Wilson's (1996) and Townsend's (1996) recent work on poverty in the US and the UK respectively, and the publication of the – admittedly problematic – official crime statistics (Povey *et al.*, 1998; Povey and Prime, 1998) and the British Crime Surveys attest to this (Mirrlees-Black *et al.*, 1996, 1998). Similarly, in the US, the perception that crime is endemic is strong (Hahn, 1998; Beckett, 1997). Moreover, these problems are far more than a linguistic construction. Equally important, though, they do not have a concrete, objective reality unconditioned by other variables such as academic theories and the language in which they are described. The unanswered, possibly unanswerable question is, in the last analysis, which dynamic underlies this? Is it the behaviour of human agents, structural processes or both of these mediated by culture?

Turning to the second issue. The ways in which poverty and the 'underclass' are conceptualised, particularly in journalistic and other sources of public commentary, are more problematic; especially in terms of the ways in which its different characteristics are articulated. Some of the links are asserted rather than demonstrated without acknowledging the sophistication of these linkages. Murray's claim that there are causal links between voluntary idleness – significantly, not unemployment *per se* – unmarried mothers and violent crime is a good example.

Thirdly, values, and the organisation of their conflicting frames of reference for explaining the above, matter. Value conflicts are an integral part of making judgements, but to reiterate an earlier point, some values have a more powerful punch than others. Some values are woven into the more permanent 'constitutive structures of everyday life' (Luckmann, 1983: 19), and as such are more enduring and in a position to exert more influence on the social construction of reality.

Before continuing it is necessary to illustrate the complex links between conceptions of crime and poverty, socio-political values and the bearing these have on policy-making, by returning to the distinction between behavioural and structural versions of the 'underclass'. At the height of its influence in the late 1980s and 1990s the values underpinning theories of the 'underclass' were of a behavioural hue, and in accord with the views of those most able to wield effective power in populist and parliamentary discourse: Murray, Murdoch, Reagan, Clinton, Thatcher and Major. Although there are rubbing points between their own values there is more than an inkling of consensus on what counts as an adequate explanation of poverty, crime and 'underclass' formation: namely behaviour that is relatively or absolutely unconditioned by the political economy. The values on which structural accounts are based contrast with the above and perhaps not surprisingly these arguments are not so well publicised.

There are individuals from unlikely quarters who one would expect, in principle, to oppose structural arguments, but whose rhetoric is similar. The example of Kenneth Clarke in Chapter 4 testifies that there is no simple relationship between political values and the socio-political perspective which sustains discourses on the 'underclass'. Clarke's statement invoked structural themes but one can rest assured that any changes in policy would not have gone against the overarching 'strategy of inequality' (Walker, 1991b). It is therefore necessary to exercise caution by being wary of the gap between the rhetoric characterising a particular conception of the 'underclass' and the reality of the policy prescriptions devised to tackle it. For example, there may be no attempt to go beyond the words used to describe the 'underclass' and to change the systemic processes underlying the social construction of an 'underclass'.

The only certainty that comes out of this is that ambiguity is the defining theme of the 'underclass' debate, a factor which is particularly evident in the context of the police service. Before examining the unique police perspectives on the 'underclass', portraits of the policing of poverty outlined in the research literature on policing and other related issues in criminal justice are sketched.

Policing the urban poverty: behavioural and structural perspectives

Academic writing on the policing of poverty reflects a wide range of views, which share several things in common with other more specific descriptions of the 'underclass'. A focus on the disproportionate concentration of certain forms of criminal behaviour in poor communities and the police service's response to this, constitutes the bulk of this work (Reiner, 1997: 1038–9). Like those aspects of the 'underclass' debate detailed throughout this narrative there are, on the one hand, material and economic (structural), and on the other hand, moral (behavioural) perspectives in historical and contemporary narratives on the policing of the 'underclass'. However, the distinction between behavioural and structural versions of the 'underclass' in this work is often implicit rather than explicit. Nevertheless, this distinction can be used as an organising principle to understand the place of the 'underclass' in interpreting aspects of policing. Secondly, the emphasis is overwhelmingly on the axiomatic link between the poverty, crime and disorder of the 'underclass'. The issues of the individual's attachment to the labour market, family structure, spatial isolation and the various other criteria that connote the 'underclass' debate are all there, but remain in the background to crime and disorder.

Before the inner city riots of the 1960s and the 1992 LA uprising in the USA, and the urban unrest in the UK in the 1980s and 1990s, the bulk of academic research into policing focused on work undertaken by rank and file. The earliest and most notable contribution of this sort of work was Banton's (1964) writing, which proved to be an invaluable teaching aid for the police service and informed their thinking about the organisation's relations with minority ethnic communities. A lot of later work in this field consisted of ethnographic research or data gleaned from the direct observation of police work, highlighting the actions of police officers coming to terms with the uncertainty and ever-changing requirements of the environment in which they work (Holdaway, 1983).

The common bond joining together this disparate range of research is the police occupational culture and the focus on patterns of police prejudice. The latter issue, explored most tellingly in Smith and Gray's (1983) work, examined the attitudes and beliefs expressed by police officers on the streets and in the canteen. A major preoccupation of this research was police officers' perceptions of the public they police. Amongst others, Smith and Gray attributed the idea of an 'underclass' to police officers suggesting that it is, in one form or another, commonly applied to represent the behaviour of some of their 'customers'. While performing the twin tasks of law enforcement and order maintenance, police officers understandably assess the merit or desert of the different sections of the public they encounter, frequently on the basis of their behaviour. Practitioners' views tend to be based on an on-the-spot judgement of an individual's character, which may be based exclusively on their behaviour or mediated with references to socially based divisions such as 'race', sex, gender, class, age and the 'underclass'.

Bearing in mind Murray's (1990: 70) caveat that 'the policeman in poor neighbourhoods may or may not bridle at the term 'underclass', but the distinction between the good folks and the underclass shines through after the first five minutes'; the police officers quoted in research on the rank and file also use some of the other terms mentioned in Chapter 5. The 'rough/respectable' and 'deserving/undeserving' distinctions are two examples, and this research is replete with examples of insulting and offensive phrases. Again, this reflects a very necessary aspect of police work, namely the allocation of desert and the fundamental role of prejudice and stereotyping in doing this. The main problem is that the use of pejorative language, in no simple way, and whether rightly or wrongly, is potentially built into action.

The perception that police officers are prejudiced may in turn prejudice some elements of the policed against certain aspects of policing. This mutual suspicion may contribute to the exaggeration and hardening of collective attitudes and the amplification of police/community conflict. Numerous examples of this were identified over the course of the 1980s and 1990s. On the one hand, there is a respectable and law abiding, generally white, police service, and on the other hand, a rough – sometimes black – criminogenic 'underclass'. The tension between these two groups has been a perennial problem affecting the police service, particularly its attempts to balance peace-keeping with law enforcement. In 1994 John Hoddinott (former Chief Constable of Hampshire and an ex-President of ACPO) wrote that 'there were circumstances where enforcement of the law had, of necessity, to be accorded a lesser priority than the maintenance of order' (1994: 163). It is when this time-honoured theme is considered that Lord Scarman's (1981: 4.11) 'policing dilemma' has had a great deal of import for everyday policing.

As shown in Chapters 7 and 8 the evidence amassed in the research reviewed above was referred to in the aftermath of the inner city riots in the US in the 1960s and in the UK in the early 1980s, particularly in academic accounts and some of it is found in the Kerner Commission (1968) and the Scarman report (1981), which in turn were touchstones for later disturbances in both countries. The existence of police prejudice, especially of a racialised (Keith, 1993) and gendered (Campbell, 1993) nature, is used to explain mutually antagonistic relations between the rank and file and a 'disreputable underclass'. It was also argued that there was more to this than the mutual hostility which characterised conflict between a white police force and black youth on the streets and in the 'hoods' of some inner city locales.

The policing of the poor was also placed into the wider context of the political economy of neo-liberalism. During the 1980s the majority of commentators wrote of unemployment, social deprivation and social exclusion, particularly the impact of these factors on minority ethnic communities. This so-called 'liberal' perspective was diametrically opposed to the 'conservative' explanation of the riots which emphasised individualised pathologies rather than socio-economic factors. The former approach has been the ascendant perspective in the academic literature, which has attempted to understand the policing of poverty in relation to the broader tendencies at work in the criminal justice process and in the context of economic recession (Lea and Young, 1993).

The legacy of racial discrimination, both attitudinal and institutional or systemic, was a black 'underclass', inhabiting the 'symbolic locations' and ghetto areas of some of the most deprived inner city areas in the world. The emergence of this substratum of the working class was an outcome of the restructuring of national economies set in the context of an increasingly competitive global economy. The transition from a Fordist to a post-Fordist mode of production and the decline of manufacturing and the rise of service industries are the key dynamics. As one economic recession follows another, particularly in urban regions which do not experience any of the advantages of periodic booms, coupled with the failure of egalitarian and welfare state based social policies and anti-discrimination legislation, other problems also arise. Poverty tends to be associated with unemployment or economic inactivity, welfare dependency, lone parents, inadequate housing and neighbourhood decline in specific geographical areas. In addition there is the formation of 'underclass-like' sub-cultural groups that are adapting to these conditions by becoming involved in crime, delinquency and disorder.

In the twenty-first century these dynamic processes are likely to continue to lead to changes throughout broad swathes of society. The police are there to pick up the pieces of the failings of the late-modern capitalist economy. The inability of successive governments to (re) incorporate marginal sub-groups into the world of work and full-scale economic, political and social citizenship have led to the formation of the exclusive society. One of these structurally excluded groups is a criminogenic 'underclass'.

These and other closely related themes are also a feature of some senior police officers' perspectives on poverty, but their perceptions of it are different to the rank and file in four ways. Following on specifically from Reiner's (1991) interviews with chief constables, their descriptions are more complex. Secondly, police perspectives on a poor 'underclass' are a unique contribution to thinking about these phenomena in general and specifically in relation to police matters. Thirdly, the 'underclass' has both material and ideological implications for police policy and practice. Fourthly, these overlapping themes have ramifications for our understanding of how social order is constructed, either through community-based strategies or through exercising the legitimate use of force. Before scrutinising these four overlapping themes it is necessary to focus on the police policy process.

The police policy process

Chapter 6 examined the police policy process. Until relatively recently, and in contrast to other public services, policy was considered to be of little or no significance in the institutional setting of the police service. When considering the tripartite structure of accountability, the view that the principle of constabulary independence and legal codes were more important than policy dominated police research. Indeed this is still the case in a lot of the criminological and socio-legal literature, in which law and procedure are prioritised above policy. Of the few studies based on the direct observation of different policy-making levels, Grimshaw and Jefferson (1987) claimed that policy, defined as a codified statement issued by the chief constable, is rarely straightforwardly translated into practice by his/her subordinates. Policy therefore either does not exist or its salience is subordinated to other facets of police work. Due to police discretion, law and policy in writing and in action respectively, are seldom the same. Due to the prevalence of selective law enforcement and the informal adaptation of policy guide-lines by different organisational groups, the codified statements intended to be policy are frequently challenged and subverted.

However, these distinctions are far too simplistic and downplay the inter-relatedness of formal and informal rhetorics and practices. Likewise the current burgeoning interest in the police policy process, although making many inroads continues to be of a limited nature. Most of this work is concerned with administrative issues and matters that affect current day-to-day police practice. This rather narrow range of concerns neglects a broader range of societal, economic, political, ideological and discursive forces which have interpenetrated the policy process.

Drawing on the literature which focuses on policy in general, police policy in particular, and the views of practitioners, the following issues were addressed: first, the role of each of the key players involved in the police policy process; second, the multidimensional nature of policy;

third, the relationship between the construction of police policy and its position in a wider context, focusing on the tension between the structural (macro-level) and cultural (micro-level) forces. Some observable patterns flow out of the various ideological and material forces which influence decision-taking and policy-making. The concepts of political power and ideology are of central importance in determining how broad patterns and general tendencies in policy emerge.

The fact that policing is an element of a society which has undergone and continues to experience rapid economic, political and ideological changes must be appreciated. Any attempt to pin down the most significant driving forces behind these changes is of course fraught with difficulties, but there are some trends that are proving to be more persistent than others. The most important transitions are probably those occurring at a macro-level which have had a top-down effect. The impact of these on the structure and culture of a particular society and the organisations within that society cannot be ascertained without taking into account the simultaneous changes at a micro-level. Thus the complexities of the links between top-down and bottom-up forces were addressed.

Innovations in police policy and practice must be situated in relation to these broad developments, paying particular attention to the unevenness of the impact of ideologies across time and space. These transformations have had serious repercussions on the police service and its location in relation to the wider societal context.

Coinciding with a reduction in the levels of public money made available to public services, the process of marketisation was set into motion. Throughout the 1980s the British police were relatively unaffected by these developments, and had the support of successive Conservative governments. As a key agency in the fight against crime and the various 'enemies within', the British police were affectionately known as Thatcher's 'boys in blue'. This did not last for long and Kenneth Clarke's NHS reforms, launched in 1989, later became the model on which fundamental reform of the police service was based. During the spell Clarke spent as Home Secretary the popularity of the police in government circles took a few hard knocks.

The analytical and theoretical issues raised by the ensuing 'reform' of the police service are three-pronged. First, the steps taken to identify 'core' and 'ancillary' functions led to a fundamental reappraisal of the police service. Secondly, this is intimately related to the introduction of the 'new public management' and market disciplines into the police service to facilitate the economic, efficient and effective delivery of police services. In addition, various incentives have been offered to entice other non-state sectors to do certain jobs that the police had tradition-ally done. Thirdly, the strong state has also flexed its muscles, particu-larly the Home Office, which has increased its level of intervention, leading to further centralisation. This trend towards centralisation oper-ates dialectically and decentralising tendencies are also significant. Pol-icy-making consists of both dimensions. Thus there is the potential for these contradictory forces to lead to the fragmentation of ideology and power and the different value systems underpinning the different asso-ciational cultures within the police service.

Amongst the most notable government-led changes of direction is the revaluation of Scarmanism. Scarman (1981) argued that the modern police service is primarily a peace-keeping organisation rather than a crime-fighting force. The quest of British governments to introduce the disciplines of the market into public sector services – efficiency, eco-nomy and effectiveness – has led to different demands being made of the police. The Home Office, bound in Walker's (1984: 117) terms by the 'Treasury brand of bureau-incrementalism', has been required to reduce expenditure like all other government departments. The import-ance of catching criminals is the best 'performance indicator' for measuring these criteria, instead of vague and unquantifiable practices such as crime prevention and keeping the Queen's peace.

Some senior police officers have questioned the wisdom of this shift of emphasis, hence the conflict of interests between some sections of the police staff associations and the Home Office. While individual members of ACPO have their own perceptions and views on this, ACPO behaves collectively and is circumscribed by an unwritten but virtually mandatory obligation to agree on any issue that affects them as a group. To maintain this united front, officers have to state in writing that they disagree with their colleagues. The focus of this book was narrowed down to look at the connections between these conflicting priorities in terms of the impact of community policing and public order policing strategies on the social construction of poverty.

Policing the 'underclass': policy, power and politics

Chapters 7, 8 and 9 indicate that some senior police officers' descrip-tions of poverty in general, and particularly the 'underclass', share many of the near universal reference points to the various other dis-courses on the topic. Firstly, the 'underclass' is used to portray practi-tioners' high level of uncertainty when looking at the complex relationship between social divisions and the structural and behavioural factors underlying crime and disorder. These findings are consistent with Reiner's (1991) interviews with chief constables. Next, because of the specific nature of the jobs police officers undertake, their perspectives on the 'underclass' are inevitably unique, reflecting their own individual perceptions as well as collectively similar views of public issues. Thirdly, the 'underclass' has both material and ideological implications for police policy and practice and the influence of political power on these interrelated processes is of cardinal importance. Finally, what is the relative significance of community policing and the more forceful response of the paramilitarist approach for understanding the 'underclass'?

Starting with the first two issues: the 'underclass' was been taken up by some police officers in the 1980s and 1990s to explain the particular social phenomena they encountered on a daily basis. In public commentary and journalistic discourse 'Murrayism' was at the top of the agenda. This version has not always found support amongst all public servants, though, and as shown earlier senior police officers in particular have given the idea different meanings, and overriding significance has been attached to structural instead of behavioural accounts. Thus senior police officers were able to deviate from the near hegemony of the behavioural perspective in public commentary and some academic descriptions of police policy and practice.

Some senior police officers have added the 'underclass' to their lexicon of social problems. Rather than uncritically adopting this concept as outlined by Murray and his protégés, it was shaped to reflect their markedly different perceptions of the multiple realities underlying police work. It is necessary to be aware that the meaning of the 'underclass' is context bound, but also that it is characterised by recurrent themes. Throughout the 1990s – and to a lesser degree in the 1980s, but with the notable exceptions of Scarman, Alderson and Newman – the behaviour of criminals and the riotous was put into a wider context. The adaptation of sub-cultural groups in 'underclass'-like positions to the pressures of social exclusion described above was pre-eminent. Turning to the third issue.

In a society in which the police service has little influence or any direct control over socio-economic conditions, and where its special pleading is ignored by an acquiescent general public, and governments disregard any of its critics, it has a limited capacity to tackle the problems which are not, in the last analysis, of its own making. In the UK, an organisation like ACPO may, in principle, come together to voice a collective viewpoint. Highlighting the structural processes underlying the emergence of an 'underclass' is one example. However, government denial of a connection between structurally driven inequality, poverty, social exclusion and crime and disorder reduces the legitimacy of their version of events. The police policy process sustains the perception that there is a structurally excluded 'underclass', but only up to a point, because the most powerful player of the tripartite system (the Home Secretary) can refute this.

Successive neo-liberal – and to a lesser extent social democratic and centre-left, governments – have to varying degrees rejected the view that changes in the political economy may have led to the creation of an excluded population which, due to becoming surplus to the requirements of the current system of production, may engage in criminal behaviour. In a market society crime is just another choice made in the market place, albeit an illegitimate and immoral one. While subcultural groups culpable for such behaviour exist, these are located in a structurally excluded sub-stratum of the population in which the choices on offer in the market place are few and far between. It is awareness of these factors which shaped the complex pattern of views and perceptions of the police officers outlined in previous chapters. The 'underclass' is used as a symbol to represent the difficult job they have in tackling intractable social problems. This may be special pleading for more resources to respond to ever increasing demands, such as rising crime and periodic outbursts of disorder, or alternatively, a cry for fundamental change to an unjust social structure.

The Scarman report explicitly restated the twin tasks of the police service: the prevention and detection of crime and keeping of the Queen's peace. These two roles are on a continuum and most operational policing is about balancing these two demands by keeping them in proportion to one another. Throughout history the demands made of the police have increased relentlessly. It is in this broad sweep of history that police policy-making has taken and continues to take place. Since the 1980s two kinds of tension have been identified in this area. The main one is the traditional balancing act embodied in the *policing dilemma*, which despite government attempts to intervene seem set to remain fundamentally unchanged. An especially significant change is the availability of resources, which have become increasingly scarce. This was recognised long before marketisation and the 'new public management'. In the UK John Alderson's communitarian model, for example, includes recognition of the potential conflicts that arise when policing a multi-cultural society with finite resources. Anticipation of these obstacles underlay his development of a philosophy of community policing. Since being incorporated into Scarman's thinking the influence of Alderson's ideas have been absorbed into police policy.

At the same time, Alderson expressed anxieties about developments in public order policing, an issue explored in greater detail by Jefferson (1990) in his work on paramilitarism. While both commentators are right about the increased capabilities of the police as a force, the inexorable logic of paramilitarism they envisaged has not been set into motion (Waddington, 1994). Although there is ongoing research in these areas, the police have not exercised the levels of force that they could exercise if they so wished. In general, various strategies of community policing, based on the principle of peace-keeping, have been the pattern of policing rather than the legitimate use of force. Furthermore, Charles Pollard (1997: 55), Chief Constable of Thames Valley police, issued a warning about the perils of pursuing 'zero tolerance' policing. When thinking about these issues it is necessary not to consider these two styles of policing as antithetical or diametrically opposed, but as part of a policing mix, consisting of communitarian and paramilitarist strategies. This is reflected by the views of most senior police officers, who claimed that the bulk of policies oriented towards the 'underclass' are generally community based, involving increasingly sophisticated techniques of intelligence gathering and surveillance. The paramilitarist response is a symbol of the 'authoritarian state' and is only there as a back-up.

What, in the last analysis are the links between the dynamic macro-economic and structural forces at work in the production of poverty and the institutional and cultural dimensions of the police policy process? How have senior police officers and the services they and their subordinates provide been affected by the demands made of them by successive governments, who are pursuing economic and social policies which are broadly in line with neo-liberalism?

While macro-economic and structural factors are important in determining the conditions under which policies are formulated these interact with human subjects. Returning to Luke's (1974) three dimensional notion of power (Chapter 6), it may be argued that actors often unconsciously follow the instructions of the most powerful groups in society, even though this goes against their particular interests. This is described as 'latent conflict, which consists of a contradiction between the interests of those exercising power and the real interests of those they exclude' (1974: 24–5). If applied to policing, the actions of ACPO in England and Wales, the other staff associations and the power structure in which they operate is organised hierarchically. In the last analysis, these groups are controlled by the Home Secretary, and by implication, central government. While agreeing with the general thrust of Lukes's thesis the various effects of power are even more nuanced than this, and there is scope for intellectual and practical resistance.

Chief constables and other senior officials may question 'the general direction imposed on life by the dominant fundamental groups' (Gramsci, 1971: 12). Some of this may be token resistance but some individuals and clusters of individuals may go against the grain for an entirely different set of reasons. Of course, wholesale social change is not feasible or even on the minds of police chiefs, but there is potential for reform, even if this is the rather modest aim of changing popular perceptions of the policing of a *perplexed society*. Furthermore there is evidence that chief constables share a similar outlook. In ACPO, for instance, there is the convention that officers must disavow guide-lines in front of their colleagues, a requirement that is suggestive of a corporate identity of sorts. This has ramifications for understanding the place of the 'underclass' in the police policy process.

There is as much evidence as it is realistically possible to obtain which shows that senior police officers collectively share the view that there is an 'underclass', founded within a structural perspective. Although the 'underclass' may not yet be an empirically defined section of the population in the social science literature, the kind of processes which would produce one are. It is therefore a powerful representation of various interlocking societal processes, such as the restructuring of the economy, the rolling back of the frontiers of the welfare state and the impact of these changes on specific poor communities. Crime and disorder have been included among these effects. According to police chiefs, it is under such circumstances that there is the likely or actual empirical realisation of an 'underclass'. Moreover, this has impacted on different aspects of police policy-making.

Final words

The first few chapters showed that the old clear-cut certainties concerning poverty and social divisions no longer ring true, if they ever did. Both in the social sciences and in wider society the concept of an 'underclass' has somehow emerged to describe and explain this confusion. In a far from straightforward way this idea entered into police thinking and ultimately informed policy and practice. The murky waters of the 'underclass' debate found in journalistic and academic discourses are even more turbid when it comes to police discourse. Although there are a variety of views there are some common perceptions concerning 'underclass' formation, especially the dominance of the structural perspective.

Various structurally generated processes led to social and economic forms of exclusion, which in turn created conditions under which crime and disorder are increasingly likely. The police service has to respond to these structural forces and the patterns of behaviour which tend to be associated with them, particularly by balancing the 'war on crime' with keeping the Queen's peace.

What are the policy implications? How do police policies and practices oriented towards the social construction of order impact on 'underclass' formation?

As an ideal type the police policy process consists of many formal, informal, institutional and cultural arrangements. In fact there is a great deal of fuzziness and many overlaps between these different dimensions. In the 1990s in the UK, for example, at a formal level (reflecting the views of central government), the Home Office rejected the structural version of the 'underclass' but was more open minded about the possible emergence of an 'underclass' or sub-group characterised by a particular type of poverty: the behavioural perspective. Informally, various arms of the Home Office such as HMIC had a more nuanced view. Here a structural version of the 'underclass' has been recognised, but due to its potential to undermine the effective, efficient and economic functioning of the police service, this argument was watered down.

The next major player in the tripartite system is the individual chief constable and the collective association to which these individuals belong, namely ACPO. Chief constables are also constrained by the same demands as those above them: the three 'Es'. These macro-level factors are reflected throughout the whole police service. They are also required to perform other duties – particularly the balancing act between law enforcement and peace-keeping – within these, cultural, institutional and systemic constraints. These macro and structural dimensions determine or influence other aspects of police work undertaken at a micro-level. The ambiguities and uncertainties in currency at a macro-level are further complicated in the police culture and at different levels of the policy process. In addition to these trends, working in the context of a social environment in which there is poverty, social exclusion, crime and disorder, there is a growing amount of police work that is left undone. In a complex late-modern society the causes of, and solutions to, the problems of a structurally excluded and impoverished 'underclass' are beyond the police. By highlighting the plight of this population and the difficult task they face, the police may expose the failure of government policies. The government, meanwhile, may turn this argument upside down, by blaming both the police and the poor for rising crime and disorder.

Appendix: the Formal Powers of Each Member of the Tripartite Structure Established by the Police Act of 1964

Home Secretary	Police Authority	Chief Constable
Statutory responsibility for approving police establishment;	Maintenance of an adequate and efficient force;	Direction and control of the force; Enforcement of the law;
Promotion of efficient policing;	Subject to the approval of the Home Secretary, the appointment of CCs; and the dismissal of CC, DCC in the interests of efficiency;	Operational control;
To control human resources and major capital expenditure and make grants of expenses;		Decision making in policy making and in law enforcement;
To make regulations concerning government administration and conditions of service as well as equipment;	The right to call for but not receive reports on any policing matters that are not covered in the CC's annual report;	CC's are required to make an annual report to the HS and the PA;
To issue circulars;	Representatives of the local community.	The PA may request supplementary ad hoc reports on matters which may concern them.
Sanctioning the appointment of CCs, and acting as broker to mediate any conflicts between CCs and the PA;		
To receive an annual report and to call for reports from the CC on any matter related to the policing of a CC's area.		

Bibliography

Abelmann, N. and Lie, J. (1995) *Blue Dreams: Korean Americans and the Los Angeles Riots* (Cambridge, Massachusetts: Harvard University Press).

Alcock, P. (1997a) *Understanding Poverty*, 2nd edition (London: Macmillan).

Alcock, P. (1997b) 'Making Welfare Work – Frank Field and New Labour's Social Policy Agenda', *Benefits*, vol. 20, September/October, pp. 34–8.

Alderson, J. (1981) *Submission to Scarman: the Case for Community Policing*, Proof of Evidence for 'Concern' at Lord Scarman's Inquiry, Part II, September, 1981.

Alderson, J. (1984) *Law and Disorder* (London: Hamish Hamilton).

Allahar, A. (1993) 'When Black First Became Worth Less', *International Journal of Comparative Sociology*, vol. 34, no. 1–2, pp. 39–55.

Althusser, L. (1971) 'Ideology and Ideological Apparatus', in *Lenin and Philosophy and Other Essays* (London: New Left Books).

Amin, A. (1994) *Post Fordism: A Reader* (Oxford: Blackwell).

Amis, M. (1995) *The Information* (London: Flamingo).

Anthias, F. (1990) 'Race and Class Revisited – Conceptualising Race and Racisms', *Sociological Review*, vol. 38, no. 1, pp. 19–42.

Anthias, F. (1998) 'Rethinking Social Divisions: Some Notes Towards A Theoretical Framework', *Sociological Review*, vol. 46, no. 3, pp. 505–35.

Aponte, R. (1990) 'Definition of the Underclass: A Critical Analysis', in H.J. Gans (ed.), *Sociology in America* (Newbury Park, California: Sage Publications).

Archaud, P. (1979) 'Vagrancy: A Literature Review', in T. Cook (ed.), *Vagrancy: Some New Perspectives* (London: Academic Press).

Ashcroft, P. (1902) *The English Poor Law System* (London: Knight and Co).

Association of Chief Police Officers (1990) *Setting the Standards For Policing: Meeting Community Expectations*, New Scotland Yard, London.

Association of Chief Police Officers, Quality of Service Committee (1993) *Getting Things Right*, ACPO, London.

Atherton, C. (1994) 'Great Expectations: Or Wither Goeth Social Policy After the Reagan-Bush Years', in R. Page and J. Baldock (eds), *Social Policy Review 6* (Canterbury: SPA).

Audit Commission (1990a) *Effective Policing – Performance Review in Police Forces*, Police Paper No. 10 (London: HMSO).

Audit Commission (1990b) *Reviewing the Organisation of Provincial Police Forces*, Police Paper No. 9 (London: HMSO).

Audit Commission (1990c) *Footing the Bill: Financing Provincial Police Forces*, Police Paper No. 6 (London: HMSO).

Audit Commission (1991a) *Pounds and Coppers: Financial Delegation in Provincial Police Forces* (London: HMSO).

Audit Commission (1991b) *Reviewing the Organisation of Provincial Police Forces*, Paper No. 9 (London: HMSO).

Audit Commission (1993) *Helping With Enquiries: Tackling Crime Effectively*, Police Paper No. 12 (London: HMSO).

Audit Commission (1994a) *Cheques and Balances: a Management Handbook on Police Planning and Financial Delegation*, Police Paper No. 13 (London: HMSO).

Audit Commission (1994b) *Cheques and Balances: a Framework for Improving Police Accountability*, Police Paper No. 14 (London: HMSO).

Audit Commission (1994c) *Staying on Course: the Second Year of the Citizen's Charter Indicators* (London: Audit Commission).

Audit Commission (1996a) *Streetwise: Effective Police Patrol* (London: HMSO).

Audit Commission (1996b) *Local Authority Performance Indicators*, Vol. 3, *Police and Fire Services* (London: HMSO).

Audit Commission for Local Authorities in England and Wales (1996c) *Misspent Youth: Young People and Crime* (London: HMSO).

Auletta, K. (1982) *The Underclass* (New York: Random House).

Bachrach, P. and Baratz, M. (1970) *Power and Poverty* (New York: Oxford University Press).

Baldwin, J. (1979) 'Ecological and Areal Studies in Great Britain and in the United States', in N. Morris and M. Tonry (eds), *Crime and Justice: an Annual Review of Research*, vol. 1 (Chicago: University of Chicago Press).

Baldwin, J. and Kinsey, R. (1982) *Police Powers and Politics* (London: Quartet).

Banting, K. (1979) *Poverty, Politics and Policy* (London: Macmillan).

Banton, M. (1964) *The Policeman in the Community* (London: Tavistock).

Banton, M. (1973) *Police-Community Relations* (London: Collins).

Barnes, B. (1976) *Interests and the Growth of Knowledge* (London: Routledge and Kegan Paul).

Barnes, B. (1982) *T.S. Kuhn and Social Science* (London: Macmillan).

Baum, S. and Hassan, R. (1993) 'Economic Restructuring and Spatial Equity – A Case Study of Adelaide', *Australian and New Zealand Journal of Sociology*, vol. 29, no. 20, pp. 151–72.

Bayley, D. (1994) *Police for the Future* (New York: Oxford University Press).

Bayley, D. (1996) 'What Do the Police Do?', in W. Saulsbury, J. Mott and T. Newburn (eds), *Themes in Contemporary Policing* (London: Police Foundation: PSI).

Bayley, D. and Mendelsohn, H. (1969) *Minorities and the Police* (New York: Free Press).

Becker, S. (1997) *Responding to Poverty: the Politics of Cash and Care* (Harlow: Addison Wesley Longman).

Beckett, K. (1997) *Making Crime Pay: Law and Order in Contemporary American Politics* (New York: Oxford University Press).

Beier, A. (1985) *Masterless Men: The Vagrancy Problem in England 1560–1640* (London: Methuen).

Bellamy, R. (1988) 'Victorian Economic Values', in E. Sigsworth (ed.), *In Search of Victorian Values: Aspects of Nineteenth Century Thought of Society* (Manchester: Manchester University Press).

Bennett, T. (1987) 'Neighbourhood Watch: Principles and Practices', in R. Mawby (ed.), *Policing Britain* (Plymouth: Plymouth Polytechnic).

Bennett, T. (1988) *Community Oriented Patrols Project*, Interim Reports Submitted to the Home Office Research and Planning Unit (London: HMSO).

Bennett, T. (1989) 'The Neighbourhood Watch Experiment', in R. Morgan and D.J. Smith (eds), *Coming to Terms With Policing: Perspectives on Policy* (London: Routledge).

Benyon, J. and Solomos, J. (eds) (1987) *The Roots of Urban Unrest* (Oxford: Pergamon).

Beresford, P. (1979) 'The Public Presentation of Vagrants', in T. Cook (ed.), *Vagrancy: Some New Perspectives* (London: Academic Press).

Berger, P. and Luckmann, T. (1966) *The Social Construction of Reality* (London: Allen and Lane).

Berger, P. and Pullberg, S. (1966) 'Reification and Social Critique of Consciousness', *History of Theory*, vol. 4, pp. 196–211.

Bergmann, B. (1996) *Saving Our Children From Poverty: What the United States Can Learn From France* (New York: Sage).

Bessant, J. (1995) 'The Discovery of an Australian "Juvenile Underclass"', *Australian and New Zealand Journal of Sociology*, vol. 31, no. 1, pp. 32–48.

Blair, T. (1997) 'Interview With Tony Blair', *The Big Issue*, 8 January.

Booth, C. (1887) 'The Inhabitants of the Tower Hamlets', *Journal of the Royal Statistical Society*.

Booth, C. (1902) *Life and Labour of the People of London* (London: Routledge).

Bouza, A.V. (1990) *The Police Mystique: an Insider's Look at Cops, Crime and the Criminal Justice System* (New York: Plenum Press).

Bovenkerk, F. (1984) 'The Rehabilitation of the Rabble', *Netherlands Journal of Sociology*, vol. 20, pp. 13–42.

Brace, C. (1872) *The Dangerous Classes of New York and Twenty Years Work Among Them* (New York: Wynskoop and Hallenbeck).

Bradshaw, J. and Millar, J. (1991) *Lone Parents in the United Kingdom*, DSS Research Report, no. 6 (London: HMSO).

Braithwaite, J. (1989) *Crime, Shame and Reintegration* (Cambridge: Cambridge University Press).

Brake, M. (1982) 'Under Heavy Manners: a Consideration of Racism, Black Youth Culture and Crime in Britain', *Crime and Social Justice*, vol. 20, pp. 1–15.

Brake, M. and Hale, C. (1992) *Public Order and Private Lives: the Politics of Law and Order* (London: Routledge).

Bratton, W. (1996) 'How We Cleared Up New York', *The Sunday Times*, 24 November.

Bratton, W. (1997) 'Crime Is Down in New York City: Blame the Police', in N. Dennis (ed.), *Zero Tolerance: Policing a Free Society*, Choice in Welfare No. 35 (London: IEA Health and Welfare Unit).

Brewer, M. (1995) quoted by E. Wilkins, 'Class Warriors Accused of Infiltrating the Animal Lobby', *The Times*, 4 February.

Briggs, A. (1988) 'Victorian Values', in E. Sigsworth (ed.), *In Search of Victorian Values: Aspects of Nineteenth Century Thought of Society* (Manchester: Manchester University Press).

Brodeur, J.P. (ed.) (1995) *Comparisons in Policing: an International Perspective* (Aldershot: Avebury).

Brogden, M. (1982) *The Police: Autonomy and Consent* (London: Academic Press).

Brogden, M., Jefferson, T. and Walklate, S. (1988) *Introducing Policework* (London: Unwin Hyman).

Brown, J. (1989) *Why Don't They Go To Work?*, Social Security Advisory Committee Research Paper, no. 2 (London: HMSO).

Brown, J. (1990) 'The Focus On Single Mothers', in C. Murray (ed.), *The Emerging British Underclass* (London: Institute of Economic Affairs).

Brueilly, J. (1994) 'From Underclass to Working Class – Germany 1800–75', *Geschichte Und Gesellschaft*, vol. 20, no. 2, pp. 251–73.

Bryson, A. and Jacobs, J. (1992) *Policing the Workshy* (Aldershot: Avebury).

Buck, N. (1996) 'Social and Economic Change in Contemporary Britain: the Emergence of an Urban Underclass?', in E. Mingione (ed.), *Urban Poverty and the Underclass* (Oxford: Blackwell).

Bursick, R. and Grasmick, H. (1993) 'Economic Deprivation and Neighbourhood Crime Rates, 1960–1980', *Law and Society Review*, vol. 27, no. 2, pp. 263–83.

Busard, R. (1987) 'The Dangerous Class of Marx and Engels', *History of European Ideas*, vol. 8, pp. 675–92.

Butcher, T. (1998) 'Managing the Welfare State', in H. Jones and S. MacGregor (eds), *Social Issues and Party Politics* (London: Routledge).

Butler, A. (1996) 'Managing the Future: a Chief Constable's View', in F. Leishman, B. Loveday and S. Savage (eds), *Core Issues in Policing* (London: Longman).

Cain, M. (1973) *Society and the Policeman's Role* (London: Routledge and Kegan Paul).

Campbell, B. (1993) *Goliath: Britain's Dangerous Places* (London: Methuen).

Campbell, B. (1994) 'Lessons from the Riots', in A. Coote (ed.), *Families, Children and Crime* (London: Institute of Public Policy Research).

Campbell, D. (1996) 'Met to Try New York Method of Crime', *The Guardian*, 19 November.

Carr, E.H. (1961) *What is History?* (London: Macmillan).

Cassels, J. (1996) *Independent Report on the Role and Responsibilities of the Police* (London: Police Foundation and Policy Studies Institute).

Castles, F., Murray, D. and Potter, D. (eds) (1971) *Decisions, Organisations and Society* (Harmondsworth: Penguin).

Cashmore, E. and McLaughlin, E. (eds) (1991) *Out of Order? Policing Black People* (London: Routledge).

Chadwick, E. (1842) *Report to Her Majesty's Principal Secretary of State for the Home Department from the Poor Law Commissioners, on an Inquiry into the Sanitary Conditions of the Labouring Populations of Great Britain* (London: Clowes).

Chambliss, W. (1969) 'The Law of Vagrancy', in W. Chambliss (ed.), *Crime and the Legal Process* (New York: McGraw Hill).

Chambliss, W. (1994) 'Policing the Ghetto Underclass: the Politics of Law Enforcement', *Social Problems*, vol. 41, no. 2, pp. 109–34.

Chaudhary, V. and Walker, M. (1996) 'The Petty Crime War', *The Guardian*, 21 November.

Checkland, S. and Checkland, O. (1973) *The Poor Law Report of 1834* (Harmondsworth: Penguin).

Chesshyre, R. (1997) 'Enough is Enough', *The Telegraph Magazine*, 1 March, pp. 20–6.

Choongh, S. (1997) *Policing As Social Discipline* (Oxford: Clarendon Press).

Clarke, J. (1996) 'The Problem of the State After the Welfare State', in M. Brundson and G. Craig (eds), *Social Policy Review 8* (Canterbury: Social Policy Association).

Clarke, J., Cochrane, A. and McLaughlin, E. (eds) (1994) *Managing Social Policy* (London: Sage).

Clegg, S. (1989) *Frameworks of Power* (London: Sage).

Cohen, P. (1979) 'Policing the Working Class City', in B. Fine, R. Kinsey, J. Lea, S. Piccioto and J. Young (eds), *Capitalism and the Rule of Law* (London: Hutchinson).

Cohen, S. (1985) *Visions of Social Control: Crime, Punishment and Classification* (Cambridge: Polity Press).

Cohen, S. (1994) 'Social Control and the Politics of Reconstruction', in D. Nelken (ed.), *The Futures of Criminology* (London: Sage).

Colman, A. and Gorman, L. (1982) 'Conservatism, Dogmatism, Authoritarianism in British Police Officers: a Comment', *Sociology*, vol. 16, pp. 1–11.

Cook, D. (1997) *Poverty, Crime and Punishment* (London: Child Poverty Action Group).

Cook, D. (1998) 'Between A Rock and a Hard Place: the Realities of Working "On the Side"', *Benefits*, vol. 21, January, pp. 11–15.

Cook, T. (1996) 'Police Claim Crime "Cover-Up"', *The Observer*, 18 February.

Cook, T.D. (ed.) (1979) *Vagrancy: Some New Perspectives* (London: Academic Press).

Coote, A. (ed.) (1994) *Families, Children and Crime* (London: Institute of Public Policy Research).

Cornish, D. and Clarke, R. (eds) (1986) *The Reasoning Criminal* (New York: Springer).

Crawford, A. (1995) 'Appeals to Community and Crime Prevention', *Crime, Law and Social Change*, vol. 22, no. 2, pp. 97–126.

Critchley, T. (1978) *A History of the Police in England and Wales* (London: Constable).

Crompton, R. (1993) *Class and Stratification: an Introduction to Current Debates* (Cambridge: Polity Press).

Crowther, C.P. (1998) 'Policing the Excluded Society', in R. Hopkins-Burke (ed.), *Zero Tolerance Policing* (Leicester: Perpetuity Press).

Currie, E. (1996) *Is America Really Winning the War on Crime and Should Britain Follow its Example?* (London: National Association for the Care and Resettlement of Offenders).

Currie, E. (1998) 'Crime and Market Society: Lessons from the United States', in Walton, P. and Young, J. (eds) (1998) *The New Criminology Revisited* (London: Macmillan).

Dahl, R.A. (1958) 'A Critique of the Ruling Elite Model', *American Political Science Review*, vol. 52, no. 1, pp. 463–9.

Dahrendorf, R. (1985) *Law and Order* (London: Stevens).

Dahrendorf, R. (1987) *The Underclass and the Future of Britain*, 10th Annual Lecture, Windsor: St George's House.

Dahrendorf, R. (1988) *The Modern Social Conflict: an Essay On the Politics of Liberty* (London: Weidenfeld and Nicholson).

Dalrymple, T. (1993) 'The Underclass: Nasty, Brutish and Short of Human Hope', *The Daily Telegraph*, 25 January.

Dangschat, J. (1994) 'Concentrations of Urban Poverty in the Landscapes of Boomtown Hamburg – the Creation of a New Urban Underclass', *Urban Studies*, vol. 31, no. 7, pp. 1133–47.

Davis, J. (1989) 'From "Rookeries" to "Communities": Race, Poverty and Policing in London, 1850–1985', *History Workshop*, vol. 27, pp. 66–85.

Davis, M. (1988) 'Nightmares in Los Angeles', *New Left Review*, 170, July/August, pp. 37–60.

Davis, M. (1990) *City of Quartz: Excavating the Future of LA* (New York: Vintage).

Davis, M. (1992) *LA Was Just the Beginning: Urban Revolt in the United States – A Thousand Points of Light* (Westfield, N.J.: Open Magazine Pamphlet Series).

Deacon, A. (1976) *In Search of the Scrounger,* Occasional Papers on Social Administration, No. 60 (Leeds: Social Administration Research Trust).

Deacon, A. and Mann, K. (1997) 'Moralism and Modernity: the Paradox of New Labour Thinking on Welfare', *Benefits,* 10, September/October, pp. 2–6.

Dean, H. and Taylor-Gooby, P. (1992) *Dependency Culture: The Explosion of a Myth* (Hemel Hempstead: Harvester Wheatsheaf).

Dean, H. (1998) 'Popular Paradigms and Welfare Values', *Critical Social Policy,* vol. 18, no. 2, pp. 131–56.

Dean, M. (1994) *Critical and Effective Histories: Foucault's Methods and Historical Sociology* (London: Routledge).

Della Porta, D. and Reiter, H. (eds) (1998) *Policing Protest: the Control of Mass Demonstrations in Western Democracies* (Minneapolis: University of Minnesota Press).

Demuth, C. (1978) *'Sus': A Report on the Vagrancy Act, 1824* (London: Runnymede Trust).

Dennis, N. (1993) *Rising Crime and the Dismembered Family: How Conformist Intellectuals Have Campaigned Against Common Sense* (London: Institute of Economic Affairs).

Dennis, N. (ed.) (1997) *Zero Tolerance: Policing a Free Society,* Choice in Welfare No. 35 (London: IEA Health and Welfare Unit).

Dennis, N. and Erdos G. (1992) *Families Without Fatherhood,* 2nd edition (London: Institute of Economic Affairs).

Dennis, N. and Mallon, R. (1997a) 'Confident Policing in Hartlepool', in N. Dennis (ed.), *Zero Tolerance: Policing a Free Society,* Choice in Welfare No. 35 (London: IEA Health and Welfare Unit).

Dennis, N. and Mallon, R. (1997b) 'Crime and Culture in Hartlepool', in N. Dennis (ed.), *Zero Tolerance: Policing a Free Society,* Choice in Welfare No. 35 (London: IEA Health and Welfare Unit).

Denzin N. (1970) *The Research Act in Sociology* (Chicago: Aldine).

Department of Social Security (1993) *Households Below Average Income 1979–1990/1* (London: HMSO).

Department of Social Security (1994) *Households Below Average Income* (London: HMSO).

Department of Social Security (1998) *New Ambitions For Our Country: a New Contract for Welfare,* Cmnd. 3805 (London: HMSO).

Devine, F. (1997) *Social Class in America and Britain* (Edinburgh: Edinburgh University Press).

Digby, A. (1978) *Pauper Palaces* (London: Routledge and Kegan Paul).

Digby, A. (1989) *British Welfare Policy: Workhouse to Workfare* (London: Faber and Faber).

Donnison, D. (1982) *The Politics of Poverty* (Oxford: Martin Robertson).

Donnison, D. (1998) 'Creating a Safer Society', in C. Jones-Finer and M. Nellis (eds), *Crime and Social Exclusion* (Oxford: Blackwell).

Donziger, S. (ed.) (1996) *The Real War on Crime: The Report of the National Criminal Justice Commission* (New York: Harper Perennial).

Driver, S. and Martell, L. (1997) 'New Labour's Communitarianisms', *Critical Social Policy,* vol. 17, no. 3, pp. 27–46.

Dunkley, P. (1982) *The Crisis of the Old Poor Law in England, 1795–1914: an Interpretive Essay* (London: Garland Publishing Inc).

Eagleton, T. (1991) *Ideology: An Introduction* (London: Verso).

Eastwood, A. (1991) quoted in *The Independent*, 4 September.

Edai, R. (1992) ' "Underclass": Problems of Conceptualisation and Measurement', *Nature*, vol. 5, no. 1, pp. 7–21.

Edin, K. and Lein, L. (1997) *Making Ends Meet: How Single Mothers Survive Welfare and Low-Wage Work* (New York: Sage).

Elliott, L. (1998) 'Circular Walk Along the Third Way', *The Guardian*, 6 July.

Ellis, W. (1996) 'Justice of the First Resort', *The Sunday Times*, 24 November.

Ellison, N. and Pierson, C. (1998) *Developments in British Social Policy* (London: Macmillan).

Ellwood, D. (1988) *Poor Support: Poverty and the American Family* (New York: Basic Books).

Emsley, C. (1996a) *Crime and Society in England 1750–1900*, 2nd edition (London: Longman).

Emsley, C. (1996b) *The English Police: A Political and Social History*, 2nd edition (London: Longman).

Engels, F. (1958) *The Condition of the Working Class in England* (Oxford: Basil Blackwell).

Ericson, R. and Carriere, K. (1994) 'The Fragmentation of Criminology', in D. Nelken (ed.), *The Futures of Criminology* (London: Sage).

Esping-Andersen, G. (1990) *The Three Worlds of Welfare Capitalism* (Cambridge: Polity).

Etzioni, A. (1993) *The Spirit of Community* (New York: Simon and Schuster).

Etzioni, A. (1997) *The New Golden Rule: Community and Morality in a Democratic Society* (London: Profile Books).

Eysenck, H. (1994) 'Much Ado About IQ', in *The Times Higher Education Supplement*, 11 November.

Fainstein, N., Gordon, I. and Harloe, M. (eds) (1992) *Divided Cities: New York and London in the Contemporary World* (Oxford: Blackwell).

Faist, T. (1993) 'From School to Work – Public Policy and Underclass Formation Among Young Turks in Germany During the 1980s', *International Migration Review*, vol. 27, no. 2, pp. 306–31.

Family Policy Studies Centre (1994) *Crime and the Family* (London: Family Policy Studies Centre).

Family Policy Studies Centre (1998) *The Crime and Disorder Bill and the Family*, Family Briefing Paper no. 3 (London: Family Policy Studies Centre).

Fanstein, N. (1996) 'A Note on Interpreting American Poverty', in E. Mingione (ed.), *Urban Poverty and the Underclass* (Oxford: Blackwell).

Farnham, D. and Horton, S. (eds) (1996) *Managing the New Public Services*, 2nd edition (London: Macmillan).

Farnworth, M. *et al.* (1994) 'Measurement in the Study of Class and Delinquency – Integrating Theory and Research', *Journal of Research in Crime and Delinquency*, vol. 31, no. 1, pp. 32–61.

Fassin, D. (1996) 'Exclusion, Underclass, Marginalisation – Contemporary Figures of Urban Poverty in France, the United States and Latin America', *Revue Française de Sociologie*, vol. 37, no. 1, p. 37.

Fattah, E. (1997) *Criminology: Past, Present and Future* (London: Macmillan).

Feeley, M and Simon, J. (1994) 'Actuarial Justice: the Emerging New Criminal Law', in D. Nelken (ed.), *The Futures of Criminology* (London: Sage).

Ferri, E. (1913) *The Positive School of Criminology* (Chicago: C.H. Kerr).

Field, F. (1989) *Losing Out: the Emergence of Britain's Underclass* (Oxford: Basil Blackwell).

Field, F. (1995) *Making Welfare Work: Reconstructing Welfare for the Millenium* (London: Institute of Community Studies).

Field, F. (1996) 'Making Welfare Work: the Underlying Principles', in A. Deacon (ed.), *Stakeholder Welfare* (London: Institute of Economic Affairs).

Field, F. (1997) *Reforming Welfare* (London: The Social Market Foundation).

Fielding, N. (1995) *Community Policing* (Oxford: Clarendon Press).

Finch, J. (1986) *Research and Policy: the Uses of Qualitative Methods in Social and Educational Research* (Barcombe, Lewes: Falmer Press).

Finer, M. (1974) *Report of the Committee on One Parent Families*, Cmnd 5269 (London: HMSO).

Finn, D. (1998) 'Welfare to Work: a New Deal for the Unemployed?', *Benefits*, 21, January, pp. 32–3.

Foster, D. (1988) 'Some Victorian Concepts of Crime' in E. Sigsworth (ed.), *In Search of Victorian Values: Aspects of Nineteenth Century Thought of Society* (Manchester: Manchester University Press).

Foucault, M. (1967) *Madness and Civilisation: a History of Insanity in the Age of Reason* (London: Tavistock Publications).

Foucault, M. (1977) *Discipline and Punish: the Birth of the Prison* (Harmondsworth: Penguin).

Fowle, T. (1881) *The Poor Law: the English Citizen, His Rights and Responsibilities* (London: Macmillan and Company).

Fox-Harding, L. (1993a) '"Alarm" Versus "Liberation"? Responses to the Increase in Lone Parents – Part I', *Journal of Social Welfare and Family Law*, vol. 2, pp. 101–12.

Fox-Harding, L. (1993b) '"Alarm" Versus "Liberation"? Responses to the Increase in Lone Parents – Part 2', *Journal of Social Welfare and Family Law*, vol. 2, pp. 174–84.

Francis, P., Davies, P. and Jupp, V. (1977) '"New Millenium Blues?": Policing Past and Policing Futures', in P. Francis, P. Davies and V. Jupp (eds), *Policing Futures: the Police, Law Enforcement and the Twenty-First Century* (London: Macmillan).

Franklin, R. (1991) *Shadows of Race and Class* (Minneapolis: University of Minneapolis Press).

Fraser, D. (1984) *The Evolution of the British Welfare State: a History of Social Policy Since the Industrial Revolution*, 2nd Edition (London: Macmillan).

Fraser, D. (ed.) (1976) *The New Poor Law in the Nineteenth Century* (London: Macmillan).

Fraser, N. and Gordon, L. (1994) 'A Genealogy of Dependency: Tracing a Keyword of the US Welfare State', *Signs*, vol. 19, no. 2, pp. 309–37.

Frazier, E.F. (1962) *Black Bourgeoisie* (New York: Collins Book).

Friedman, M. (1980) *Free To Choose* (London: Penguin).

Fryer, P. (1984) *Staying Power: the History of Black People in Britain* (London: Pluto Press).

Fukuyama, F. (1992) *The End of History and the Last Man* (London: Heinemann).

Gallie, D. (1994) 'Are the Unemployed an Underclass: Some Evidence from the Social Change and Economic Life Initiative', *Sociology*, vol. 28, no. 3, pp. 737–57.

Gamble, A. (1988) *The Free Economy and the Strong State* (London: Macmillan).

Gans, H. (1990) 'Deconstructing the Underclass: The Term's Danger as a Planning Concept', *Journal of American Planning Association*, vol. 56, no. 27, pp. 272–7.

Gans, H. (1993) 'From "Underclass" to "Undercaste"': Some Observations About the Future of the Post-Industrial Economy and Its Major Victims', *International Journal of Urban and Regional Research*, vol. 17, no. 3, pp. 327–35.

Garafalo, R. (1914) *Criminology* (Boston, Mass.: Little Brown).

Gardiner, S. (1995) 'Criminal Justice Act 1991 – Management of the Underclass and the Potentiality of Community', in L. Noaks, M. Levi and M. Maguire (eds), *Contemporary Issues in Criminology* (Cardiff: University of Wales Press).

Garfinkel, I. and McLanahan, S. (1986) *Single Mothers and Their Children* (Washington: Urban Institute).

Garland, D. (1997) 'Of Crime and Criminals: The Development of Criminology in Britain', in M. Maguire, R. Morgan, and R. Reiner (eds), *The Oxford Handbook of Criminology* (Oxford: Clarendon Press).

Gaskell, P. (1968) *Artisans and Machinery* (London: Frank Cass).

Gattrell, V. (1990) 'Crime, Authority and the Policeman State', in F.M.L. Thompson (ed.), *Cambridge Social History of Britain, 1750–1950, Volume 3: Social Agencies and Institutions* (Cambridge: Cambridge University Press).

Giddens, A. (1973) *The Class Structure of Advanced Societies* (London: Hutchinson).

Giddens, A. (1974) 'Elites in the British Class Structure', in P. Stanworth and A. Giddens (eds), *Elites and Power in British Society* (Cambridge: Cambridge University Press).

Giddens, Anthony (1990) *The Consequences of Modernity* (Cambridge: Polity Press).

Giddens, A. (1994) *Beyond Left and Right: the Future of Radical Politics* (Cambridge: Polity Press).

Gilder, G. (1982) *Wealth and Poverty* (London: Buchan and Enright).

Gilroy, P. (1987a) *There Ain't No Black in the Union Jack* (London: Hutchinson).

Gilroy, P. (1987b) 'The Myth of Black Criminality', in P. Scraton (ed.), *Law, Order and the Authoritarian State: Readings in Critical Criminology* (Milton Keynes: Open University Press).

Gilroy, P. and Sim, J. (1987) 'Law, Order and the State of the Left', in P. Scraton (ed.), *Law, Order and the Authoritarian State: Readings in Critical Criminology* (Milton Keynes: Open University Press).

Ginsburg, N. (1992) *Divisions of Welfare* (London: Sage).

Glazer, N. (1995) 'Making Work Work: Welfare Reform in the 1990s', in D. Nighthingale and R. Haveman (eds), *The Work Alternative: Welfare Reform and the Realities of the Job Market* (Washington: Urban Institute Press).

Goddard, M. (1995) 'The Rascal Road – Crime, Prestige and Development in New Papau Guinea', *Contemporary Pacific*, vol. 7, no. 1, pp. 55–80.

Golding, P. and Middleton, S. (1982) *Images of Welfare* (Oxford: Martin Robertson).

Goldstein, H. (1990) *Problem Oriented Policing* (Philadelphia: Temple University Press).

Gordon, D. and Pantazis, C. (1997) *Breadline Britain in the 1990s* (Aldershot: Aldgate).

Gordon, R. (1992) *The Bushman Myth: the Making of a Namibian Underclass* (Boulder: Westview Press).

Gorer, G. (1969) 'Modification of National Character: The Role of the Police in England', in W. Chambliss (ed.), *Crime and the Legal Process* (New York: McGraw Hill).

Gouldner, A. (1973) 'Introduction', in I. Taylor, P. Walton and J. Young (eds), *The New Criminology* (London: Routledge and Kegan Paul).

Graef, R. (1989) *Talking the Blues* (London: Fontana).

Graham, P. and Clarke, J. (1996) 'Dangerous Places: Crime and the City', in J. Muncie and E. McLaughlin (eds), *The Problem of Crime* (London: Sage).

Gramsci, A. (1971) *Selections from the Prison Notebooks* (London: Lawrence and Wishart).

Gray, A. (1998) 'New Labour – New Labour Discipline', *Capital and Class*, no. 65, pp. 1–8.

Green, A. and Owen, D. (1998) *Where Are the Jobless? Changing Unemployment and Non-Employment in Cities and Regions* (Bristol: Policy Press).

Greenwood, J. (1873) *In Strange Company: the Experiences of Being a Roving Respondent* (London: Henry King and Co).

Gregg, P. and Wadsworth, J. (1998) *Unemployment and Non-Employment: Unpacking Economic Inactivity* (London: Employment Policy Institute).

Grimshaw, R. and Jefferson, T. (1987) *Interpreting Policework: Problems and Practice in Forms of Beat Policing* (London: Allen and Unwin).

Gross, B. (1982) 'Reagan's Criminal Anti-Crime Fix', in A. Gartner, C. Greer and F. Reisman (eds), *What Is Reagan Doing To Us* (New York: Harper and Row).

Hadfield, R. (1996) 'Police Claim Crime "Cover-Up"', *The Observer*, 18 February.

Hagan, J. and Palloni, A. (1990) 'The Social Reproduction of a Criminal Class in Working Class London, Circa 1950–1980', *American Journal of Sociology*, vol. 96, no. 2, pp. 265–99.

Hagedorn, J. (1988) *People and Folks: Gangs, Crime and the Underclass in a Rust Belt City* (Chicago: Lake View Press).

Hagedorn, J. (1991) 'Gangs, Neighbourhoods and Public Policy', *Social Problems*, vol. 38, no. 4, pp. 529–42.

Hahn, P. (1998) *Emerging Criminal Justice: Three Pillars of Proactive Justice* (London: Sage).

Halsey, C. (1989) 'Social Trends Since World War II', in I. McDowell, P. Sarre and C. Hamnett (eds), *Divided Nation: Social and Cultural Change in Britain* (London: Hodder and Stoughton).

Halsey, C. (1993) 'The Head of the Family – An Interview with Melanie Phillips', *The Guardian*, 23 February.

Ham, C. and Hill, M. (1993) *The Policy Process in the Modern Capitalist State*, 2nd edition (London: Harvester Wheatsheaf).

Handler, J. (1996) *The Poverty of Welfare Reform* (New Haven: Yale University Press).

Handler, J. and Hasenfeld, Y. (1997) *We the Poor People: Work, Poverty and Welfare* (London: Yale University Press).

Handler, J. and Hasenfeld, Y. (1997) *We the Poor People: Work, Poverty and Welfare* (London: Yale University Press).

Handler, J. and Hollingworth, E. (1971) *The Deserving Poor: a Study of Welfare Administration*, Institute for Research on Poverty Monograph Series (Chicago: Markam).

Handler, J.F. and Hollingworth, E.J. (1971) *The Deserving Poor: a Study of Welfare Administration*, Institute for Research on Poverty Monograph Series (Chicago: Markham).

Hardey, M. and Crow, G. (eds) (1991) *Lone Parenthood: Coping With Constraints and Making Opportunities* (Hemel Hempstead: Harvester Wheatsheaf).

Harris, K.M. (1993) 'Work and Welfare Among Single Mothers in Poverty', *American Journal of Sociology*, vol. 99, no. 2, pp. 317–52.

Häussermann, H. and Kazepov, Y. (1996) 'Urban Poverty in Germany: A Comparative Analysis of the Poor in Stuttgart and Berlin', in E. Mingione (ed.), *Urban Poverty and the Underclass* (Oxford: Blackwell).

Hayek, F. (1973) *Law, Legislation and Liberty*, vols. 1–2 (London: Routledge).

Hayek, F. (1986) *The Road to Serfdom* (London: Routledge and Kegan Paul).

Heidensohn, F. (1998) 'Criminal Justice: Security, Social Control and the Hidden Agenda', in H. Jones and S. MacGregor (eds), *Social Issues and Social Politics* (London: Routledge).

Henry, S. and Milovanovic, D. (1996) *Constitutive Criminology: Beyond Postmodernism* (London: Sage).

Hernstein, R. and Murray, C. (1994) *The Bell Curve* (New York: Free Press).

Hewitt, M. (1992) *Welfare, Ideology and Need* (Hemel Hempstead: Harvester Wheatsheaf).

Hill, M. (1996) *Social Policy: a Comparative Perspective* (Hemel Hempstead: Harvester Wheatsheaf).

Hill, M. (1997) *Understanding Social Policy*, 5th edition (Oxford: Blackwell).

Hill, M. (ed.) (1993) *New Agendas in the Study of the Policy Process* (London: Harvester Wheatsheaf).

Hills, J. (ed.) (1996) *New Inequalities: the Changing Distribution of Income and Wealth in the UK* (Cambridge: Cambridge University Press).

Hills, J. (1998) *Income and Wealth: the Latest Evidence* (York: Joseph Rowntree Foundation).

Hobbs, D. (1988) *Doing the Business* (Oxford: Clarendon Press).

Hobsbawm, E. (1959) *Primitive Rebels: Studies in Archaic Forms of Social Movement in the Nineteenth and Twentieth Centuries* (Manchester: Manchester University Press).

Hoddinott, J. (1994) 'Public Safety and Private Security', *Policing*, vol. 10, no. 3, pp. 158–65.

Hoggett, P. (1994) 'The Politics of Modernisation of the UK Welfare State, in R. Burrows and B. Loader (eds), *Towards a Post-Fordist Welfare State* (London: Routledge).

Hogwood, B. (1992) Trends in British Public Policy (Buckingham: Open University Press).

Hogwood, B. and Gunn, L. (1981) *The Policy Orientation* (Centre for the Study of Public Policy: University of Strathclyde).

Hogwood, B. and Gunn, L. (1984) *Policy Analysis for the Real World* (Oxford: Oxford University Press).

Hogwood, B. and Peters, B. (1983) *Policy Dynamics* (Brighton: Harvester Wheatsheaf).

Holdaway, S. (1982) 'The Scarman Report: Some Sociological Aspects', *New Community*, vol. 9, no. 3, pp. 366–70.

Holdaway, S. (1983) *Inside the British Police Force: A Force at Work* (Oxford: Basil Blackwell).

Holdaway, S. (1989) 'Discovering Structure: Studies of the British Police Occupational Culture', in M. Weatheritt (ed.), *Police Research: Some Future Prospects* (Aldershot: Avebury).

Holdaway, S. (1996) *The Racialisation of British Policing* (Basingstoke: Macmillan).

Hollingshead, J. (1986) *Ragged London in 1861*, with an introduction by A. Wohl (London: Dent).

Holman, B. (1970) *Unsupported Mothers* (London: Mothers in Action).

Holman, B. (1978) *Poverty: Explanations of Social Deprivation* (London: Martin Robertson).

Home Office (1967) *Police Manpower, Equipment and Efficiency* (London: Home Office).

Home Office (1983a) Circular 114/1983 *Manpower, Effectiveness and Efficiency in the Police Service*, November (London: Home Office).

Home Office (1983b) *Crime Statistics for the Metropolitan Police District*, Statistical Bulletin, no. 22 (London: Home Office Research and Statistics Department).

Home Office (1984) *Crime Statistics for the Metropolitan Police District Analysed by Ethnic Group*, Statistical Bulletin, no. (London: Home Office Research and Statistics Department).

Home Office (1988) Circular 114/88, *Tackling Public Disorder Outside of Metropolitan Areas* (London: HMSO).

Home Office (1989) *Crime Statistics for the Metropolitan Police District Analysed by Ethnic Group: Victims, Suspects and Those Arrested*, Statistical Bulletin, no. 5 (London: Home Office Research and Statistics Department).

Home Office (1993a) *Report of Her Majesty's Chief Inspector of Constabulary for the Year 1992* (London: HMSO).

Home Office (1993b) *Police Reform: A Police Service for the 21st Century*, Cmnd 2281 (London: HMSO).

Home Office (1995a) *The Role of HM Inspectorate of Constabulary for England and Wales* (London: Home Office Public Relations Branch).

Home Office (1995b) *Review of the Police Core and Ancillary Tasks*, Final Report (London: HMSO).

Home Office (1998) *Notifiable Offences in England and Wales, 1997* (London: Home Office Research and Statistics Department).

Hopkins-Burke, R. (ed.), *Zero Tolerance Policing* (Leicester: Perpetuity Press).

Hough, M. and Mayhew, P. (1983) *The British Crime Survey*, First Report, Home Office Research Study, no. 147 (London: Home Office Research and Statistics Department).

House of Commons (1980) *Race Relations and the 'Sus' Law*, Second Report from the Home Affairs Committee, Session 1979–80, HC 559 (London: HMSO).

House of Commons (1981a) *Racial Disadvantage*, Fifth Report from the Home Affairs Committee, Session 1980–81, HC 424 (London: HMSO).

House of Commons (1981b) *Commission for Racial Equality*, First Report from the Home Affairs Committee, Session 1981–2, HC 46 (London: HMSO).

House of Commons (1982) *Efficiency and Effectiveness in the Civil Service*, Report of the Treasury and Civil Service Select Committee (London: HMSO).

House of Commons (1983) *Ethnic and Racial Questions in the Census*, Second Report from the Home Affairs Committee, Session 1982–3, HC 33 (London: HMSO).

Howe, L. (1985) ' The "Deserving" and the "Undeserving": Practice in the Urban, Local Social Security Office', *Journal of Social Policy*, vol. 14, no. 1, pp. 49–72.

Hughes, G. (1996) 'Communitarianism and Law and Order', *Critical Social Policy*, vol. 16, no. 4, pp. 17–42.

Hutton, W. (1995) *The State We're In* (London: Jonathan Cape).

Imbert, Sir P. (1988) *Report of the Commissioner of the Metropolitan Police for the Year 1987*, Cmnd. 389 (London: HMSO).

Imbert, Sir P. (1989) *Report of the Commissioner of the Metropolitan Police for the Year 1988*, Cmnd. 670 (London: HMSO).

Imbert, Sir P. (1991) *Report of the Commissioner of the Metropolitan Police for the Year 1990* (London: HMSO).

Imbert, Sir P. (1992) *Report of the Commissioner of the Metropolitan Police for the Year 1991/2* (London: HMSO).

Institute of Race Relations (1987) *Policing Against Black People* (London: Institute of Race Relations).

Irwin, J. (1986) *The Jail: Managing the Underclass in American Society* (Chicago: University of Chicago Press).

James, A. and Raine, J. (1998) *The New Politics of Criminal Justice* (London: Longman).

Janssen, B. (1993) *The Reluctant Welfare State*, 2nd edition (Pacific Grove, Ca: Brooks Cole).

Jefferson, T. (1987) 'Beyond Paramilitarism', *British Journal of Criminology*, vol. 27, pp. 47–53.

Jefferson, T. (1988) 'Race, Class, Crime and Policing: Empirical, Theoretical and Methodological Issues', *International Journal of the Sociology of Law*, vol. 16, pp. 521–39.

Jefferson, T. (1990) *The Case Against Paramilitary Policing Considered* (Milton Keynes: Open University Press).

Jefferson, T. (1993a) 'Pondering Paramilitarism: A Question of Viewpoints', *British Journal of Criminology*, vol. 33, no. 3, pp. 374–88.

Jefferson, T. (1993b) 'The Racism of Criminalisation: Policing and the Reproduction of the Criminal Other' in L. Gelsthorpe (ed.), *Minority Ethnic Groups in the Criminal Justice System* (Cambridge: Cambridge University Press).

Jefferson, T. and Walker, M. (1992) 'Ethnic Minorities in the Criminal Justice System', *Criminal Law Review*, pp. 83–95.

Jefferson, T. and Walker, M. (1993) 'Attitudes to the Police of Ethnic Minorities in a Provincial City', *British Journal of Criminology*, vol. 33, no. 2, pp. 251–66.

Jencks, C. (1992) *Rethinking Social Policy: Race, Poverty and the Underclass*, (Cambridge, MA: Harvard University Press).

Johnson, R. (1970) 'Educational Policy and Social Control in Early Victorian England', *Past and Present*, no. 49, pp. 96–119.

Johnston, L. (1992) *The Rebirth of Private Policing* (London: Routledge).

Johnston, L. (1993) 'Privatisation and Protection: Spatial and Sectoral Ideologies in British Policing and Crime Prevention', *Modern Law Review*, vol. 56, no. 6, pp. 771–92.

Johnston, P. (1997) 'Mean Streets Where They Test the Zero Option', *The Daily Telegraph*, 8 January.

Joint Consultative Committee (1990) *The Operational Policing Review* (Surbiton: The Joint Consultative Committee of the Three Staff Associations of England and Wales).

Jones, D. (1988) *Crime and Protest: Community and Police in Nineteenth Century Britain* (London: Routledge and Kegan Paul).

Jones, H. (ed.) (1997) *Towards a Classless Society?* (London: Routledge).

Jones, K. (1991) *The Making of Social Policy in Britain, 1830–1990* (London: Athlone).

Jones, M. (1993) 'Wedded to Welfare', *The Sunday Times*, 11 July.

Jones, T., Newburn, T. and Smith, D.J. (1994) *Democracy and Policing* (London: Policy Studies Institute).

Jones-Finer, C. and Nellis, M. (eds) (1998) *Crime and Social Exclusion* (Oxford: Blackwell).

Jordan, B. (1973) *Paupers: the Making of a New Claiming Class* (London: Routledge and Kegan Paul).

Jordan, B. (1996) *A Theory of Poverty and Social Exclusion* (Cambridge: Polity Press).

Katz, M. (1986) *In the Shadow of the Poorhouse: a Social History of Welfare in America* (New York: Basic Books).

Katz, M. (1989) *The Undeserving Poor: From the War on Poverty to the War on Welfare* (New York: Pantheon Books).

Katz, M. (ed.) (1993) *The Underclass Debate: Views from History* (Princeton, New Jersey: Princeton University Press).

Kay, J. (1850) *Education of the Poor People: the Social Condition and Education of People*, vols. 1 and 2 (London: Longman Brown, Green and Longmans).

Kay, J. (1969) *The Moral Condition of the Working Class Employed in the Cotton Manufacture in Manchester* (Didsbury: E.J. Moten Publishers).

Keith, M. (1988) 'Squaring Circles: Consultation and Inner City Policing', New Community, vol. 15, no. 1, pp. 63–77.

Keith, M. (1991) 'Policing a Perplexed Society: No Go Areas and the Mystification of Police-Black Conflict', in E. Cashmore and E. McLaughlin (eds), *Out of Order? Policing Black People* (London: Routledge).

Keith, M. (1992) 'The 1948 "Race Riots" in Liverpool', *Migration*, vol. 13, pp. 5–31.

Keith, M. (1993) *Race, Riots and Policing: Lore and Disorder in a Multi-racist Society* (London: University College of London Press).

Kerner, O. (1968) *Report of the National Advisory Commission on Civil Disorders* (New York: Bantam Books).

King, D. (1995) *Actively Seeking Work? The Politics of Unemployment and Welfare Policy in the United States and Great Britain* (London: University of Chicago Press).

King, M. and Brearley, N. (1996) *Public Order Policing: Contemporary Perspectives on Strategy and Tactics* (Leicester: Perpetuity Press).

Kinsey, R. (1985) *Merseyside and Crime and Police Survey*, Final Report, October 1985 (Liverpool: Merseyside County Council).

Kinsey, R. and Young, J. (1982) 'Police Autonomy and the Politics of Discretion', in D. Cowell, T. Jones and J. Young (eds), *Policing the Riots* (London: Junction Books).

Kinsey, R., Lea, J. and Young, J. (1986) *Losing the Fight Against Crime* (Oxford: Blackwell).

Koch, B. and Bennett, T. (1993) *Community Policing in Canada and Britain*, Home Office Research Bulletin, no. 34 (London: Home Office Research and Statistics Directorate).

Labour Party (1996a) *Protecting Our Community* (London: Labour Party).

Labour Party (1996b) *Tackling Youth Crime: Reforming Youth Justice* (London: Labour Party).

Labour Party (1997) *New Labour Leading Britain into the Future*, election manifesto (London: Labour Party).

Labour Party (1998) *Local Policy Forum 1998: Crime and Justice*, Consultation Paper (London: Labour Party).

Lacey, N. and Zedner, L. (1995) 'Locating the Appeal to "Community" in Contemporary Criminal Justice', *Journal of Law and Society*, vol. 22, no. 3, pp. 301–25.

Laclau, E. (1990) *New Reflections on the Revolution of Our Time* (London: Verso).

Lane, R. (1992) 'Urban Police and Crime in Nineteenth Century America', in M. Tonry and N. Norris (eds), *Modern Policing, Crime and Justice: A Review of Research*, vol. 15 (Chicago: Chicago University Press).

Layder, D. (1994) *Understanding Social Theory* (London: Sage).

Layder, D. (1997) *Modern Social Theory: Key Debates and New Directions* (London: University College of London Press).

Lea, J. (1986) 'Police Racism: Some Theories and Their Policy Implications', in R. Matthews and J. Young (eds), *Confronting Crime* (London: Sage).

Lea, J. and Young, J. (1982) 'The Riots in 1981: Urban Violence and Political Marginalisation', in D. Cowell, T. Jones and J. Young (eds), *Policing the Riots* (London: Junction Books).

Lea, J. and Young, J. (1984) *What's to be Done About Law and Order?* (Harmondsworth: Penguin).

Lea, J. and Young, J. (1993) *What's to be Done About Law and Order?: Crisis in the Nineties* (London: Pluto Press).

Lee, J. (1981) 'Some Aspects of Police Deviance in Relations With Minority Groups', in C. Shearing (ed.), *Organisational Police Deviance* (Toronto: Butterworth).

Lee, M. (1995) 'Pre-Court Diversion and Youth Justice', in L. Noaks, M. Levi and M. Maguire (eds), *Contemporary Issues in Criminology* (Cardiff: University of Wales Press).

Leeds, A. (1977) 'The Concept of "Culture of Poverty": Conceptual, Logical and Empirical Problems With Perspectives From Brazil and Peru', in E. Lennock (ed.), *The Culture of Poverty: a Critique* (New York: Simon and Schuster).

Leigh, L. (1979) 'Vagrancy and the Criminal Law', in T. Cook (ed.), *Vagrancy: Some New Perspectives* (London: Academic Press).

Leishman, F., Cope, S. and Starie, P. (1996) 'Reinventing and Restructuring: Towards a New Policing Order', in F. Leishman, B. Loveday and S. Savage (eds), *Core Issues in Policing* (London: Longman).

Letts, Q. (1997) 'Joining the Resistance in the Big Apple', *The Times*, 24 January.

Levitas, R. (1996) 'The Concept of Social Exclusion and the New Durkheimian Hegemony', *Critical Social Policy*, vol. 16, no. 1, pp. 5–20.

Lewis, O. (1968) 'The Culture of Poverty', in D.P. Moynihan (ed.), *Understanding Poverty* (New York: Basic Books).

Lindblom, C. (1959) 'The Science of "Muddling Through"', *Public Administration*, vol. 19, pp. 79–99.

Lipsky, M. (1980) *Street Level Bureaucracy* (New York: Russell Sage).

Lister, R. (ed.) (1996) *Charles Murray and the Underclass* (London: Institute of Economic Affairs).

Lister, R. (1997) 'In Search of the Underclass', in Socio-Legal Studies Association (eds), *In Search of the 'Underclass' Working Papers from the SLSA One-day Conference in Queen's University Belfast 1997* (Belfast: Queen's University of Belfast).

Lister, R. (1998) 'From Equality to Social Inclusion: New Labour and the Welfare State', *Critical Social Policy*, vol. 18, no. 2, pp. 215–25.

Loader, I. (1996) *Youth, Democracy and Policing* (London: Macmillan).

Loveday, B. (1996) 'Crime at the Core', in F. Leishman, B. Loveday and S. Savage (eds), *Core Issues in Policing* (London: Longman).

Luckmann, T. (1983) *Life World and Social Realities* (London: Heinemann).

Lukes, S. (1974) *Power* (London: Macmillan).

Lukes, S. (ed.) (1986) *Power: Readings in Social and Political Theory* (Oxford: Basil Blackwell).

Lustgarten. L. (1986) *The Governance of the Police* (London: Sweet and Maxwell).

Lynn, R. (1994) 'Is Man Breeding Himself Back to the Age of the Apes', *The Times*, 24 October.

MacClure, J. (1965) *Educational Documents: England and Wales, 1816 to the Present Day* (London: Methuen).

MacDonald, R. (ed.) (1997) *Youth, the 'Underclass' and Social Exclusion* (London: Routledge).

Macnicol, J. (1987) 'In Pursuit of the Underclass', *Journal of Social Policy*, vol. 16, no. 3, pp. 293–318.

MacGregor, S. (1998) 'A New Deal For Britain', in H. Jones and S. MacGregor (eds) *Social Issues and Social Politics* (London: Routledge).

Mandelson, P. (1997) *Labour's Next Step: Tackling Social Exclusion*, Fabian Pamphlet no. 581 (London: Fabian Society).

Mandelson, P. and Liddle, R. (1996) *The Blair Revolution* (London: Faber and Faber).

Mann, C.R. (1993) *Unequal Justice: a Question of Colour* (Bloomington, Ind.: Indianna University Press).

Mann, K. (1992) *The Making of an English Underclass? The Social Divisions of Welfare and Labour* (Buckingham: Open University Press).

Manning, P. (1977) *Police Work* (Cambridge, Massachusetts: MIT Press).

Marcuse, P. (1996) 'Space and Race in the Post-Fordist City: the Outcast Ghetto and Advanced Homelessness in the United States Today', in E. Mingione (ed.), *Urban Poverty and the Underclass: A Reader* (Oxford: Blackwell).

Margolis, J. (1993) 'Are Our Children Out of Control', *The Sunday Times*, 21 February.

Marsden, D. (1976) *Mothers Alone: Poverty and the Fatherless Family*, Revised Edition (Harmondsworth: Penguin).

Marshall, G. *et al.* (1996) 'Social Class and the Underclass in Britain and the USA', *British Journal of Sociology*, vol. 47, no. 1, pp. 22–44.

Marshall, T. (ed.) (1992) *Community Disorders and Policing: Conflict Management in Action* (London: Whiting and Birch).

Marshall, T.H. (1972) 'Value Problems of Welfare Capitalism', *Journal of Social Policy*, vol. 1, no. 1, pp. 18–32.

Marx, K. (1930) *Capital*, vol. 2 (London: J. M. Dent).

Mason, D. (1982) 'After Scarman: A Note on Institutional Racism', *New Community*, vol. 10, no. 1.

Massey, D. (1993) 'Latinos, Poverty and the Underclass – A New Agenda for Research', *Hispanic Journal of Behavioural Sciences*, vol. 15, no. 4, pp. 449–75.

Matza, D. (1964) *Delinquency and Drift* (New York: John Wiley and Sons).

Matza, D. (1966) 'The Disreputable Poor', in R. Bendix and S. Lipsett (eds), *Class, Status and Power* (London: Routledge and Kegan Paul).

Mawby, R. (1990) *Comparative Policing Issues: the British and American Experience in International Perspective* (London: Unwin Hyman).

Mayhew, H. (1861) *London Labour and the London Poor* (London: Dover Publications).

Mayhew, P. and Mirlees-Black, C. (1993) The 1992 British Crime Survey, Home Office Research Study, no. 132 (London: HMSO).

Mayhew, P., Elliot, D. and Dowds, L. (1989) *The 1988 British Crime Survey* (London: HMSO).

McConville, M. and Shepherd, D. (1992) *Watching Police, Watching Communities* (London: Routledge).

McKay, S. and Oppenheim, S. (1997) 'Rethinking Welfare', *Benefits*, vol. 20, September/October, p. 1.

McKenzie, I. and Gallagher, G. (1989) *Behind the Uniform: Policing in Britain and America* (Hemel Hempstead: Harvester Wheatsheaf).

McLanahan, S. and Garfinkel, I. (1989) 'Single Mothers, the Underclass and Social Policy', *Annals*, no. 501, January, pp. 92–104.

McLaughlin, E. (1990) *Community, Policing and Accountability: a Case Study of Manchester 1981–88* (PhD. Thesis: Faculty of Law, University of Sheffield).

McLaughlin, E. (1994) *Community Policing and Accountability: the Politics of Policing in Manchester in the 1980s* (Aldershot: Avebury).

McLaughlin, E. and Murji, K. (1995) 'The End of Public Policing: Police Reform and the "New Managerialism"', in L. Noaks and M. Maguire (eds), *Contemporary Issues in Criminology* (Cardiff: University of Wales Press).

McLaughlin, E. and Murji, K. (1997) 'The Future Lasts a Long Time: Public Policework and the Managerialist Paradox', in P. Francis, P. Davies and V. Jupp (eds), *Policing Futures: the Police, Law Enforcement and the Twenty-First Century* (London: Macmillan).

McPhail, C., Schweingruber, D. and McCarthy, J. (1998) 'Policing Protest in the United States: 1960–1995', in D. Della Porta and H. Reiter (eds), *Policing Protest: The Control of Demonstrations in Western Democracies* (Minneapolis: University of Minnesota Press).

Marx, K. (1970) *The German Ideology* (London: Lawrence and Wishart).

Mead, L. (1986) *Beyond Entitlement: The Social Obligations of Citizenship* (New York: Free Press).

Mead, L (1992) *The New Politics of Poverty: the Nonworking Poor in America* (New York: Basic Books).

Mead, L. and Deacon, A. (eds) (1997) *From Welfare to Work: Lessons From America* (London: Institute of Economic Affairs, Health and Welfare Unit).

Messerschmidt, J. (1993) *Masculinities and Crime: Critique and Reconceptualisation of Theory* (Lanham, Maryland: Rowman and Littlefield).

Metropolitan Police (1995) *Policing Plan 1995/96* (Scotland Yard: Metropolitan Police).

Michael, A. (1997) *First Steps in Consultation on Crime and Disorder*, Home Office News Release, 149/97, 12 June.

Michael, A. (1998a) *Towards A Radical Century*, Speech Presented at New Statesman and London School of Economics Annual Conference (London: Home Office).

Michael, A. (1998b) *Clear Guidance for Cutting Crime*, Home Office News Release, 325/98, 13 August.

Miles, R. (1989) *Racism* (London: Routledge).

Mill, J.S. (1962) *Utilitarianism, On Liberty, Essay on Bentham*, edited with an introduction by Mary Warnock (London: Collins).

Millar, J. (1994) 'State, Family and Personal Responsibility: the Changing Balance
for Lone Mothers in the United Kingdom', *Feminist Review*, vol. 48, pp. 24–39.

Miller, J. (1993) Estate Betrayed By Its Fathers', *The Sunday Times*, 11 July.

Miller, W. (1977) *Cops and Bobbies: Police Authority in New York and London,
1830–1870* (Chicago: Chicago University Press).

Miller, W. (1979) 'London's Police Tradition in a Changing Society', in S. Holdaway (ed.), *The British Police* (London: Edward Arnold).

Mills, C. Wright (1956) *The Power Elite* (Oxford: Oxford University Press).

Mincey, R. (1988) *Is There A White Underclass?* (Washington DC: Brookings
Urban Institute).

Mingione, E. (1996) 'Urban Poverty in the Advanced Industrial World: Concepts,
Analysis and Debates', in E. Mingione (ed.), *Urban Poverty and the Underclass: a
Reader* (Oxford: Blackwell).

Mirrlees-Black, C., Mayhew, P. and Percy, A. (1996) *The 1996 British Crime Survey*,
Home Office Statistical Bulletin, Issue 19/96 (London: Government Statistical
Service).

Mirrlees-Black, C., Budd, T., Partridge, S. and Mayhew, P. (1998) *The 1998 British
Crime Survey, England and Wales*, Home Office Statistical Bulletin, Issue 21/98
(London: Government Statistical Service).

Mizen, P. (1998) '"Work-Welfare" and the Regulation of the Poor: the Pessimism
of Post-Structuralism', *Capital and Class*, no. 65, pp. 35–53.

Monkonnen, E. (1981) *Police in Urban America, 1860–1920* (Cambridge: Cambridge University Press).

Monkonnen, E. (1991) *Hands Up: American Policing, 1920–1960* (Cambridge:
Cambridge University Press).

Monkonnen, E. (1992) 'History of Urban Police', in M. Tonry and N. Norris (eds)
Modern Policing, Crime and Justice, vol. 15 (Chicago: University of Chicago
Press).

Monkonnen, E. (1993) 'Nineteenth Century Institutions: Dealing With the
Urban "Underclass"', in M. Katz (ed.), *The Underclass Debate* (New Jersey: Princeton University Press).

Morgan, R. (1992) 'Talking About Policing', in D. Downes (ed.), *Unravelling Criminal Justice* (London: Macmillan).

Morgan, R. (1997) 'Swept Along by Zero Option', *The Guardian*, 22 January.

Morgan, R. and Newburn, T. (1997) *The Future of Policing* (Oxford: Clarendon
Press).

Morris, L. (1994) *Dangerous Classes: the Underclass and Social Citizenship* (London:
Routledge).

Morris, L. (1995) *Social Divisions* (London: University College of London Press).

Morris, L. and Irwin, S. (1992) 'Employment Histories and the Concept of the
Underclass', *Sociology*, vol. 26, no. 3, pp. 401–20.

Morrison, W. (1995) *Theoretical Criminology: From Modernity to Post-modernism*
(London: Cavendish).

Morrison, W.D. (1891) *Crime and Its Causes* (London:).

Moynihan, D.P. (1965) *The Negro Family: the Case for National Action* (United
States Department of Labour: Office of Policy Planning and Research).

Moynihan, D.P. (1969) *Maximum Feasible Understanding: Community Action in the War on Poverty* (New York: Free Press).

Murphy, P., Williams, J. and Dunning, E. (1989) *Football on Trial: Spectator Violence and Development in the Football World* (London: Routledge and Kegan Paul).

Murray, C. (1984) *Losing Ground: American Social Policy 1950–1980* (New York: Basic Books).

Murray, C. (1990) *The Emerging British Underclass* (London: Institute of Economic Affairs).

Murray, C. (1992) quoted in L. Lightfoot and T. Rayment 'Police Study Videos to Catch Riot Ringleaders', *The Sunday Times*, 26 July.

Murray, C. (1994) *The Underclass: the Crisis Deepens* (London: Institute of Economic Affairs).

Murray, C. (1997) *Does Prison Work?* (London: Institute of Economic Affairs Health and Welfare Unit).

Murray, R. (1929) *Studies in English Social and Political Thinkers of the Nineteenth Century* (Cambridge: W. Heffer and Sons Ltd).

Myrdal, G. (1964) *The Challenge to Affluence* (Chicago: Victor Gollancz).

Nash, M. and Savage, S. (1994) 'A Criminal Record? Law, Order and Conservative Policy', in S. Savage, R. Atkinson and L. Robins (eds), *Public Policy in Britain* (London: Macmillan).

Newman, Sir K. (1983) *Policing London: Post Scarman*, Sir George Bean Memorial Lecture, 30 October.

Newman, Sir K. (1984) *Report of the Commissioner of the Metropolis for the Year 1983* (London: HMSO).

Newman, Sir K. (1985) *Report of the Commissioner of the Metropolis for the Year 1984* (London: HMSO).

Northam, G. (1988) *Shooting in the Dark* (London: Faber).

O'Connor, J. (1998) 'US Welfare Policy: The Reagan Record and Legacy', *Journal of Social Policy*, vol. 27, no, 1, pp. 37–62.

O'Hare, W. and Curry-White, B. (1992) 'Is There a Rural Underclass?', *Population*, vol. 20, no. 6.

O'Malley, C. (ed.) (1966) *London Street Life: Selections from the Writings of Henry Mayhew* (London: Chatto and Windus).

Office of Population Censuses and Surveys (1995) Figures quoted in *The Daily Telegraph*, 16 November.

Oppenheim, C. (1994) *The Welfare State: Putting the Record Straight* (London: CPAG).

Oppenheim, C. (1998a) 'Changing the Storyline', *The Guardian*, 1 April.

Oppenheim, C. (1998b) 'Poverty and Social Security in a Changing Britain', in H. Jones and S. MacGregor (eds), *Social Issues and Party Politics* (London: Routledge and Kegan Paul).

Oppenheim, C. and Harker, L. (1996) *Poverty: the Facts* (London: CPAG).

Orr, J. (1997) 'Strathclyde's Spotlight Initiative', in N. Dennis (ed.), *Zero Tolerance: Policing a Free Society*, Choice in Welfare No. 35 (London: IEA Health and Welfare Unit).

Pahl, R. (1988) 'Some Remarks on Informal Work, Social Polarisation and Social Structure', *International Journal of Urban and Regional Research*, vol. 12, pp. 247–67.

Pakulski, J. and Waters, M. (1996) *The Death of Class* (London: Sage).

Pearson, G. (1983) *Hooligan: a History of Respectable Fears* (London: Macmillan).

Phillips, D. (1977) *Crime and Authority in Victorian England: the Black Country 1835–60* (London: Croom Helm).

Phillips, D. (1980) 'A New Engine of Power and Authority: the Institutionalisation of Law Enforcement in England 1780–1830' in V. Gatrell *et al.* (eds), *Crime and the Law* (London: Europa).

Phillips, D. (1983) 'A Just Measure of Crime, Authority, Hunters and Blue Locusts: the Revisionist Social History of Crime and Law in Britain 1780–1850', in S. Cohen and A. Scull (eds), *Social Control and the State* (Oxford: Martin Robertson).

Phillips, M. (1993) 'The Head of the Family', *The Guardian*, 23 February.

Philo, C. (ed.) (1995) *Off the Map: the Social Geography of Poverty in the UK* (London: Child Poverty Action Group).

Pilkington E. (1995) 'Japan's "Untouchables Locked Into Disadvantage By Collective Amnesia', *The Guardian*, 2 August.

Pierson, P. (1994) *Dismantling the Welfare State? Reagan, Thatcher and the Politics of Retrenchment* (Cambridge: Cambridge University Press).

Pitts, J. and Hope, T. (1998) 'The Local Politics of Inclusion: The State and Community Safety', in C. Jones-Finer and M. Nellis (eds), *Crime and Social Exclusion* (Oxford: Blackwell).

Piven, F. and Cloward, R. (1993) *Regulating the Poor* (New York: Vintage Books).

Policy Studies Institute (1983) *Police and People in London*, 4 volumes (London: Policy Studies Institute).

Pollard, C. (1997) 'Short Term Fix, Long-Term Liability?', in N. Dennis (ed.), *Zero Tolerance: Policing a Free Society*, Choice in Welfare No. 35 (London: IEA Health and Welfare Unit).

Popov, O. (1991) 'Towards a Theory of "Underclass" Review', *Stanford Law Review*, vol. 43, no. 5, pp. 1095–132.

Povey, D., Prime, J. and Taylor, P. (1998) *Notifiable Offences, England and Wales, 1997*, Home Office Statistical Bulletin, issue 7/98 (London: HMSO).

Povey, D. and Prime, J. (1998) *Notifiable Offences, England and Wales, April 1997 to March 1998*, Home Office Statistical Bulletin, issue 22/98 (London: Government Statistical Service).

President's Commission on Law Enforcement and the Administration of Justice (1968) *The Challenge of Crime in a Free Society* (New York: Dutton Books).

Pryce, K. (1979) *Endless Pressure* (Harmondsworth: Penguin).

Rainwater, L. (ed.) (1970) *Behind Ghetto Walls: Black Families in a London Slum* (London: Allen Lane, Penguin Press).

Rainwater, L. and Yancey, W. (1967) *The Moynihan Report and the Politics of Controversy* (Cambridge, Mass.: MIT Press).

Read, S. (1997) 'Below Zero', *Police Review*, 17 January.

Reagan, R. (1981) 'Presidential Address', in E. Sandoz and C. Crabb (eds), *A Tide of Discontent: The 1980 Election and Their Meaning* (Washington DC: Congressional Quarterly Press).

Rein, M. (1970) 'The Welfare Crisis', in L. Rainwater (ed.), *Behind Ghetto Walls: Black Families in a London Slum*, (London: Allen Lane, Penguin Press).

Rein, M. (1983) *From Policy to Practice* (London: Macmillan).

Reiner, R. (1985) *The Politics of the Police* (Hemel Hempstead: Harvester Wheatsheaf).

Reiner, R. (1991) *Chief Constables: Bosses, Bobbies or Bureaucrats* (Oxford: Oxford University Press).

Reiner, R. (1992a) 'Police Research in the United Kingdom: A Critical Review', in N. Tonry and N. Morris (eds), *Modern Policing: Crime and Justice, A Review of Research*, vol. 15 (Chicago: University of Chicago Press).

Reiner, R. (1992b) *The Politics of the Police*, 2nd edition (Hemel Hempstead: Harvester Wheatsheaf).

Reiner, R. (1994) 'Policing and the Police', in M. Maguire, R. Morgan, and R. Reiner (eds), *The Oxford Handbook of Criminology* (Oxford: Clarendon Press).

Reiner, R. (1995a) 'Community Policing in England and Wales', in J-P. Brodeur (ed.), *Comparisons in Policing: An International Perspective* (Aldershot: Avebury).

Reiner, R. (1995b) 'Selling the Family Copper: the British Police plc', *The Independent*, 12 October.

Reiner, R. (1997) 'Policing and the Police', in M. Maguire, R. Morgan and R. Reiner (eds), *The Oxford Handbook of Criminology*, 2nd edition (Oxford: Clarendon Press).

Reiner, R. (1998) 'Policing, Protest and Disorder in Britain', in D. Della Porta and H. Reiter (eds), *Policing Protest: The Control of Demonstrations in Western Democracies* (Minneapolis: University of Minnesota Press).

Renvoize, J. (1985) *Going Solo: Single Mothers By Choice* (London: Routledge and Kegan Paul).

Reuss-Ianni, E. and Ianni, F. (1983) 'Street Cops and Management Cops: the Two Cultures in Policing', in M. Punch (ed.), *Control in the Police Organisation* (Cambridge, Mass.: MIT Press).

Rex, J. (1973) *Race, Colonialism and the City* (London: Routledge and Kegan Paul).

Rex, J. (1988) *The Ghetto Underclass: Essays on Race and Social Policy* (Aldershot: Avebury).

Rex, J. and Tomlinson, S. (1979) *Colonial Immigrants in a British City: a Class Analysis* (London: Routledge and Kegan Paul).

Richards, F. (1991) 'The Underclass: a Race Apart', *Living Marxism*, November, pp. 30–4.

Roche, M. (1992) *Rethinking Citizenship: Welfare, Ideology and Change in Modern Society* (Cambridge: Polity Press).

Rock, P. (1990) *Helping Victims of Crime: the Home Office and the Rise of Victim Support in England and Wales* (Oxford: Clarendon Press).

Rock, P. (1995) 'The Opening Stages of Criminal Justice Policy Making', *British Journal of Criminology*, vol. 35, pp. 1–16.

Roelandt, T. and Veenman, J. (1992) 'An Emerging Ethnic Underclass in the Netherlands?: Some Empirical Evidence', *New Community*, vol. 19, no. 1, pp. 121–41.

Rolison, G. (1991) 'An Exploration of the Term Underclass as it Relates to African-Americans', *Journal of Black Studies*, vol. 21, no. 3, pp. 287–301.

Romeanes, T. (1998) 'A Question of Confidence: Zero Tolerance and Problem Oriented Policing', in R. Hopkins-Burke (ed.), *Zero Tolerance Policing* (Leicester: Perpetuity Press).

Room, G. (ed.) (1995) *Beyond the Threshold: the Measurement and Analysis of Social Exclusion* (Bristol: The Policy Press).

Rose, D. (1996) *In the Name of the Law: the Collapse of Criminal Justice* (London: Jonathan Cape).

Rose, L. (1988) *Rouges and Vagabonds: the Vagrant Underworld in Britain, 1815–1985* (London: Routledge).

Rose, M. (1971) *The English Poor Law, 1780–1930* (Newton Abbot: David and Charles).

Rose, M. (1985) *The Poor and the City: the English and the Poor Laws in its Urban Context* (Leicester: University of Leicester Press).

Rose, M. (1986) *The Relief of Poverty, 1834–1914* (London: Macmillan).

Roshier, B. (1989) *Controlling Crime: the Classical Perspective in Criminology* (Chicago: Lyceum Books).

Rowntree, S. (1901) *Poverty, a Study of Town Life* (London: Macmillan).

Rude, G. (1985) *Criminal and Victim: Crime and Society in Early Eighteenth Century Britain* (Oxford: Clarendon Press).

Ruggles, P. and Marton, W. (1986) *Measuring the Size and Characteristics of the Underclass: How Much Do We Know?* (Washington DC: Urban Institute).

Runciman, W.G. (1989) *A Treatise on Social Theory: Volume II: Substantive Social Theory* (Cambridge: Cambridge University Press).

Runciman, W.G. (1990) 'How Many Classes Are There in Contemporary in British Society', *Sociology*, vol. 24, no. 3, pp. 377–96.

Runciman, W.G. (1994) 'An Outsiders View of the Criminal Justice System', *Modern Law Review*, vol. 57, no. 1, pp. 1–9.

Rutherford, A. (1998) 'Criminal Policy and the Eliminative Ideal', in C. Jones-Finer and M. Nellis (eds), *Crime and Social Exclusion* (Oxford: Blackwell).

Rutter, M. and Madge, N. (1976) *Cycles of Disadvantage* (London: Heinemann).

Sampson, A. *et al.* (1988) 'Crime Localities and the Multi-Agency Approach', *British Journal of Criminology*, vol. 28, no, 4, pp. 478–93.

Sampson, R. and Lamb, R. (1993) 'Structural Variations in Juvenile Court Processing: Inequality, the Underclass and Social Control', *Law and Society Review*, vol. 27, no. 2, pp. 285–311.

Sampson, R. and Laub, J. (1994) 'Urban Poverty and the Family in the Context of the Family – a New Look at Structure and Process in a Classic Study', *Child Development*, vol. 65, no. 2, pp. 523–40.

Sampson, R. and Wilson, W.J. (1993) 'Towards a Theory of Race, Crime and Urban Poverty' in J. Hagan and R. Peterson (eds), *Crime and Inequality* (Stanford, Cal.: Stanford University Press).

Saulsbury, W. Mott, J. and Newburn, T. (eds), *Themes in Contemporary Policing* (London: Police Foundation: PSI).

Savage, S. and Charman, S. (1996) 'Managing Change', in F. Leishman, S. Cope and P. Starie (eds), *Core Issues in Policing* (London: Longman).

Savage, S. Charman and Cope, S. (1996) 'Police Governance: the Association of Chief Police Officers and Constitutional Change', *Public Policy and Administration*, vol. 11, no. 2, pp. 92–106.

Scarman, Lord (1981) *The Brixton Disorders 10–12 April, Report of an Inquiry by the Rt Honorable Lord Scarman*, Cmnd 8427 (London: Home Office).

Scarman, Lord (1992) quoted in L. Lightfoot and T. Rayment 'Police Study Videos to Catch Riot Ringleaders', *The Sunday Times*, 26 July.

Schneider, J. (1980) *Detroit and the Problem of Order, 1830–80: a Geography of Crime, Riot and Policing* (Lincoln: University of Nebraska Press).

Sennett, R. (1990) *The Conscience of the Eye* (London: Faber and Faber).

Shields, R. (1991) *Places On the Margin* (London: Routledge).

Sigsworth, E. (ed.) (1988) *In Search of Victorian Values: Aspects of Nineteenth Century Thought and Society* (Manchester: Manchester University Press).

Silver, H. (1965) *The Concept of Popular Education: a Study of Ideas and Social Movements in the Early Nineteenth Century* (London: Macgibbon and Kee).

Silver, H. (1993) 'National Conceptions of the New Urban Poverty: Social Structural Change in Britain, France and the United States', *International Journal of Urban and Regional Research*, vol. 17, no. 3, pp. 336–54.

Silver, H. (1996) 'Culture, Politics and National Discourses of the New Urban Poverty', in E. Mingione (ed.), *Urban Poverty and the Underclass* (Oxford: Blackwell).

Silver, A. (1967) 'The Demand for Civil Order in Society', in Bordua, D. (ed.), *The Police* (New York: Wiley).

Silverman, E.B. (1998) 'Below Zero Tolerance: The New York Experience', in R. Burke (ed.), *Zero Tolerance Policing* (Leicester: Perpetuity Press).

Simey, M. (1988) *Democracy Revisited* (London: Pluto Press).

Simon, J. (1993) *Poor Discipline: Parole and the Social Control of the Underclass, 1890–1990* (Chicago: University of Chicago Press).

Sivanandan, A. (1982) *A Different Hunger: Writings on Black Resistance* (London: Pluto Press).

Skogan, W. (1995) 'Community Policing in the United States', in J-P. Brodeur (ed.), *Comparisons in Policing: an International Perspective* (Aldershot: Avebury).

Skolnick, J. (1966) *Justice Without Trial* (New York: John Wiley and Sons).

Small, S. (1994) *Racialised Barriers: the Black Experience in the United States and England in the 1980s* (London: Routledge).

Smiles, S. (1958) *Self Help* (London: John Murray).

Smith, D.J. (1983a) *A Survey of Londoners*, Police and People in London, vol. 1, no. 618 (London: PSI).

Smith, D.J. (1983b) *A Survey of Police Officers*, Police and People in London, vol. 3, no. 620 (London: PSI).

Smith, D.J. (1992) *Understanding the Underclass* (London: PSI).

Smith, D.J. and Gray, J. (1983) *Police and People in London*, vol. 4, no. 621 (London: PSI).

Solomos, J. (1986) *Riots, Urban Protest and Social Policy: the Interplay of Reform and Social Control*, Policy Papers in Ethnic Relations (University of Warwick: Centre for Research in Ethnic Relations).

Solomos, J. and Back, L. (1996) *Racism and Society* (London: Macmillan).

South, N. (1988) *Policing for Profit* (London: Sage).

Southgate, P. and Ekblom, P. (1984) *Contacts Between the Police and Public*, Home Office Research and Planning Unit, Home Office Research Study, no. 58 (London: HMSO).

Southgate, P. and Ekblom, P. (1986) *Police Public Encounters*, Home Office Research Study, no. 90 (London: HMSO).

Srivnas, K. (1992) 'Underclass, Hi-Tech and the Los-Angeles Uprising', *Economic and Political Weekly*, vol. 27, pp. 43–4.

Stacey, M. (1960) *Tradition and Change: a Study of Banbury* (Oxford: Oxford University Press).

Stedman-Jones, G. (1971) *Outcast London* (London: Penguin).

Stedman-Jones, G. (1983) *Languages of Class* (Cambridge: Cambridge University Press).

Steedman, C. (1984) *Policing the Victorian Community* (London: Routledge).

Stenson, K. (1993) 'Community Policing as a Government Technology', *Economy and Society*, vol. 22, no. 3, pp. 373–89.

Stevens, P. and Willis, C. (1979) *Race, Crime and Arrests*, Home Office Research Study, no. 58 (London: HMSO).

Stevenson, J. (1977) 'Social Control and the Prevention of Riots in England 1889–1829', in A. Donajgrodski (ed.), *Social Control in Nineteenth Century Britain* (London: Croom Helm).

Storch, R. (1975) 'The Plague of Blue Locusts: Police Reform and Popular Resistance in the North of England, 1840–1857', *Journal of Social History*, vol. 9, pp. 61–90.

Sudo, P. (1994) 'The Underclass', *Scholastic Update*, 126, pp. 4–5.

Taylor, I. (1995) 'Critical Criminology and the Free Market: Theoretical and Practical Issues in Everyday Social Life and Everyday Crime', in L. Noaks, M. Levi and M. Maguire (eds), *Contemporary Issues in Criminology* (Cardiff: University of Wales Press).

Taylor, I., Evans, K. and Fraser, P. (1996) *A Tale of Two Cities: a Study in Manchester in Sheffield* (London: Routledge).

Taylor, I. (1997) 'The Political Economy of Crime', in M. Maguire, R. Morgan and R. Reiner (eds), *The Oxford Handbook of Criminology* (Oxford: Clarendon Press).

Taylor, I. (1998) 'Free Markets and the Costs of Crime: An Audit of England and Wales', in P. Walton and J. Young (eds) *The New Criminology Revisited* (London: Macmillan).

Taylor, I. (ed.) (1991) *The Social Effects of Free Market Policies* (Hemel Hempstead: Harvester Wheatsheaf).

The Times (1996) 'Zero Tolerance: There Should Be No Blind Eye to Crime', 19 November.

The Times (1997) 'American Zero: Why Blair and Howard Are Both Drawn to US Models', 8 January.

Tobias, J. (1967) *Crime and Industrial Society in the Nineteenth Century* (London: Batsford).

Tonry, M. (1995) *Malign Neglect: Race, Crime and Punishment* (New York: Oxford University Press).

Townsend, P. (1979) *Poverty in the United Kingdom* (Harmondsworth: Penguin).

Townsend, P. (1990) 'Underclass and Overclass: the Widening Gulf Between the Social Classes in Britain in the 1980s', in G. Payne and M. Cross (eds), *Sociology in Action* (London: Macmillan).

Townsend, P. (1996) *A Poor Future*, London: Lemos and Crane.

Trattner, W.I. (1974) *From the Poor Law to the Welfare State* (New York: Free Press).

Travis, A. (1996) 'Atlantic Cuffings', *The Guardian*, 21 November.

US Department of Justice (1993) *Highlights from 20 Years of Surveying Crime Victims – the National Crime Victimisation Survey*, Bureau of Justice Statistics (Washington DC: US Department of Justice).

Utting, D. (1994) 'Family Factors and the Rise of Crime', in A. Coote (ed.), *Families, Children and Crime* (London: Institute of Public Policy Research).

Valentine, C. (1968) *Culture and Poverty: Critique and Counter Proposals* (Chicago: University of Chicago Press).

Vallely, P. (1994) 'A Search for Hope in the Wasteland', *The Daily Telegraph*, 18 March.

Wacquant, L. (1996) 'Red Belt, Black Belt: Racial Division, Class Inequality and the State in the French Urban Periphery and the American Ghetto', in E. Mingione (ed.), *Urban Poverty and the Underclass: a Reader* (Oxford: Blackwell).

Waddington, D. *et al.* (1989) *Flashpoints: Studies in Public Disorder* (London: Routledge).

Waddington, D. (1992) *Contemporary Issues in Public Disorder* (London: Routledge).

Waddington, P.A.J. (1987) 'Towards Paramilitarism? Dilemmas in Policing Civil Disorder', *British Journal of Criminology*, vol. 27, pp. 37–46.

Waddington, P.A.J. (1991) *The Strong Arm of the Law: Armed and Public Order Policing* (Oxford: Clarendon Press).

Waddington, P.A.J. (1993) 'The Case Against Paramilitary Policing Considered', *British Journal of Sociology*, vol. 33, no. 3, pp. 353–73.

Waddington, P.A.J. (1994) *Liberty and Order: Public Order Policing in the Capital* (London: University College of London Press).

Waddington, P.A.J. (1997) 'Policing With Gloves Off', *Police Review*, 25 April, pp. 26–7.

Wagner, P., Weiss, C., Wittrock, B. and Wollmann, H. (1991) 'The Policy Orientation: Legacy and Promise', in P. Wagner *et al.* (eds), *Social Sciences and Modern States: National Experiences and Theoretical Cross-roads* (Cambridge: Cambridge University Press).

Waldfogel, J. (1997) 'Ending Welfare As We Know It: The Personal Responsibility and Work Opportunity Act Of 1996', *Benefits*, Issue 20, September/October, pp. 11–15.

Walker, A. (1984) *Social Planning* (Oxford: Blackwell).

Walker, A. (1990a) 'Blaming the Victims', in C. Murray (1990), *The Emerging British Underclass* (London: Institute of Economic Affairs).

Walker, A. (1991a) 'Poverty and the Underclass', in H. Haralambos (ed.), *Developments in Sociology*, vol. 7 (Ormskirk: Causeway Press).

Walker, A. (1991b) 'The Strategy of Inequality: Poverty and Income Distribution in Britain 1979–89', in I Taylor (ed.), *The Social Effects of Free Market Policies* (Hemel Hempstead: Harvester Wheatsheaf).

Walker, A. and Walker, C. (eds) (1997) *Britain Divided: the Growth of Social Exclusion in the 1980s and 1990s* (London: CPAG).

Walker, S. (1977) *A Critical History of Police Reform* (New York: Lexington).

Walker, R. (1995) 'The Dynamics of Poverty and Social Exclusion', in G. Room (ed.), *Beyond the Threshold: the Measurement and Analysis of Social Exclusion* (Bristol: The Policy Press).

Wall, D. (1998) *The Chief Constables of England and Wales: the Socio-Legal History of a Criminal Justice Elite* (Dartmouth: Ashgate).

Walton, P. and Young, J. (eds) (1998) *The New Criminology Revisited* (London: Macmillan).

Walvin, J. (1987) *Victorian Values* (London: Andre Deutsch).

Ward, C. (1989) *Welcome Thinner City: Urban Survival in the 1990s* (London: Bedford Square Press).

Warner, W.L. and Srole, L. (1945) *The Social Systems of American Ethnic Groups* (New Haven: Yale University Press).

Waxman, T. (1977) *The Stigma of Poverty: a Critique of Poverty Theories and Policies* (New York: Random House).

Westergaard, J. (1992) 'About and Beyond the "Underclass": Some Notes on Influences of Social Climate on Sociology Today – BSA Address 1992, *Sociology*, vol. 26, no.4, pp. 575–87.

Westergaard, J. (1995) *Who Gets What?: The Hardening of Class Inequality in the Late Twentieth Century* (Cambridge: Cambridge University Press).

Westergaard, J. and Resler, H. (1975) *Class in a Capitalist Society* (Harmondsworth: Penguin).

Whelan, C. (1996) 'Marginalisation, Deprivation and Fatalism in the Republic of Ireland: Class and Underclass Perspectives', *European Sociological Review*, vol. 12, no.1, pp. 33–51.

Wiener, M. (1990) *Reconstructing the Criminal: Culture, Law and Policy in England 1830–1914* (Cambridge: Cambridge University Press).

Willetts, D. (1992) 'Theories and Explanations of the Underclass', in D.J. Smith (ed.), *Understanding the Underclass* (London: PSI).

Williams, J., Murphy, P. and Dunning, E. (1987) *The Roots of Football Hooliganism* (London: Routledge).

Wilson, J.Q. (1975) *Thinking About Crime* (New York: Basic Books).

Wilson, J.Q. and Kelling, G. (1982) 'Broken Windows: the Police and Neighbourhood Safety', *Atlantic Monthly*, March, pp. 29–38.

Wilson, W.J. (1978) *The Declining Significance of Race: Blacks and Changing American Institutions* (Chicago: University of Chicago Press).

Wilson, W.J. (1987) *The Truly Disadvantaged* (Chicago: Chicago University Press).

Wilson, W.J. (1991a) 'Studying Inner City Dislocation: the Challenge of Public Agenda Research – 1990 Presidential Address', *American Sociological Review*, vol. 56, pp. 1–14.

Wilson, W.J. (1991b) 'Public Policy Research and the Truly Disadvantaged', in C. Jencks and P. Petersen (eds), *The Urban Underclass* (Washington DC: Brookings Institute).

Wilson, W.J. (1993) *The Ghetto Underclass: Updated Version* (Newbury Park: Sage).

Wilson, W.J. (1996a) *When Work Disappears: the World of the New Urban Poor* (New York: Knopf).

Wilson, W.J. (1996b) 'The Poorest of the Urban Poor: Race, Class and Social Isolation in America's Inner City Ghettos', in M. Bulmer and A. Rees (eds), *Citizenship Today: the Contemporary Relevance of T.H. Marshall* (London: University College of London Press).

Wohl, A. (1977) *The Eternal Slum: Housing and Social Policy in Victorian England* (London: Edward Arnold).

Wood Report (1929) *Report of Mental Deficiency Committee* (London: HMSO).

Wood, P. (1991) *Poverty and the Workhouse in Victorian Britain* (London: Allen Sutton).

Woodcock, Sir J. (1992) 'Why We Need A Revolution', *Police Review*, vol. 100, no. 5187, 16 October, pp. 1929–32.

Wootton, B. (1959) *Social Science and Social Pathology* (London: George Allen and Unwin).

Wrigley, C. (1973) *Political Economy and the Whig Reforms, 1815–37* (London: Gregg International Publishers Limited).

Yang, J. (1992) 'Listening to the Voiceless and Silent (Los Angeles Underclass People)', *Amerasia Journal*, vol. 18, no. 1, pp. 121–4.

Young, A. (1996) *Imagining Crime* (London: Sage).

Young, G. and Handcock, W. (1956) *English Historical Documents, 1833–1874* (London: Eyre and Spottiswoode).

Young, J. (1981) 'Thinking Seriously About Crime: Some Models of Criminology', in M. Fitzgerald, G. McLennan and J. Pawson (eds), *Crime and Society* (London: Routledge and Kegan Paul).

Young, J. (1997) 'Left Realist Criminology', in M. Maguire, R. Morgan, and R. Reiner (eds), *The Oxford Handbook of Criminology* (Oxford: Clarendon Press).

Young, J. (1998) 'Writing on the Cusp of Change: A New Criminology for an Age of Late Modernity', in P. Walton and J. Young (eds), *The New Criminology Revisited* (London: Macmillan).

Zedner, L. (1995) 'Comparative Research in Criminal Justice', in L. Noaks, M. Levi and M. Maguire (eds), *Contemporary Issues in Criminology* (Cardiff: University of Wales Press).

Index

abandoned neighbourhoods, 167, 180
Abelmann, N. and Lie, J., 101
actuarial justice, 180
age, 136, 146, 182, 212
    see also social divisions
agency, 15, 80, 182
    see also structure
Aid for Families with Dependent
    Children (AFDC), 41, 44–8, 53–7
Alcock, P., 1, 10
Alderson, J., 94, 100–4, 121, 132–3,
    145–51, 155, 157, 164, 167,
    179, 200, 218–20
Althusser, L., 168
altruism, 193
Amin, A., 183
Amis, M., 9
Anthias, F., 101, 205
anti-poverty policies, 50, 191
Aponte, R., 3
Archaud, P., 25
Arendt, H., 182
Association of Chief Police Officers
    (ACPO) *see* chief constables
Atherton, C., 56
Audit Commission, 111, 114,
    123, 125, 143, 195
Auletta, K., 51–2

Bachrach, P. and Baratz, M., 16,
    126–7, 129, 159–60
Baldwin, J. and Kinsey, R., 93
Banting, K., 117
Banton, M., 92–3, 212
Barnes, B., 65
Baum, S. and Hassan, R., 6
Bayley, D., 8, 10
Bayley, D. and Mendelsohn, H., 96
Beckett, K., 14, 42, 51, 60–1, 210
beggars, begging, 24, 197–9, 201–2
behavioural conceptions of poverty,
    social exclusion and the

underclass, 3–6, 14–7, 19–20,
    27, 31, 42, 44, 48, 53–4, 64,
    70, 75–7, 82, 87–8, 106–8,
    128, 131, 133–5, 153–6,
    163–4, 177, 180–1, 188–9,
    191–2, 201–2, 203–4, 206–9,
    211–12, 217–22
Beier, A., 23
Bellamy, R., 29
Bennett, T., 152
Benyon, J. and Solomos, J., 132
Beresford, P., 25
Berger, P. and Luckmann, T., 15,
    88–90, 117, 205
Berger, P. and Pullberg, S., 88
Bessant, J., 6
Big Issue, 198
Blair, T., 83, 190, 192, 194, 198
Booth, C., 22
bourgeois law, 37
Bouza, A.V., 60
Bowling, B., 197
Brace, C., 44
Bradshaw, J. and Millar, J., 78–9
Braithwaite, J., 192
Brake, M., 136, 139
Brake, M. and Hale, C., 139
Bratton, W., 42, 197, 199
Briggs, A., 21, 29–30
British Crime Survey, 7, 210
Brodeur, J.P., 8
Brogden, M., 33, 116, 121
Brogden, M., Jefferson, T. and
    Walklate, S., 33
broken windows hypothesis, 197
    see also zero tolerance policing
Brown, J., 49, 54, 78–9
Bryson, A. and Jacobs, J., 194
Buck, N., 6, 182
Bush, George, 14, 42, 57, 60
Butcher, T., 133, 143
Butler, R., 83

251